Irish Literature, History, and Culture

THE IRISH PLAY

ON THE

NEW YORK STAGE

1874-1966

John P. Harrington

THE UNIVERSITY PRESS OF KENTUCKY

Publication of this volume was made possible in part
by a grant from the National Endowment for the Humanities.

Scholarly publisher for the Commonwealth,
serving Bellarmine College, Berea College, Centre
College of Kentucky, Eastern Kentucky University,
The Filson Club Historical Society, Georgetown College,
Kentucky Historical Society, Kentucky State University,
Morehead State University, Murray State University,
Northern Kentucky University, Transylvania University,
University of Kentucky, University of Louisville,
and Western Kentucky University.

Editorial and Sales Offices: The University Press of Kentucky
663 South Limestone Street, Lexington, Kentucky 40508-4008

01 00 99 98 97   5 4 3 2 1

Library of Congress Cataloging-in-Publication Data

Harrington, John P.
      The Irish play on the New York stage, 1874-1966 / John P. Harrington
      p.   cm. — (Irish literature, history and culture)
      Includes bibliographical references (p.) and index.
      ISBN 0-8131-2033-0 (alk. paper)
      1. English drama—Irish authors—History and criticism. 2. English drama—
Irish authors—Appreciation—United States. 3. Theater—New York (State)—
New York—History—20th century. 4. Theater—New York (State)—New York—
History—19th century. 5. Public opinion—New York (State)—New York—
History. 6. Ireland—Foreign public opinion, American. 7. Irish—Travel—
United States—History. 8. Ireland—Relations—United States. 9. United States—
Relations—Ireland. 10. Ireland—In literature. I. Title. II. Series.
PR8789.H37   1997
792.9'5'09747109034—dc21   97-17688

This book is printed on acid-free recycled paper
meeting the requirements of the American National Standard
for Permanence of Paper for Printed Library Materials.

Manufactured in the United States of America

for Janet

CONTENTS

INTRODUCTION

In the lovely "Metalogue to the Magic Flute," written for the bicentenary of Mozart's birth in 1956, W.H. Auden celebrates the tribulations and triumphs of performing arts. He attributes a large part of the kind of appreciation accorded an artist to shifting expectations:

> Each age has its own mode of listening.
> We know the *Mozart* of our fathers' time
> Was gay, rococo, sweet, but not sublime,
> A Viennese Italian; that is changed
> Since music critics learned to feel 'estranged'.

Auden also counts the fashions of an age for many of the tribulations put upon a work of art, and in this poem he imagines that the characteristic *Magic Flute* of 1956 would include a Queen of the Night cast as a college dean, a Sarastro as a professor of history, Tamino as a Ph.D. candidate, and Papageno as a juke-box boy. In addition, Auden acknowledges the many intermediaries of the artist as a test of a work of art's resilience:

> The Diva whose
> Fioriture and climactic note
> The silly old composer never wrote,
> Conductor *X*, that over-rated bore
> Who alters tempi and who cuts the score,
> Director *Y* who with ingenious wit
> Places his wretched singers in the pit
> While dancers mime their roles, *Z* the Designer
> Who sets the whole thing on an ocean liner,

The girls in shorts, the men in yachting caps;
Yet Genius triumphs over all mishaps.

The last line states Auden's conviction throughout the poem. It is
immediately reiterated and punctuated for emphasis: "It soothes the
Frank, it stimulates the *Greek:* / Genius surpasses all things, even Chic."[1]
Mozart certainly has unusual status in the arts, Auden's poem was for a
celebratory function, and the poet has qualified this notion elsewhere.
But this idea of artistic genius transcending circumstance appears consistently in the mid twentieth century. For example, George Steiner, in
a quite different context, insists that "only genius can elaborate a vision so intense and specific that it will come across the intervening
barrier of broken syntax or private meaning."[2] Steiner's confidence is
no less than Auden's, and without the humor. His assertion is that artistic genius transmits its vision against all forms of interference, the
"things" that Auden has genius surpassing.

Genius is a much-abused word, but even so the frequent abuse of
that term in conjunction with the word *Irish* is striking. The artists
themselves are not shy of the term, or even of its power over impedi-
ments. When Sean O'Casey departed from the realistic and specifically
Irish *mise en scène* of his first plays, Bernard Shaw pleaded his colleague's
case to Lady Astor as follows: "Sean O'Casey's all right now that his
shift from Dublin slums to Hyde Park has shown his genius is not limited by frontiers."[3] The chapter that follows on O'Casey's Hyde Park
play, *Within the Gates,* shows that those frontiers, the cultural differences and contemporary expectations that hinder vision, were not negligible when O'Casey came to New York in 1934. In America, before and
after O'Casey's visit, the notion of *Irish genius* has special resonance.
Apart from the innumerable appearances of that phrase in the following chapters, it is worth noting here that *The Genius of Irish Theater*
was published in New York in 1960 as a companion to *The Irish Genius,*
an anthology of poems and stories. These were very literate antholo-
gies, and the genius of the title no doubt had more to do with publisher's
packaging than with editorial policy. But in the large number of related
publications, there was no *Genius of French Theater,* for example, but a
Landmarks of French Theater. Nor was there any volume called *The Dutch
Genius.* This phenomenon is interesting because the whole celebration
of Irish genius in America frequently patronizes and so departs from
the sense of Auden or Steiner.

In 1914, or three years after Lady Gregory led a company of Abbey Theatre players on a first tour of America, Emma Goldman gave lectures on the "Social Significance of Modern Drama" at the Berkeley Theatre in New York. Only in reference to Ireland did she depart from her ordinarily rigorous and revolutionary critique. On the topic of Irish drama she celebrated how "only a people unspoiled by the dulling hand of civilization and free from artifice can retain such simplicity of faith and remain so imaginative, so full of fancy and dreams, wild and fiery, which have kindled the creative spark in the Irish dramatists of our time."[4] The same very patronizing notion of Irish genius can be seen in 1929, when Hallie Flanagan, product of George Pierce Baker's drama workshop at Harvard, and later head of the Federal Theatre Project, went to Ireland, scornfully made a pilgrimage to sites associated with Boucicault's *Colleen Bawn,* and then reported back to American readers this formula: "St. Patrick . . . the Tara brooch . . . the Ardagh chalice . . . the Abbey Theatre."[5] This very selective and simplistic American view of Ireland, in proclamation of its genius, is one instance of "things" intervening with genius and barriers interfering with visions. Because it is more exotic in America than in Ireland, Irish drama as performed in New York, the center of the American theater world, demonstrates especially well how these factors compete. In some instances "genius triumphs over all mishaps." In some mishaps prevail. The extravagant mythology of what George Jean Nathan called "the Celtic's poetic impulse" ("the rich singing humor and beauty of an O'Casey, the mordant lyric passion of a Synge . . ."[6]) is a quite formidable test of the power of genius to transcend frontiers and elaborate a specific vision. The chapters that follow record the formidable tests given Irish genius in New York from Dion Boucicault to Brian Friel.

W.B. Yeats, consistently a figure in the background of the productions described in this book, was always very articulate about the theater's resistance to individual genius and the high probability in production of mishap. His essay "A People's Theatre," first published in 1919, was a reflection on Irish drama after his tours in America as advance publicity for the Abbey company. "We had not set out to create this sort of theatre," he wrote, lamenting the popularity of work not of his first choice, "and its success has been to me a discouragement and a defeat."[7] Even earlier, he had described the theater's resistance to genius in these famous lines from "The Fascination of What's Difficult":

> The fascination of what's difficult
> Has dried the sap out of my veins, and rent
> Spontaneous joy and natural content
> Out of my heart. There's something ails our colt
> That must, as if it had not holy blood
> Nor on Olympus leaped from cloud to cloud,
> Shiver under the lash, strain, sweat and jolt
> As though it dragged road-metal.

The thing that ailed his colt, introduced as only possibly a Pegasus emblem of grandeur in triumph and control, is "Theatre business, management of men."[8] A whole body of theatre studies has developed in the last few decades as a contemporary corroboration of Yeats's sentiment. This work admits the force of audience, and particularly its expectations, to the study of theatrical genius and the things that lash it in practice. One representative example is Loren Kruger's *The National Stage,* with its intention to expand "the field of critique or critical entertainment beyond the limited realm of the work itself to include the place and occasion of its production and reception" and so to provide in its study of autonomy and engagement "an analysis of theatre's exemplary articulation of art and society."[9] In addition to place and occasion of production, study of the history of theater is now more attentive to the factors of "theatre business" implied by Yeats. Marvin Carlson's work identifies a number of useful resources for expanding study beyond the limits of the individual play text. Among these factors, and in addition to the written script, Carlson numbers "lines of business," "the phenomenon of publicity and programs," and "the effect of institutionalized readers—dramaturgs and reviewers."[10] This study of the Irish play on the New York stage draws on all these materials as well as the play text to place art, artist, and audience in relation to each other at a particular time. My intention is not to argue another theory of reception, or even to labor a slight adjustment of existing ones, but to set a record of exemplary transactions between art and society. This record of what Yeats called "lash, strain, sweat and jolt" is descriptive and anecdotal because only those means allow for the unpredictability of expectations, fashions, and intermediaries meeting the written play in production.

Instead of a comprehensive survey, I have concentrated on seven individual productions, from Boucicault's *The Shaughraun* in 1874 to

Friel's *Philadelphia, Here I Come!* in 1966. These seven productions are articulate because they include some public disagreement when staged in New York, such as the confrontation of *Mrs Warren's Profession* and the Society for the Suppression of Vice in 1905, the vocal demonstrations that greeted *The Playboy of the Western World* in 1911, and the general debate on artistic innovation and artistic fraud surrounding *Waiting for Godot* in 1956. All of these plays have prior histories, but the New York productions are especially valuable instances of art meeting society because the situation of art as export product, facing external evaluation, emphasizes barriers and interference, all theater business. That element of distance between artist and audience also minimizes factors like foundational allegiances and proximity to the dramatic material that can obscure the fundamental transaction between art and audience. Last, the meeting of American audience with Irish drama has teh clarifying effect of exoticism, of foreign and cosmopolitan innovation, however humble or peasant-like its guise. For example, after attending productions by the Irish Players in 1911, Eugene O'Neill, at this point having finished touring with his father's revivals of *The Count of Monte Cristo* and begun composition of his own first plays, wrote that "the work of the Irish Players on their first trip over here, was what opened my eyes to the existence of a real theatre, as opposed to the unreal—and to me, then—hateful theatre of my father."[11] For "real" O'Neill did not mean anthropological and documentary accuracy, which, along with the role of a national theater, dominated the debate over the *Playboy* in Dublin in 1907. Rather, he meant really theatrical in new ways unlike the practice of his father's theater, which was an Americanized version of European melodrama. In the Irish Players, O'Neill, as a member of the audience, found a drama of aesthetic ambition unlike his father's or previous productions in New York of plays like Boucicault's *Shaughraun* or Shaw's *John Bull's Other Island,* both of which revise melodrama in their own way and for their own time. O'Neill saw the precedent set by the Irish Players as the assertion of the privilege of art and artist, and the possibility of a theater less directly addressed to the audience than a theater of cultural engagement like Boucicault's or a theater of political reform like Shaw's. O'Neill saw and endorsed Lady Gregory's quite calculated resolve to select a chosen audience and to estrange a popular one, a resolve that can be seen in the 1911 New York production history as analogous to the action of the Playboy, Christy Mahon, against the Mayo villagers in the play and so as essential to the broader scene of production and reception of this play, its predecessors, and its successors as Irish plays in New York. All these factors of art in practice make the study of the Irish play as a foreign product on the New York stage a useful complement to textual criticism of the plays and to textual histories of Irish drama as a tradition.

To emphasize that clarifying effect of cultural contrast between Irish play and New York stage, I have not attempted a chronicle of hybridized Irish American theater. There certainly is a valuable history in that subject, but it is an American history and so only a background element in this story. The Irish American theater audience in New York is part of the audience for Irish plays, not the whole of that audience. The Irish playwrights presented here alternatively cultivate the Irish American audience (like Boucicault) or disparage it (like Shaw), but only as a part of their audience no more fundamental than any other. Likewise, the Irish American theater in New York or elsewhere is an occasional but not essential part of the story of the seven productions described here. O'Neill appears and reappears as an appreciative spectator and fellow playwright in these chapters through O'Casey's *Within the Gates* in 1934, but only as an interesting barometer of taste, not as an Irish American artist. Less extraordinary examples also figure in the background: James Pilgrim's antebellum Paddy plays, Harrigan and Hart, *Abie's Irish Rose,* and William Alfred's *Hogan's Goat.* But these figure here no more—and no less—significantly than other contextual developments like the rise of the "little" theater or agitprop in the Depression era. There are also many prominent figures associated with Irish American theater and performance without any particular relevance to my subject who consequently go unmentioned but for here: Chauncey Olcott, Victor Herbert, George M. Cohan, James Gleason, Philip Barry, and so forth.

The specific subject of this study is what these seven productions individually and collectively reveal about playwright, play, Irish drama, and New York theater. These playwrights as artists qualify the kind of image Auden gave Mozart as a silent and transcendent figure above the fray of fashion. The playwrights here assume a particular role somewhere on the range from Shaw's extremely aggressive and manipulative taunt to the audience and Boucicault's or Friel's more submissive but no less calculated appeal to the audience. The playwright, it proves, can cause considerable damage to the ideal transmission of vision and become, in fact, one of the things to be surpassed. The audience itself always constructs an image of the playwright out of fashionable expectations, and this image may or may not follow the image the playwright actively or passively cultivates. Sean O'Casey cultivated his rough-hewn image against all logic, because it was not compatible with his attempt in *Within the Gates* to elaborate a new kind of drama. Though O'Casey's play failed, his elaboration of the Irish playwright was so successful that it entirely offset other available images, like that of Shaw, for example, or Joyce, and established a role that successors, like Friel, would find restrictive. These early and formative productions also reveal dimensions of the plays later obscured by conventions established in subsequent productions. For example, Shaw's personal taunts to the audience have parallels in *Mrs Warren's Profession,* and the sometimes hilarious episode of *Waiting for Godot* in Miami and on Broadway demonstrates features of the play lost after it became an object of international reverence.

One of the most persistent factors in this series of productions over nearly a century is an evolving but consistent set of expectations for an "Irish play." Boucicault first defined that genre by the criterion of Irish subject matter, but from the beginning of this century to the present, the "Irish play" has come to imply a specific kind of Irish subject matter, invariably rural and Catholic. When the Irish Players visited New York in 1911, the *Gaelic American,* unhappy with the image of Ireland being broadcast throughout New York, called them the "Anti-Irish Irish Players." Just so, there is in New York a history of Irish Irish plays and non-Irish Irish plays, or plays by Irish playwrights outside the form and content of the narrowest expectations. The same playwright can be known for both at the same time. In 1905, Shaw's attempt to surpass Boucicault's Irish stereotypes, *John Bull's Other Island,* opened in the same month, with the same company, as *Mrs Warren's Profession,* with its entirely English scene and characters. In 1934, O'Casey's non-Irish Irish play *Within the Gates* opened in competition with a revival of his *Juno and the Paycock,* which is frequently adverted to as the quintessential Irish Irish play. These expectations are stronger in New York than in Dublin, and the fact that there could be a single selective and reductive notion of an Irish play is a feature of New York cultural history. This is what Irish drama reveals about New York. At the same time, however, Irish drama, particularly as presented in New York, lends itself to simplification and reduction to a formulaic "Irish play." This, insofar as it has a useful clarifying effect, is what New York reveals about Irish drama. The seven productions described here all confront the competing desires to fulfill expectations and, by innovation, to shatter them. In the beginning and the end of this account of the Irish play on the New York stage, Boucicault and Friel can be seen attempting with mixed success to revise audience expectations. In between those points in time, Shaw, Lady Gregory with the Irish Players, Joyce, O'Casey, and Beckett can all be seen attempting, with equally mixed success, a more radical renovation of audience expectations. One indication of the outcome of this dynamic over time is that Irish Irish play expectations remain in effect in New York and have the self-perpetuating effect of influencing what kind of Irish play will be produced there. In fact, non-Irish Irish plays have an impressive historical record in New York. In the record, though not in the general perception that governs the theater marketplace, the Irish plays of Shaw, Joyce, and Beckett have had at least as much influence as those of Boucicault, Synge, O'Casey, and Friel.

These generalizations are retrospective, and the historical as distinct from the textual study of drama offers the opportunity for comparisons of different attempts at different times to transmit genius through interference. In these seven examples, there is in the first, Boucicault, and the last, Friel, an active engagement of artist with audience in works that hope to revise assumptions and expectations by degree. The whole trajectory between those two is a mid twentieth century phenomenon of artistic arrogance and narcissism that is sometimes humorous and sometimes discouraging. To further complicate matters, the work of art has sometimes benefitted from consummate arrogance, and sometimes subtle revision has had no effect or even proved counterproductive. The audience of the artist might seem a likely villain: a mass project that despite generous instruction consistently fails to improve itself. In fact, the record shows that the audience responds positively to challenge and deplores formula and repetition. Moreover, the audience regularly ignores the advice of professional spectators—dramaturgs and reviewers. All these complications resist reduction to a single, simple theory of reception. However, it can be said that the story of the Irish play on the New York stage does not instill confidence that "Genius surpasses all things." Instead, the story suggests the hopeful possibility that there is a much more complex and so more responsive collaboration of many "things" with genius in theater.

1

DION BOUCICAULT,
THE IRISH PLAY, AND THE
POLITICS OF RECONCILIATION

In 1972, on March 17, or St. Patrick's Day, the *Times Literary Supplement* published a special Irish issue, with contributions from Thomas Kilroy, Maire Cruise O'Brien, John Montague, Liam Miller, and others. Though all the essays and unsigned reviews did not advert to sectarian violence in Northern Ireland, the occasion for the issue plainly was the worsening situation there. Denis Donoghue, as introducer, discussed the unionist and the nationalist positions in order to formulate their literary import. "Irish literature is a story of fracture," Donoghue wrote, "the death of one language, so far as it is dead or dying or maintained as an antiquity, and the victory of another; the broken relationship of one religion to another, both claiming to be Christian; the divergence of one Irishman from another."[1] To the same issue, Brian Friel contributed one of his rare essays on drama, an essay no more optimistic than Donoghue's. Friel was then identified as the author of *Philadelphia, Here I Come!*, which had opened in Dublin eight years before and then succeeded both in London and in New York. The title of Friel's essay was "Plays Peasant and Unpeasant," an allusion to Shaw's *Plays Pleasant and Unpleasant*, with the latter including *Mrs Warren's Profession*, which had one of the most eventful of world premieres in New York. Friel's purpose was to extract a particularly faithful tradition of Irish drama, the sort neglected by Shaw, from those multiple political, social, and literary fractures. His procedure was to "scrap all those men who wrote within the English tradition, for the English stage and for the English people, and . . . go back no further than 1899, on the night of May 9, the opening of the Irish Literary Theater." The casualties were Farquhar,

Steele, Sheridan, Goldsmith, Wilde, and Shaw, all charged with pur-
veying pleasantries and unpleasantries for the foreign stage. Friel did
not note that the night of 1899 he memorialized consisted of one Irish
play by W.B. Yeats, which the Irish audience denounced, and one rather
un-Irish play by Edward Martyn on the Ibsenite model, both in productions by English people trained on and for the English stage. But
the aim of selecting and creating one's own tradition was, for Friel in
1972, recognition "that the theatre was an important social element that
not only reflected but shaped the society it served." The obstacles were
demands for fashion and formula: chic. Much more interested in the
shaping power of drama than in its obligation to society, Friel admired
theater riots, specifically those concerning Synge and O'Casey in Dublin:
"The robust technique was at least an indication of rude involvement."
What he deplored in 1972 was epitomized when "the Abbey still goes on
offering Boucicault. . . . Irish audiences laugh tolerantly, whether at the
play or the Abbey directors does not really matter much." This point was
worth repeating in conclusion, where among irrelevancies the pride of
place was given to the fact that "Boucicault capers on the Abbey stage."[2]

Since 1972 both Friel and Donoghue have admitted complications
and refinements to these opinions, which is a good indication of the
effect of time on opinion. Nor could any Irish spokesperson be assumed
to be under oath on St. Patrick's Day in the *Times Literary Supplement,*
which is a good parallel indication of the effect of place on opinion.
However, it is striking that at this moment in 1972 Dion Boucicault
could epitomize the enemies of Irish drama. It was, of course, not his
intention. In 1860 Boucicault stood on the stage of Wallack's Theatre in
New York City, greeting curtain calls after *The Colleen Bawn,* which
was based on a Limerick murder case and opened in New York, and
told the audience: "I had long thought of writing a play from material
gathered from my native country but this is the first time I ever tried
it. I hope that the play will lead other greater men, of finer genius and
talents than I possess, to give you plenty of Irish plays."[3] The playwright on curtain call is not under oath, either, but in such a short
statement the proportion of fabrication here is rather high. More than a
century of change has given different edges to words like *genius, talent, Irish,* and even *play.* Over the century following his death in 1890,
Boucicault increasingly became a figure of fun or even contempt, as
evident in 1972. However, the transformation of a fixed body of work
obviously has more to do with the subsequent course of drama than

with any alteration in the work itself. Boucicault's reputation has suffered as the relation of artist to audience progressed through the twentieth century. The course of this relation is especially evident in the circumstances of openings in New York of works by Boucicault, Shaw, J.M. Synge, James Joyce, Sean O'Casey, Samuel Beckett, and Friel. To use Brian Friel's terms, this change is away from a conception of art that "reflects" society to one in which art "shapes" society. In the twentieth century, the artist increasingly expects the audience to desire this shaping action, and the audience consistently fails to prove malleable. Despite Friel's afternote that art "serves," this change sets in place different prerogatives and degrees of control for audience and artist. The twentieth century has seen the rise of the latter, with a consequent fall for a figure like Boucicault.

Unhappiness with defectors to the English stage and discussions of the story of Irish literature in *TLS* help illustrate how at least part of that story is about the fortunes of Irish literature as export, of the effect of place on opinion. Study of the Irish play in New York has the benefits of eliminating the "racy of the soil" sorts of foundational allegiances that dominate, for better and for worse, domestic literature and culture, Irish or other. Boucicault is an especially good example because he at least posed in a subordinate relation to audience that is almost unthinkable in the late twentieth century. His performance in New York required relation with a foreign audience, and the cultural difference helps isolate and define the kind of relation. His work also presents reconciliation as a real possibility, and this possibility apparently vanished and was replaced by an emphasis on fracture by 1972. These factors are especially evident in the opening of *The Shaughraun* in New York in 1874. It is a play about reconciliation between warring parties, the colonists and the colonized, written by a playwright willing to appear as unctuous as in the speech quoted above, built around a character, Conn the Shaughraun, equally unctuous and equally agent of reconciliation. It was the play that disappointed Friel, and one that has subsequently been revived in Ireland and elsewhere to general praise. It is an example of a work needing recovery of the historical from the contemporary—another "thing" to trouble genius.

Boucicault is known as a melodramatist, and his own life had actual near-operatic scenes. He obscured the specifics of his birth, which is now generally accepted as December 26, 1820, in Dublin, to Dionysius Lardner, a writer of science articles, and to Anne Darley Boursiquot,

separated from her husband, a Huguenot who favored a spelling that
Boucicault later adjusted to English convention. After a "dark period,"
which like Shakespeare's is filled with conjecture, including a rumored
ride on the first steam engine from Liverpool to Manchester, Boucicault
appeared in London in 1837 as an actor and playwright under the name
Lee Moreton. He also appeared with a play called *Out of Town,* which
was reminiscent of *School for Scandal.* Retitled *London Assurance,* the
play was an enormous success when produced by Charles Mathews
and Madame Vestris at Covent Garden in 1841. As would happen
throughout his career, Boucicault's authorship was challenged, in this
case by one John Brougham, whose claim, before theatrical productions enjoyed the slightest copyright protection, was eventually decided, in New York, for Brougham and against Boucicault. After
additional London successes, and another "dark period," rumored to
include marriage in France and an unexplained disappearance of the
wife during mountain climbing in the Alps, Boucicault arrived in New
York in 1853. As Sean O'Casey would later, Boucicault wrote his autobiography in the third person. In retrospect, he recalled his arrival in
New York as a breaking dawn of great opportunity, especially after
"finding himself defeated and disregarded by the London managers":

> Boucicault turned his face to the West, and on the 18th
> September, 1853, landed in New York. It was not a city. It
> was a theatre. It was a huge fair. Bunting of all nationalities
> and of no nationality was flaunting over the streets. Poles of
> liberty accentuated the "Rights of Man." Bands of music
> preceded processions of a dozen boys bearing flags and
> tattered targets. Irish was spoken at the wharves, German in
> the saloons, French in the restaurants. But the chiefest feature
> in this polyglot city was its boyhood. A boy in heart, but a
> man, and a very shrewd one, in the head![4]

Though of course a reconstruction, the reminiscence is interesting in its emphasis on variety of ethnicity, for Boucicault, unlike others, would be selective and do little with ethnicities other than Irish,
and in its emphasis on marching guards, an element of New York that
will provide the violence of the Orange Riots shortly before the opening of *The Shaughraun* and simultaneously the comedy of Harrigan and
Hart's various performances as The Mulligan Guards. Reconstructing

his arrival, Boucicault identified himself as the author of *London Assurance*, without mention of Brougham. He also failed to mention his new wife, the well-known actress Agnes Robertson. He did mention the superiority of American theaters to London ones, a plainly embittered sentiment reissued in various forms by Irish playwrights including Shaw, Joyce, O'Casey, and Beckett.

John Brougham provides a very interesting counterpoint to Boucicault. Born in Dublin ten years before Boucicault, he also preceded Boucicault to London and to America by about ten years. His first impressions of New York, also written in retrospect, were rather different:

> Came to America, October, 1842. Opened at Park Theatre, in the palmy days of light houses and heavy gas bills . . . . The city was, of course, entirely new to me, in climate, people, and surroundings. I particularly remember the fireflies, which I thought were the result of an atmosphere charged with flashes of lightning. At that time, too, the barbarous custom was prevalent of beating a gong to tell the animals that the feed was ready. . . . As viewed from the Astor House, New York was bounded on the North by Union Square, then a great pile of dirt, with one or two dwellings in the vicinity, and a few farms nearby.[5]

Not much source material evident there, and Brougham's work for the American stage differed radically from Boucicault's. Neither had important influences or precedents for the predicament of the Irish playwright in New York. The theater historian Margaret G. Mayorga's comment that "the stage Irishman is as old as American drama itself"[6] is often quoted, but most appearances of the figure Boucicault would revise were by American or English playwrights. One important exception was Tyrone Power, whose tours of America in the 1830s were extremely popular, and who became, after his death at sea and upon a revival of his *O'Flannigan and the Fairies,* the first Irish playwright to be hissed by the Irish American audience unhappy with the representation of their homeland on the New York stage.[7] A more common case, and a contributing factor to unhappiness with the stage Irishman, was an Irish play with a non-Irish author, such as James Pilgrim's *Paddy the Piper* (1850) and *Shandy Maguire* (1851), which were performed by the Irish comedian Barney Williams. Without a demonstrably successful precedent, Brougham concentrated on solo performances of Irish historical programs, such as the temperance advocate Father Matthew or as Daniel O'Connell, that drew an almost exclusively Irish and Irish American audience and pleased them with the heroic representation of their people. Brougham also created a number of American historical programs, especially *The Declaration of Independence* (1844), for long solo tours before Boucicault had introduced the practice of touring companies. His first dramas were comical and entirely acceptable comedies of the American Irish: *The Game of Love* (1855) portrays the Irish family Murphy, whom most New Yorkers believe to be Greek, experimenting with the social advantage in the New World of adopting the name De Merfie. Brougham was known as a performer more than as a playwright, and because his work was tailored for the American Irish, his work lacks the revealing contrast of the Irish play in New York. He also had the misfortune to be pioneering for Boucicault and consistently losing in the transaction. Brougham's play *Emerald Ring* was plundered by Boucicault for his *The Rapparee; or, The Treaty of Limerick,* to much greater success. Late in life Brougham was best known for playing the role of Dazzle in *London Assurance,* which always remained associated with Boucicault, and as Colonel O'Grady in Boucicault's *Arrah-na-Pogue,* on occasion opposite his rival as Shaun the Post. Brougham's losing record was extended to off-stage business endeavors. He opened the Lyceum Theatre on Broadway at Broome Street in 1850, lost the lease two years later, and had it taken over by James W. Wallack, who succeeded in making it a successful legitimate theater. On that bankroll, Wallack's Theatre moved uptown, where it became the scene of Boucicault's greatest successes in New York, including *The Shaughraun* in 1874.[8]

Boucicault's course after arrival in New York was rather different from Brougham's. Rather than impersonate familiar Irish figures, he wrote plays on current events. There were many exceptions, as he was both prolific and a well-known plagiarist, but the first phase of his work after *London Assurance* was primarily the topical play on politics of interest to the general American public. In his own words, after arrival in New York: "Boucicault had used these three years in study of the American people, their tastes, and the direction of their intellectual appetites. The poetic and romantic drama had no longer its old charm; the actual, the contemporaneous, the photographic had replaced the works of imagination. It was in turning over the *Illustrated Journal* that the idea struck him that the stage might be employed in a similar manner to embody and illustrate the moving events of the period."[9] Among his major successes in this vein were *Jessie Brown: or, The Relief of Lucknow* (1858), which was about the Sepoy rebellion in India and which was first produced while the siege was in progress. Another was *The Octoroon* (1859), about slavery in America. Now generally dismissed as less political than commercial because it appears by contemporary standards equivocal on the issue of slavery, the play was at its time considered incendiary. The *New York Post* ran an article called "John Brown on the Stage" that noted that the play "abounds in scenes which, however artfully contrived for the purpose of concealing the more repulsive characteristics of slavery, bring out its necessary evils, such as the slave auction, the severance of families, and the cruel operation of the prejudice against color, more effectively even than the play of 'Uncle Tom's Cabin.'"[10] Boucicault was especially proud that the play was in production in New York on the day John Brown made his raid on Harper's Ferry. As always in Boucicault, there is the note of the ridiculous: he played the role of an Indian, Wah-no-tee. But in Boucicault's work there is also much in contrast to Brougham's limitations and much in line with Friel's demand for "robust technique" and "rude involvement."

Sean O'Casey's work begins with recognizable Irish dramas in identifiable Irish settings and then attempts less localized non-Irish dramas such as *Within the Gates*. O'Casey's context in the 1920s made that probable. Boucicault's progress was the reverse. He came to the Irish drama as a novelty and a stage innovation late in his career, thus creating the precedents that influenced O'Casey. By his own account, Boucicault was in 1860 in a five-month engagement with Laura Keene at the Olympic Theatre in New York when a comic vehicle for both failed. His version of the breakthrough is perfectly melodramatic:

> "Have you nothing—no subject, no play half written? Can
> you think of nothing to replace this unlooked-for collapse?"
> pleaded Miss Keene.
> "I have nothing," replied Boucicault.

Then he wandered darkened streets, "on a bitter night, and the sleet driven by a northerly blast [that] lashed the author's face as he turned up Broadway." He found a lonely light above a bookshop run by a poor but noble clerk named Brentano (before that family became New York bookstore magnates). He took one dozen "cheap novels," hoping to find one worth plagiarizing that night in his hotel room. Fortunately, one was worthy, and it was Gerald Griffin's *The Collegians*. In the morning he was able to dash off to Miss Keene a letter perfectly in character with himself and his enterprise:

> My Dear Laura:
>
> I have it! I send you seven steel engravings of scenes around Killarney. Get your scene-painter to work on them at once. I also send a book of Irish melodies, with those marked I desire Baker to score for the orchestra. I shall read act one of my new Irish play on Friday; we rehearse that while I am writing the second, which will be ready on Monday; and we rehearse the second while I am doing the third. We can get the play out within a fortnight.
>
> Yours,
> D.B.[11]

The novel was based on a famous Limerick murder case of 1819, and Boucicault kept this intact. His staging put the emphasis much more on innocent women, the parish priest, the evil attorney with his hunchbacked assistant, and the lovable Irish rogue, Myles-na-Coppaleen, which he played himself. He was also able to organize everything around a spectacular drowning scene, requiring twenty boys shaking blue fabric, and *The Colleen Bawn* was an enormous success. Boucicault claimed that its importance was "the revolution effected by this play in what may be termed the Irish drama and the representation of Irish character."[12] However, the letter to Laura Keene, which Boucicault himself published, includes those qualities that have always conspired against his reputation: the plagiarism (or at best adaptation), the borrowing of clichés (Irish melodies), the emphasis on the visible (scene paintings) over the text, and the willingness to rewrite. Chic at the moment of his "invention," these are qualities that became obsolete quickly and utterly. By 1904, when his *John Bull's Other Island* was staged in New York, Shaw was especially satirical of generic Irish scenery and stage decoration. By 1955, when *Waiting for Godot* was planned for tryouts before New York, the director Alan Schneider thought that a producer's proposal of rewrites was hilarious and patiently pointed out that "Beckett's particular blend of purity and intellect was not exactly suited to sitting in a hotel room in Philadelphia rewriting the second act."[13] Boucicault's was, and in his time he could with justification claim, as he did: "When I wrote 'The Colleen Bawn,' I invented the Irish Drama. It was original in form, in material, in treatment, and in dialogue."[14] Without question, as an image of Ireland rather than Irish America, it was original to the New York stage and fundamental to the representation of Ireland on the American stage.

The Colleen Bawn episode was true to a pattern of success followed hard by failure that characterizes all of Boucicault's career. The success that salvaged the engagement with Laura Keene was followed by the collapse in 1863 of an enterprise in London known as the Theatre Royal, which attempted to transfer theater control from manager to playwright. Boucicault's fortunes, however, were restored by his next Irish play, *Arrah-na-Pogue,* about the 1798 rising. The title is an Irish Gaelic phrase for the maiden, Arrah of the Kiss, played by Mrs. Boucicault, Agnes Robertson, opposite Boucicault in another comic rogue role, Shaun the Post. The play opened in Dublin in 1864, and this example of "rude involvement" included a particularly strident rewording of "The Wearing of the Green," the song about the defiant wearing of the nationalist color, with new lyrics that were later banned from performance in Great Britain. True to the pattern, Boucicault again quickly moved from this success to failure. From Dublin, where he was performing in a revival of *The Colleen Bawn,* he produced a theatrical spectacular called *Babil and Bijou* at Covent Garden in the summer of 1872. Despite a long run, the extravaganza could never recover production costs, and Boucicault, with Agnes, returned to America.

In New York, he would again rebound with a new Irish play, *The Shaughraun,* with himself in the title role as wastrel rogue. He had offered a new Irish play to Lester Wallack and completed at least some of a script called "Boyne Water." At a first reading, however, Wallack revealed that in London he had just purchased a historical drama of the same period, *Clancarty,* another Irish play by a non-Irish playwright. "Nothing that I can see," replied Boucicault, again by his own account and with his own peculiar blend of naiveté and opportunism, "but to change the period of my play, say, to the present day."[15] The result was a play that was melodramatic and included sensation scenes (in a dungeon, atop a cliff), but also, as set in the present time, like *The Octoroon,* had a more immediate political edge than a historical piece was likely to provide. Played out against a backdrop of Sligo ruins, the plot follows the return to Ireland of Robert Ffolliott, who was transported to Australia for Fenian crimes. His return is expected by his fiancée, Arte O'Neal, and by his sister, Claire Ffolliott, as well as by the young and well-intentioned Captain Molineux of the English army. The Ffolliott family estate is being usurped by Corry Kinchela, the villain who caused Ffolliott's transportation and also has designs on his fiancée. The catalyst to subsequent developments is Conn the Shaughraun, whose combination of charm and delinquency vexes both his mother and his love, Moya. As was true of actual negotiations at the time of the production, in the play some convicted Fenians are eligible for pardon, and in a suitably complicated series of complications, Ffolliott, in order to be free, must reconstitute himself a prisoner, while Kinchela, to complete his designs, must appear to free Ffolliott. Conn guides Ffolliott through myriad perils and apparently sacrifices his own life. At Conn's wake, Molineux exposes Kinchela. Ffolliott is pardoned and wed to Arte O'Neale. Molineux and Claire Ffolliott receive permission from Robert to marry. Conn, not dead after all, rises from his funeral bier, implores advice from the audience, and vows to mend his ways by beginning family life with Moya.

The comic structure and reuse of his own well-established stage persona might suggest willful escapism and commercial pandering, but only by very narrow contemporary criteria. Boucicault published his own justification. Shortly after the success of *The Shaughraun,* he described his position on art and audience in an essay on "The Decline of the Drama" in the influential *North American Review.* There he reiterated his lifelong complaint about newspaper critics, a position much like the contemporary one, in familiar terms. If drama "has descended below the level at which it ought to have rested," he wrote, "it owes its further decline to the destructive influence of the newspaper press."[16] On this occasion he based his complaint on the plausible ground of conflict of interest: "the theatres occupy a large space in the advertising columns of the press, and the newspaper is a commercial, not a literary enterprise. So the proprietor must take care of his customers, and the hired scribe writes as he is bid" (243). What is not at all contemporary about his position, however, is his belief in drama as an indicator rather than instigator of public sentiment, a product rather than a producer of social consensus. "Critics have failed to reflect," he wrote, "that drama is the necessary product of the age in which it lives, of which it is the moral, social, and physical expression" (236). In Boucicault's age comedy and formula did not prohibit political commentary any more than the propriety of *The Octoroon* prevented the contemporary critic from understanding its indictment of slavery. The figure of Boucicault is a useful reminder that placing audience over the artist does not prohibit political provocation. Boucicault understood this in terms that were from the marketplace, not romance: "There are three constituent factors in the drama; the author who writes, the actor who performs, and the public that receives. Of these three the public is the most important, for it calls into existence the other two as infallibly as demand creates supply" (245).

The age and scene help explain Boucicault's role and the importance of *The Shaughraun*. From the distance of half a century, the theater historian Montrose J. Moses characterized American theater in the 1870s as dominated by a small group of managers, including Lester Wallack; of having a small number of male stars, including H.J. Montague, who would play Captain Molineux; and as having as its "most spectacular playwright" Dion Boucicault, "who was turning out plays with surprising ease." He described legitimate theater fare in New York as balanced between melodrama, mainly French, and domestic comedies, mainly English.[17] None of this suggests a market for Fenian plays, but Boucicault's relish for contemporary events may help explain why "The Boyne Water" became *The Shaughraun*. In 1870 and in 1871, the Irish population in New York erupted into violence greater than any since the Draft Riots during the American Civil War. Against a scene of spreading American nativism, the Irish rioted in both years on July 12, the anniversary of William of Orange's crossing of the Boyne River and rout of Stuart protectors of Catholic Ireland. In 1870 the Protestant celebratory parade, from The Cooper Union on the Bowery uptown to Elm Park on the upper West Side, was chased by Catholic laborers, widely termed "armed Fenians," who eventually fired guns on the paraders, causing eight deaths. In 1871 the same parade was guarded by a large police force that fired into rioting spectators and caused a general uproar that left sixty-eight dead.[18] Thus a Fenian play had a place if a playwright was, as Boucicault claimed in his autobiographical essay, more interested in "the actual, the contemporaneous" than in "the poetic and romantic." Nor, in New York, did such a play have to take its most obvious theatrical form. One contemporary not mentioned by

Moses was Ned Harrigan, who in the 1880s was praised by William Dean Howells, then in search of an American drama, as "our one original."[19] The original had among his earliest works a burlesque parody of Boucicault called "Arrah-na-Brogue." On July 15, 1873, roughly the anniversary of the Orange Riots, Harrigan performed in his first Mulligan Guard sketch, launching a long cycle of sketches and plays, performed with his partner Tony Hart, that parodied the whole notion of parades and concomitant loyalties. Harrigan and Hart, both Americans, were popular for Irish American roles, but they had just as many sketches about other ethnicities, especially German, and roles for blackface. Harrigan was a solo performer when he built a theater of his own in 1890. No more successful than Brougham, he leased it away five years later, and as the Garrick Theatre it became homebase for the "Shaw cult" after the turn of the century.[20]

Boucicault's treatment of Fenians, *The Shaughraun*, opened on Saturday night, November 14, 1874. On the side of low culture, this was the date of the widely noted extension into its thirtieth week of P.T. Barnum's "entertainment" at the Hippodrome on Sixth Avenue. On the side of high culture, this date marked a performance of a *Merchant of Venice* at the Fifth Avenue Theatre by Edwin Booth as part of his engagement in a number of Shakespearean roles. Against these, Wallack's Theatre promised in its playbill "an entirely New and Original Play, in 3 Acts, illustrative of Irish Life and Character." The outline of the action promised fifteen scenes in those three acts, along with some original Irish airs, some familiar ones, and Strauss's new waltz "Du Du."[21] In the days following his "Dear Laura" letter to Miss Keene, Boucicault defended the title of the play, which Wallack found mystifying, and insisted on this Hiberno-English neologism about vagrancy. Further, he created a production that was particularly impressive in stage machinery, notably a descending mechanism to create the illusion of Conn ascending a prison tower wall. This device was physically demanding on himself. His first biographer, Townsend Walsh, describes how in this production Boucicault, "at the age of fifty-five or thereabout," was required

> to jump in and out of cabin windows, to scale prison walls
> that revolved in full view of the audience apparently without
> human agency (would that all Irish prisons were constructed
> on this plan!), to climb over abbey ruins and execute a "back

fall" down a precipitous "run" after being "stretched out" and "waked" as a genuine corpse, to come to life for a hand-to-hand encounter with a pair of ruffians; and finally, from the inside of a barrel, shoot through the bung-hole at the arch villain Corry Kinchela, and afterward place the barrel over the colleen Moya, thereby concealing her from view.[22]

All this action was performed at a very brisk pace, and the performance was repeated 143 times in this world-premiere run. On opening night, according to a frequently repeated tale, Boucicault discovered himself to have attended to all details except his own costume. In one of his several versions of this story, two hours before curtain (five hours before in another version), Boucicault demanded of his dresser:

> "Have you got an old red hunting-coat? Where is your *Tony Lumpkin* dress? Surely you have a Goldfinch coat?"
> "But, sir, they will not fit."
> "That is just what I want. Tear the arms to make them shorter; slit up the back—so. What have you there? *Tony Lumpkin's* hunting cap?—black velvet—the very thing! Tear the lining out. I see a splendid pair of old boots yonder."
> "Those are not a pair, sir."
> "So much the better."[23]

Thus was dressed the stage Irishman, and this was much better received than Ada Dyas's entrance as Arte O'Neal in costume that seemed to most rather grand even for genteel poverty. By all accounts Boucicault received a standing ovation when he entered with the words, "There's somebody talking about me,"[24] and proceeded into a long speech about how Conn had not stolen Squire Foley's horse, as it might appear, but how Squire Foley's horse had stolen Conn's character. On opening night there were special problems in the final scene of Act II, a short one at "the ruins of St. Bridget's Abbey" (220) designed to resolve the action before an intermission. First, the generic Celtic scene of moonlight and shimmering waters, actually sequined fabric reflecting stage lights, the sort of scene Shaw deplored, was marred when the stagehands broke the glass moon. The audience, however, applauded in amusement when the screen rose and the waters shimmered beneath a total lunar eclipse. Second, the end of the scene did not resolve the action plainly enough.

Boucicault wanted the curtain to fall on two gunshots, already established—and well, he thought—to signify that Robert Ffolliott had escaped. On opening night, the shots rang out, but the curtain fell on silence. In subsequent performances the scene was lengthened with some dialogue allowing Kinchela to groan helpfully, "Tis Robert Ffolliott escaped!" (221) and "the curtain thereupon descended upon deafening applause."[25] The final curtain on opening night got that sort of applause, and Boucicault as both star and playwright gave a speech humbly thanking all associated with the production, especially the scenic designers, and all who attended.

These reports on illusionism, including costume, scenic machinery, and timing, in reference to an effort to introduce Irish material to the American stage constitute a consistent problem that the Irish play in New York illustrates especially well. It is the problem of distinguishing what is "real" from what is not, and this difficulty will underlie many disagreements and disturbances in the reception, for example, of Synge's *Playboy of the Western World* in New York. Boucicault's announced purpose, as declared long ago on the opening of *The Colleen Bawn,* was to introduce "material gathered from my native country." The manner in which he introduced it, however, was the "sensation scene," in that play a spectacular rescue from drowning in a sea of blue cloth, which was fundamentally at odds with communication of documentary information. The contrary quality of this effort to provide the real and the unreal was evident in the newspaper notices for *The Shaughraun.* For the *New York Times,* Boucicault's praiseworthy accomplishment was in realism, and that was an innovation: "He has created an Irish drama, and almost driven the old-fashioned rough-and-tumble Irishman from the stage. The caricature has gone. The portrait from nature has been substituted in its stead." In the mind of this newspaper, Boucicault had "depicted to us Ireland and Irishmen as they are," and this accuracy was especially welcome because "here we chiefly know the Irish through the medium of very bad domestic servants and political followers of 'Boss Kelly.'"[26] However, to the *New York Daily Tribune,* Boucicault's praiseworthy accomplishment was in romance, and that was an exercise in embellishment.

> Its story, characters, and treatment are Irish. Its persons are ten in number, exclusive of soldiers and other mechanic figures, and these are contrasted with equal force and skill.

The types of character are old, but they are generic, and they are presented in a novel manner. The framework of the plot is also old, but this too is so garlanded with the fresh flowers of Mr. Boucicault's invention that nobody sees its ancient rafters, or, on seeing them, would ask for new ones.

To this newspaper, the "material" of Boucicault's native land was incidental, and the sprucing up of familiar roles welcome: "The story is one of adventure: the characters typify virtue and vice in violent opposition, and those of the heroic mold are softened and endeared by generosity, quaintness, and sweetness."[27]

To no less a witness than Henry James, whose notice appeared near the end of the run of *The Shaughraun,* the play was equally realist and romanticist, and the question of aesthetic preference was superseded by the importance of entertainment. James appeared to lament the disinterest of the public in realism: in "the expectation of seeing the mirror held up to nature as it knows nature—of seeing a reflection of its actual, local, immediate physiognomy." Instead, James reported, "the images may be true to an original or not; the public doesn't care. It has gone to look and listen, to laugh and cry—not to think." Yet he, too, ceased to care. Commenting that dramatists seeking "types" seek "first of all in the land of brogue and 'bulls,'" James observed that "a cynic," though apparently not him, "might say that it is our privilege to see Irish types enough in the sacred glow of our domestic hearths, and that it is therefore rather cruel to condemn us to find them so inveterately in that consoling glamour of the footlights." James, in his lofty fashion, chose to join the general public in expectations and in verdict. "There is no particular writing in it, but there is an infinite amount of acting, of scene-shifting, and of liveliness generally, and all this goes on to the tune of the finest feelings possible. Love, devotion, self-sacrifice, humble but heroic bravery, and brimming Irish *bonhomie* and irony, are the chords that are touched. . . . It was his happy thought to devise a figure which should absolutely, consummately, and irresistibly please. It has pleased."[28]

Boucicault thought his endeavor much more in line with the one described in the *Times,* and he thought this was a matter of importance greater than entertainment. He remembered James's comments, and seven years later in the *Boston Gazette* described his continuing efforts to raise Irish characters above a "low sensational class" of play because

"there is no force in nature so great as the *vis inertia* of concrete ignorance." He used as example when "Mr. James said, 'we have quite
enough of Ireland and the Irish in reality, without requiring the aid of
fiction to bring the subject to our minds.'"[29] In the century since, New
York has been schooled in the vexed question of "the Irish in reality"
by a succession of Irish playwrights, each revising the previous lesson,
and by a succession of critical responses, each revising the idea of the
"real" on stage. As both the immediate and the subsequent reception
of *The Shaughraun* shows, Boucicault's combination of the sensational
and the documentary, the unreal and the real, made it possible to ig-
nore one or the other, and most often in the nineteenth century the
sensational proved the superior attraction. Boucicault, by example more
than by dictum, demonstrated the impasse between realism and ro-
manticism and so established in wary successors a suspicion of clash-
ing elements.

The *Shaughraun*'s immediate reception was totally positive, even
from camps as different as competing newspapers and the imperious
Henry James. Among his own playwright competitors, the play was
noteworthy enough to inspire two plagiarized versions during Boucicault's own first run. In January, John F. Poole opened *The Shockraun*
at the Olympic Theatre on Broadway, a house that was formerly Laura
Keene's Varieties and was at that moment in its last days as a musical
and variety theater. On the same night, at the Comique, Josh Hart, a
noted vaudeville manager, opened *The Skibbeah,* or "hangman," with
Ned Harrigan and Tony Hart in the cast. The result was another lawsuit, eventually decided in Boucicault's favor because the copies were
so close they could not claim to be burlesques. Little of particular interest emerged from the proceedings other than Harrigan's song on the
subject:

> We'll find out who wrote Shakespeare
> If we don't it isn't our fault
> Twas wrote by Poole and Buffalo Bill
> And claimed by Boucicault.[30]

In general significance, however, the imitations are good indications of
Boucicault's success with segments of the audience other than reviewers.

George Odell's cautious *Annals* put the New York receipts at about a quarter million dollars, with many records for single-show profits. Townsend Walsh, an ardent advocate, put Boucicault's personal profits in New York and elsewhere at more than half a million.[31] Another sort of praise appeared in the form of an the extravagant ceremony at Wallack's on the night of the last performance, Saturday, March 6, 1875. Joined by local dignitaries and presided over by a Judge Brady, the company was given a post-performance banquet onstage that lasted until after midnight, with the audience patiently waiting in the seats for presentations. Nearby was a gift to Boucicault shrouded in a green cloth decorated with the Celtic harp; unveiled later, it proved to be a statue of Tatters, Conn's offstage dog. After many introductions and a long speech from the Judge, Boucicault, in his own long speech to a packed audience, said, "You offer me the most honorable distinction to which any artist can aspire, and that is the assurance of his fellow citizens that they perceive in his works, together with something that is sweet, something that is good." Later, in appropriately high melodramatic style, he added, "Let me disclaim any pretension as an actor to excel others in the delineation of the Irish character. It is the Irish character as misrepresented by the English dramatists that I convict as a libel."[32] Boucicault's position as an artist here is wholly contemporary in literary Anglophobia and implicit condemnation of critics who praise English dramatists, or, for that matter, American imitators. However, the opinion is distinctly antique in its celebration of audience and audience support. Subsequent Irish playwrights in New York, beginning with Shaw, favored the method of instructing the audience by antagonizing it. In subsequent chapters, particularly the reception in New York of Shaw, Synge, and Joyce, the justice department, successors to Judge Brady, will appear, but as enemies, not masters of ceremony.

By contemporary standards, instruction by ingratiation rather than by antagonism is proof positive of the banal and the mercenary. Very recently, such performances as Boucicault's at Wallacks on the closing in 1875 have been called "premeditated blarney" and "bootlicking." The question of Finianism in *The Shaughraun* has been dismissed because "the story turns less on the Fenian movement . . . than it does on the extrication of love from mortgage payments."[33] But this is anachronistic criticism. The place of *The Shaughraun* in the tradition is the addition of a Fenian plot, a contemporary controversy, to the conventions of love and money, and thus the direct address of the work to current events and the immediate concerns of the audience, Irish, Irish

American, or American, all of whom were witnesses to the Orange Riots in New York and to international news. David Krause seems fairer when he observes of the Fenian plot that "if any playwright had dared to treat this incendiary subject seriously in 1874, he and his play would certainly have been suppressed as an incitement to riot."[34] Boucicault was at pains to articulate his belief that introduction of current political issues in ingratiating rather than confrontational terms *was* serious. This engagement with audience expectations was, incidentally, a manner Boucicault limited to theater. He was much more confrontational in personal style and in extratheatrical forms of publicity. For the London production of 1876, he published an open letter to Prime Minister Benjamin Disraeli noting that "the work is founded on an episode in the Fenian insurrection of 1866" and that a general pardon for Fenians "is the *Deus ex machina* of the drama." Stating in the letter that "the theatre has been acknowledged a sensitive test of public opinion," Boucicault attributed his play to the question of whether "the English people have begun to forgive the offense" of the Fenian campaign and attributed its success to an audience answer to the question in the affirmative.[35] That is the particular political intent of *The Shaughraun,* and it is presented, in the denouement of the play, as an action asked of England without reciprocal concession by Ireland. The conclusion is not assimilation of Irish into British society, but absorption of the British presence (Molineux) into Irish society. The story turns on the Fenian movement, a subject that did not lend itself to bootlicking.

Moreover, the politics of the text of *The Shaughraun* were especially pointed for the New York audience, which, as an effect of its predominantly Irish Catholic demography, tended to expect in Irish works a republican sentiment. Early in Act I, Molineux, improbably enough for a British officer, announces the imminent landing of a "distinguished Fenian hero" (177). Early in Act II, the villainous Corry Kinchela announces his confidence that Ffolliott's guard will respond quickly and brutally to any escape: "The late attack on the police-van at Manchester, and the explosion at Clerkenwell prison in London will warrant extreme measures" (200). These fabled names of Fenian attacks, Manchester and Clerkenwell, could expect to arouse in New York a frightened but steadfastly pro-Irish, anti-British response. In Boucicault's play, however, the melodrama is not intent on casting political issues into English/Irish divisions or on underscoring the sense of fracture that at a later date may be, for many, requisite. *The Shaughraun* is, instead, intent on melodramatizing forms of internal betrayal, of Irish betrayal of Irish, which is for many, both now and then, politically incorrect. Kinchela, pure villain, is an Irish squire, and his loathsome assistant, Harvey Duff, is a local perjurer. Kinchela's comment on Manchester and Clerkenwell predicts extreme measures, not from the British army, but from the Royal Irish Constabulary, the local police. This distinction between the soldiers, including Molineux, and the constabulary runs throughout the play text. When Conn's mother believes him dead, she says, "It is the polis, not the sodgers, murthered him" (22). In the end, it proves that Ffolliott's real enemy, and presumably the enemy of his cause, is not the soldiery, and not even the constabulary. Conn is clearest: "those smugglin' thieves, Mangan, Sullivan, and Reilly; they are guidin' the polis—the mongrel curs go do that!" (217). Though it has political absurdities enough, such as Ffolliott's un-Fenian disdain for violence, *The Shaughraun* is quite effective as portrayal of internal betrayal. Whether seen as compromising the Irish cause for foreign consumption, or as elevating Irish heroism by emphasizing obstacles, the result is a melodramatic representation of more than love and mortgage payments and a representation rather different from ones most likely to please the local audience

There are other forms of complexity in *The Shaughraun* that bear comparison with contemporary Irish plays. The opening scene, in which Molineux introduces himself to Claire Ffolliott, is a good example of comic reversal of advantage and power: using a churn as prop, the British officer, politically and militarily in command, is rendered foolish, while the Irish woman, dispossessed, is rendered authoritative. *The Shaughraun* makes much of perceived stereotypes, usually in Molineux's commentaries on "you Irish," but equally often by Irish characters, such as Claire, referring to Molineux: "How confused he is. That's a good fellow, although he is an Englishman" (178). In this fashion the play does establish divisions, ones that are quite contemporary in sensibility of images, projections, and alterity. One prominent form of division is language. In the first scene Claire plays peasant to the stranger:

MOLINEUX: Is this place called Swillabeg?
CLAIRE: No; it is called Shoolabeg.
MOLINEUX: Beg pardon; your Irish names are so unpronounceable. You see, I'm an Englishman.

CLAIRE: I remarked your misfortune. Poor creature, you couldn't help it.
MOLINEUX: I do not regard it as a misfortune.
CLAIRE: Got accustomed to it, I suppose. Were you born so?

.   .   .

CLAIRE (*starting away*): What are you doing?
MOLINEUX: Tasting the brogue. Stop, my dear; you forget the crown I promised you. Here it is. (*he hands her the money*) Don't hide your blushes, they become you.
CLAIRE: Never fear—I'll be even wid your honour yet. Don't let—(*up to porch*)—the butther spoil while I'm gone. (*going, and looking at card*) What's your name again—Milligrubs?
MOLINEUX: No; Molineux.
CLAIRE: I ax your pardon. You see, I'm Irish, and the English names are so unpronounceable. [176]

These divisions are ultimately resolved in the play. Claire marries Molineux. Rapprochement on the stage does not in itself prevent representation of cultural relations, such as colonizer and colonized, with some complexity. Nor does reconciliation as an ending prove the drama a simple sop to the audience on artistic and on political levels.

That passage suggests some of the similarities between *The Shaughraun* and Brian Friel's *Translations*. Set in Donegal in a historical past, 1833, *Translations* takes as issue the English ordinance survey and its project to Anglicize Irish place names. In *Translations,* the Irish characters are peasants, the British are soldiers, and the divisions could not be more clearly marked. In Friel's play the young and well-intentioned British role is taken by Lieutenant Yolland, who, like Molineux, is rendered comical and foolish against the superior powers of the Irish, whose qualifications are demonstrated in purloined equipment, wit, and especially in polylinguality (Greek and Latin, though no English). Yolland (English only, no Latin, no Greek, no Irish) plays a role like that of Molineux, as in this conversation with Owen, the local son now in service to the Anglicizers:

OWEN: Now. We have we got to? Yes—the point where the stream enters the sea—that tiny little beach there. George!
YOLLAND: Yes. I'm listening. What do you call it? Say the

Irish name again?

OWEN: Bun na hAbhann.

YOLLAND: Again.

OWEN: Bun na hAbhann.

YOLLAND: Bun na hAbhann.

OWEN: That's terrible, George.

YOLLAND: I know. I'm sorry. Say it again.

OWEN: Bun na hAbhann.

YOLLAND: Bun na hAbhann.

OWEN: That's better. Bun is the Irish word for bottom. And Abha means river. So it's literally the mouth of the river.

YOLLAND: Let's leave it alone. There's no English equivalent for a sound like that.[36]

In *Translations,* the form of betrayal is not Irish deceit to other Irish but English seduction of Irish, of Irish-speaking characters aiding the English campaign. The weak include Owen and Maire, whose ambitions make the bilingual status of English and Irish more valuable than the Irish alone. Thus Yolland, who speaks no Irish, walks out with Maire, who speaks no English, in a romantic scene scarcely less melodramatic than any in Boucicault's play. The obvious difference between the plays is the outcome. Whereas in *The Shaughraun* the Fenian pardon is obtained and the pairs of characters are betrothed, in *Translations* punishment swiftly follows the moment of apparent reconciliation between English male and Irish female: Yolland dies for romancing a local woman, the British army responds brutally, and the figure of local responsibility throughout, Hugh the schoolmaster, capitulates to the new order: "We must learn those new names." The final resolution in *Translations* is a defeat, and the final word is "downfall."[37] The final line in *The Shaughraun* is "Hurroo! Hurroo!" (238).

The Irish dramatist of victory has only with difficulty been assimilated into a subsequent dramatic tradition that celebrates fracture. Over time, Boucicault has been increasingly a troubling presence, at once admirable and deplorable, much like Conn the Shaughraun. In Oscar Wilde's time, Boucicault was a desirable association. Wilde's first production in America, *Vera,* was to have been managed by Boucicault, but it was postponed in a period of wariness of plays about rebellion and assassination, Boucicault's *metier.* During his tour in America in 1881-82, ostensibly to explain the phenomenon of aestheticism, Wilde made some fuss over "my friend" Dion Boucicault, sought his help in managing the journalistic press, and took a lesson in ingratiating the audience by consistently referring to Ireland as "Niobe of nations" and adding to his repertoire of lectures a very positive exposition on "The Irish Poets of 1848."[38] Shaw, in his turn, famously derided Boucicault's representation of Ireland while borrowing stage devices, most conspicuously importing courtroom devices from *Arrah-na-Pogue* into *The Devil's Disciple*. For John Millington Synge, *The Shaughraun*, in particular, illuminates the whole project of the Irish Literary Theatre and its descendants. On a revival in 1904, Synge wrote that "some recent performances of *The Shaughraun* at the Queen's Theatre in Dublin have enabled local playgoers to make an interesting comparison between the methods of the early Irish melodrama and those of the Irish National Theatre Society. It is unfortunate for Dion Boucicault's fame that the absurdity of his plots and pathos has gradually driven people of taste away from his plays." Against these "people of taste," Synge praised the influence of Boucicault for preserving "traditional comedy of the Irish stage" and countering "the reaction against the careless Irish humour of which everyone has had too much."[39] One acknowledged landmark of modern Irish drama, cited by Brian Friel as epitomizing "rude involvement" of exactly the kind Boucicault lacked, was the first performance of *The Playboy of the Western World* in 1907. In fact, the Abbey Theatre had opened that season with a *conversatione* that featured Frank Fay reading W.B. Yeats's "Death of Cuchulain" and a performance by Joseph Holloway, noted diarist of the Irish national theater, of Conn the Shaughraun's set piece about Squire Foley's stolen horse and his own stolen character. In the audience was Synge's nephew Edward Stephens, who favored the Boucicault piece and recalled wondering "whether laughing could become dangerous."[40]

In his autobiographies, Sean O'Casey, also cited by Friel, frequently charts developments in his own literary life against Boucicault, beginning with his description in *Pictures in the Hallway* of playing Father Dolan in *The Shaughraun* at Mechanics Hall, the building that would become the Abbey Theatre. For O'Casey, as for Synge, Boucicault was a furtive allegiance opposed to "people of taste." Later, in *Inishfallen Fare Thee Well*, when lionized by party-goers as representing the new tradition in Irish drama, "Sean whispered the names of Shaw and Strindberg, which they didn't seem to catch, though he instinctively kept firm silence about Dion Boucicault, whose works he knew as well as Shakespeare's." When subsequently condemned as traitor to tradition, O'Casey leaves Dublin between the opposing landmarks of the Irish Literary Theatre and Boucicault: "wheeling into Brunswick Street, passing the Queen's Theatre where Sean had seen his first play *The Shaughraun;* past the Ancient Concert Rooms, where the National Theatre performed some of its early plays, before it had a habitation or even a name. It was this street that had been Sean's via dolorosa."[41] Synge in 1904 and O'Casey in retrospect indicate a particular and long-standing ambivalence toward the Irish National Theatre and the enterprise that has come to dominate the national drama. That is an element in the history of modern Irish drama that is lost when Boucicault is excluded from the tradition. It is an element of subversiveness, of allegiance to low culture rather than high culture, and greater interest in the engaged audience than in the purity of high art.

This silent and secretive reference of things to Boucicault and to his taboo success are especially well rendered by James Joyce in *Ulysses,* where Leopold Bloom, authority on low culture, including "The Wearing of the Green," *Lily of Killarney,* and other ephemera and by-products of Boucicault, thinks, while wandering Dublin in the Lestrygonians episode, that "Corny Kelleher he has Harvey Duff in his eye" and later fondly recalls the Queen's Theatre and the "Dion Boucicault business with his harvestmoon face."[42] Things change, and after a general decline in the eyes of Irish writers, Boucicault has made something of a comeback. After the 1970s, in the 1990s, with its twenty years of difference in local political context, Boucicault has reappeared in Irish cultural politics as a politicist, full of rude involvement, and enemy of colonialism. In *The Field Day Anthology of Irish Literature* of 1991, Boucicault reappears as a playwright whose "underlying political rationale in his work is confirmed by his strong nationalist sentiments." His "spectacular scenes" have also been rediscovered: "Bouci-cault's Irish plays were characterized by spectacular stage-settings which allowed him to exploit the dramatic—and subversive—potential of Irish scenery with its many historical and political associations."[43] The suggestion of the word *exploit* preserves the suspicion of Boucicault's success, of "the Dion Boucicault business." But the dimension of reconciliation—both in *The Shaughraun,* between the English and the Irish, and in the playwright, between the artist and the audience—remains obscure in the 1990s. Boucicault's utility has been rediscovered by making him over in the image of contemporary Irish politics, which, despite widespread rhetoric, accepts only adversarial relations and does not conceive reconciliation as anything but a myth.

Back in New York in 1899, the year that the Irish Literary Theatre was launched in Dublin, Townsend Walsh was eulogizing Boucicault, who died in 1890, for the readers of *The Gael*. Walsh insisted that "these plays, in spite of the sneers of the litterateurs, constitute our national Irish drama. While Mr. W.B. Yeats and Mr. John Eglinton are discussing literary ideals in Ireland, the crown still belongs to Boucicault." The whole question of Yeats, Eglinton, others, and the essays circulated as *Literary Ideals in Ireland* will underlie the reception of the Abbey players in New York in 1911. But in 1899, for Walsh, what constituted the literary accomplishments of Boucicault plays in New York were not flatteries for the local audience but challenges, "rude involvement." In the course of praising Boucicault, Walsh told his readers that "*The Shaughraun* will always give offense, not because the wake is such an outrageous caricature, but because it tends to ridicule a sincere Celtic rite." Similarly, Boucicault "was not blind to the faults of his countrymen, and some of his best art was expended on the delineation of the dark and tragic figure of the traitor and informer," especially Harvey Duff, "the type of informer common during Fenian times."[44] For Walsh, Boucicault's accomplishment was not nationalist sentiment but direct engagement of his audience on terms that were not platitudes.

In New York, over time, neither the plays nor the playwright fared any better than in Dublin. The things that the plays could not surpass were the tendencies to force work to its lowest level by imitation. Boucicault gave New York the Irish play, and Henry James's worst fears were fulfilled: the Irish types were inveterately on stage. One good example of how they appeared on stage is *Emerald Isle; or, The Caves of Carrig-Cleena,* a production at the Herald Square Theatre in 1902 that was written by Arthur Sullivan and Edward German and so was another in the tradition of Irish plays by non-Irish authors. Brooks McNamara's book *The Shuberts of Broadway* reproduces the opening page of the prompt-book. The first chorus begins with whispers:

Have ye heard the brave news that is goin' around?
Do ye mane that Blind Murphy's owld pig has been
    found?
Sure, it's better than what ye mane, I'll be bound—
Are ye spakin' of Terence O'Brian at all?

The "girls" of the chorus then dance to the lyric: "And it's Terence has sent us a warnin' to say / He is secretly coming among us to-day." The "men" then come forward, snapping fingers, "shillelaghs up," and sing: "And the Saxons may send us to Botany Bay, / But it's Ireland that's ready to answer his call!"[45] Such were the fortunes of that Irish type, the rebel, descended from Robert Ffolliott. He had come up in the world, for Terence O'Brian returns to woo the daughter of the Lord Lieutenant of Ireland, but has also become rather distant from the Irish "materials" Boucicault took as inspiration. Two years later, in 1904, when Shaw brought *John Bull's Other Island* to New York, there was good reason to explode the Irish types that proliferated far beyond Bouci-cault's direct influence. The reputation of the playwright suffered, not from what he had done, but from the effect of what he had done. The influential American critic William Winter's opinion of Boucicault's reputation is a brief paradigm of the larger pattern of reconciliation and repudiation apparent in his career and in his posthumous career. Boucicault actively courted Winter, thus violating the law against consorting with the enemy. He wrote Winter poems: "O Winter, thou'rt well nam'd, for thou dost come / But once a year. How, in these piping times, / Have we not long'd for thee, thou Genial Soul!" In response, Winter alternately patronized and condemned. Shortly after quoting that poem, Winter, in 1908, commented that Boucicault's "voice was singularly dry and hard, and yet it could well convey the accent of bland, persuasive, sagacious Irish blarney." In the same context, Winter wrote: "Dion Boucicault, as a man, was vain, self-indulgent, shallow, fickle, and weak. Also, like some other Irishmen of renown, he was unfortunate in a propensity to strife."[46] Curiously, the description fits Conn the Shaughraun quite well, and so what was acceptable in New York in an Irish stage character was not acceptable in an Irish man. There was a boundary beyond which subversiveness was not to extend. Boucicault was content to live within that limit. His successors as Irish playwrights in New York were not. There would be a rising trend in vanity and self-indulgence, a victory of sorts for the playwright, and a narrowing of audience, surely a loss of sorts for all involved.

2

THE BERNARD SHAW CULT,
NEW YORK, 1905

In the fall of 1905, Bernard Shaw was one of the most newsworthy names in New York. The man remained in England, but the figure of the playwright was well established in America as that "Irish smut dealer." He was widely cited in New York as the object of a cult, and from abroad Shaw managed his affairs to cultivate the cult. Within a single month, he discovered on the New York stage the liabilities of departing from Irish stereotypes and the benefits of courting infamy. The first lesson was learned from a production of *John Bull's Other Island,* a play with Irish subject matter, and the second from a production of *Mrs Warren's Profession,* the world premiere of an Irish playwright's work on non-Irish material. Both productions illustrate very well Shaw's advance, of sorts, over Boucicault. In New York Boucicault labored to satisfy and to engage the largely Irish American audience he found flocking to his Irish plays. A quarter century later, Shaw manipulated and titillated an audience he planned, at least, to recruit selectively and to screen. As it happened, an unintended result of that selection process was attraction of a rather louche segment of the American audience with which Shaw did not wish to be associated. Nevertheless, thanks to Shaw the process of selecting an audience was well along on its evolution to what would become the active recruitment of a mostly upper-crust American audience by the Irish Players on their first exploration of the New World in 1911.

The Shaw episode of 1905 has sometimes been reconstructed differently—often as a grave conflict between the forces of repression with the iconoclastic and ultimately victorious artist. The record is otherwise. It suggests, instead, a very conventional, rather than Shavian, comedy. The forces of repression were led by Anthony Comstock, who dubbed Shaw the "Irish smut dealer." But Comstock resembles the representatives of the older generation of comedy, feeble and finally unsuccessful in opposition. Shaw himself claimed to be representative of youth against Comstock as age, and his cause was ultimately rewarded. But, as in the comic denouement, the vindication of the Shaw play largely defanged and institutionalized it, neutralizing its proclaimed reformist intention. The artist antagonizing the audience did not achieve his desired effect. The New York Court of the Special Sessions, which would later deliberate over a subsequent Irish playwright in New York, James Joyce, presented the best general verdict on Shaw's work as staged in New York in October 1905. The court found, in a decision to be examined later in this chapter, that "the reforming influence of the play is minimized by the method of attack."

The year 1905 began auspiciously for the Shaw play in New York. In January, *You Never Can Tell* was produced at the Garrick Theatre by Arnold Daly, a born New Yorker, a former office boy for Charles Frohman, and, in this production, the player of Valentine. It was Daly's fourth Shaw production in four years and his first at the Garrick, a newer and more imposing site than his previous ones. Shaw was very well received, Daly reasonably well received, and the rest of the production dismissed. The *New York Times* called the production "distinctly a triumph for Bernard Shaw" and noted that Daly excelled at a task "made especially difficult by reason of the fact that the actress cast for the opposite role was utterly lacking int he requisite experience." The review offered a general exposition on Shaw and quoted with approval Shaw's explanation in the preface to *Plays Pleasant and Unpleasant:* "It is one thing to give the theatre what it wants and quite another for the theatre to do what it wants." The *Times* reviewer then attempted a comparable aphorism: "In the laws of the drama, there is none which is more important than that which demands that the people on the stage and not the audience shall be the ones in doubt as to motive and action."[1] In retrospect, both remarks seem prescient about Shaw productions in New York in this year. The theater would find itself able but momentarily prohibited from doing what it wanted precisely because the audience was not in any doubt as to motive and action on the stage.

By 1905 Shaw was already a known and rather revered figure in the American theater world, especially in New York. There, according to his first American biographer, Archibald Henderson, Shaw's work drew two kinds of spectators: "regular playgoers who sought and found amusement and entertainment; and genuine lovers of the higher forms of drama."[2] In 1894 the mercurial and controversial Richard Mansfield salvaged his own career with the first American production of Shaw, of *Arms and the Man,* and in 1897 Mansfield had a subsequent success performing Dick Dudgeon in *The Devil's Disciple.* Brooks Atkinson's history of Broadway attributes Shaw's commitment to become a professional dramatist to the profits from these American productions. Flush with their success, Mansfield had taken over Harrigan's Theatre on Thirty-fifth Street and, against the agreement with financially troubled Ned Harrigan, renamed it the Garrick both to flatter himself and to minimize signage redesign. His career was collapsing, however, and with it the exclusive American access to Shaw's work. As Atkinson recounts it: "Although Shaw wrote *The Man of Destiny* for Mansfield, he reserved it for Ellen Terry and Henry Irving at the time when Mansfield was being patronizing towards Shaw. The association of Shaw and Mansfield was pleasant in the beginning, but it got chilly when Mansfield decided to have a life of his own. Shaw was not only prolific but voracious; he consumed useful people."[3]

That left an opening for Daly, who succeeded Mansfield as the principal Shaw representative in New York and as a principal tenant of the Garrick. Daly's acting career had begun with a very successful role as Chambers in a dramatization of *Pudd'nhead Wilson* in 1895. Reversing the course of Boucicault and John Brougham, Daly went to London and made his West End debut at the Garrick Theatre there. There he also discovered Shaw's *Plays Pleasant and Unpleasant,* which was published in 1898. It inspired the founding member of the New York Shaw cult. By 1903 Daly was back in New York, performing in Clyde Fitch's *Major Andre* and organizing a group of performers interested in the kind of intellectual, literary theater associated with Shaw. He joined with Winchell Smith as business manager and staged as trial matinees, on his own personal investment, *Candide.* Daly played Marchbanks, according to one notice, in a fashion "suggestive of Shelley in social sentiments and of Keats in appearance."[4] Truly a former apprentice to Frohman, Daly saw matters in terms other than purely aesthetic: "At the first matinee I lost all my $350, but we didn't stop. We gave another matinee. This time our losses were lighter. At the next performance we were richer by $80. Another netted $110. Then we wandered from one theatre to another, then to town-halls, above livery stables, until we could get the Berkeley Lyceum — which I rented from my old employer,

Charles Frohman — into shape for performances. Then the tide turned."[5] The production became a sensation and had an unusually long run of 150 performances at the Berkeley Lyceum, followed by a road company.

On return to New York, Daly followed *Candida* with a successful production of *Man of Destiny* in February 1904. At that point the major theatrical force Liebler and Company became Daly's producer. During the summer, he returned to England to visit Shaw and plan productions. By his own account, Daly presented Shaw with the suggestion that he write a play about Cromwell for New York: "Shaw said he thought it good, but then he raced on to suggest that we might have Charles the First come on with his head under his arm. I pointed out to Shaw that it would be highly inconvenient for a man to come on the stage with his head under his arm, even if he were an acrobat. Shaw, however, said he thought it could be done. In the end he said he would compromise: 'Write the first thirty-five minutes of that play yourself,' he said, 'and let me write the last five minutes.'"[6] Again, one sees Shaw's "advance" over Boucicault, who would rewrite it all himself, and progress toward Beckett, for whom rewrites were unthinkable. The final result of this encounter differed from the original inspiration as much as Boucicault's *Shaughraun* differed from his "Boyne Water." It was *How He Lied to Her Husband,* which Daly produced at the Berkeley Lyceum in New York in the fall of 1904. By the beginning of 1905, the *New York Evening Post,* in reference to Daly's production of *John Bull's Other Island,* referred confidently to "the most ardent worshippers of Bernard Shaw" and to "the Shaw cult in this city."[7]

Even without Cromwell as a subject, Shaw was perceived in New York as an Irish playwright. The partnership with Daly, an Irish American, reinforced the perception. One of the first attempts to describe this playwright/producer collaboration, Henderson's "Arnold Daly and Bernard Shaw" in *Arena* in 1904, introduced Shaw to American readers by reference to W.B. Yeats's denunciation of the "theatre of commerce."[8] Evocation of Yeats and association with the theater of art would become the usual introduction to New York audiences of Irish playwrights, especially Synge, Joyce, and O'Casey. It was Shaw's opponent in the debate over *Mrs Warren's Profession,* Anthony Comstock, secretary for the Society for the Suppression of Vice, who identified the playwright, in a letter to Daly, as the "Irish Smut Dealer."[9] B.H. Goldsmith's early monograph on Daly describes how "in the summer of 1904 Mr. Daly went abroad to consult with Mr. Shaw about further productions. It was only natural that the personal meeting of the two brilliant Irishmen should produce quite a lot of intellectual fireworks." Goldsmith also records Daly's later remark, after the collaboration ended, on Shaw: "Being an Irishman, he couldn't help being brilliant."[10] The reading segment of the New York Shaw cult would also know Shaw's statement in his "Preface: Mainly about Myself" to the unpleasant volume of *Plays Pleasant and Unpleasant:* "As an Irishman I could pretend to patriotism neither for the country I had abandoned nor the country that had ruined it."[11] The next Shaw-Daly collaboration in New York would take up both of these disappointments to Shaw.

The two brilliant Irishmen opened *John Bull's Other Island* at the Garrick Theatre on October 10, 1905, with Daly in the role of Larry Doyle. By the title and by construction of the play around English and Irish stereotypes, Shaw addressed the long line of plays descended from George Colman's *John Bull; or, the Englishman's Fireside* (1803). It was a line to which Boucicault had contributed his own *John Bull* in 1872 as well as his Irish plays leading to *The Shaughraun*. Until Shaw, the stereotypes were exploited cheerfully; Shaw hoped to expose them as frauds. He wrote the play for the Abbey Theatre in Dublin, but it was by various accounts either unmanageable or unacceptable for the Irish venue. Hence it found its first production in London, at the Court Theatre, in the initial 1904-5 season of the partnership of Harley Granville-Barker and John Eugene Vedrenne. On Shaw's advice, that production delayed its opening until Parliament was in session, because, as Shaw put it, "you will sell a lot of stalls to the political people; and the Irish M.P.'s will fill the pit."[12] That local audience was as pleased by Shaw's reversal of roles, of his dreamy Saxon and pragmatic Celtic characters, as previous ones had been by stereotypes fulfilled. After its scheduled run, the production was revived in February 1905 and again in September 1905, a month before Daly's New York production. The New York audience knew that in London Prime Minister Balfour attended four performances and that Edward VII, at a command performance, had in gales of laughter famously broken his chair. Apart from the contrast in the play between Broadbent the Englishman and Doyle the Irishman, the idea of a specific audience seems central to the conception of the play as Shaw described it in his "Preface for Politicians": "Writing the play for an Irish audience, I thought it would be good for them to be shewn very clearly that the loudest laugh they could raise at the expense of the absurdist Englishman was not really a laugh on their side. . . . English audiences very naturally swallowed it eagerly and smacked their lips over it, laughing all the more heartily because they felt they were taking a caricature of themselves with the most tolerant and large-minded good humor."[13] The English laughter was great enough that when the play was revived in London in 1912, Shaw distributed a statement asking the audience to laugh a little less and so stop interrupting the performance. New York City would provide a different context for the play, where the humor of the text would not work the same as for the Irish, who rejected the play, or the English, who adored it. As a neutral ground, New York could absorb the general point about stereotypes.

Intended as exposure of unexamined delusions, in this case both romantic Ireland and industrious England, *John Bull* opens in striking fashion with the appearance of Tim Haffigan, who appears to be a sly Irish rogue, much like Boucicault's Conn the Shaughraun. Then it is revealed that Haffigan is a scrounger, born in Glasgow, completely unacquainted with actual Ireland, and making a career of mugging Irishness for English providers. Haffigan is quite consciously a stage Irishman, and the first act of the play exposes the role as a fiction. It was a fiction perhaps even more epidemic in New York—onstage and offstage—than in London. It was one that Shaw associated with Boucicault, particularly with the character Myles-na-Coppaleen in *The Colleen Bawn* and the title character in *The Shaughraun,* both of which originated in New York. Writing in 1896 about a touring production of *The Colleen Bawn,* Shaw insisted: "What I mean is that Dion Boucicault, when he invented Myles, was not holding the mirror up to nature, but blarneying the British public precisely as the Irish car-driver, when he is 'cute' enough, blarneys the English tourist."[14] For Shaw, it was imperative to expose realities, and he held his mirror up to the sly rogue as well as to the priest, in this play a philosophical defrocked curate not at all like Father Dolan, and to the maiden, who in Shaw's play abandons her Irish lover for an English one. All this was essential to a project Shaw described in the preface to the play as "a very uncompromising presentment of the real old Ireland" (7).

The opening of *John Bull's Other Island* was a new phase in the continuing attempt to present the "real" Ireland on the New York stage. When John Millington Synge's *Playboy of the Western World* alarmed New York audiences in 1911 with its "realism," Shaw would repeat the point of Tim Haffigan for the *New York The Evening Sun:* "The stage Irishman of the nineteenth century, generous, drunken, thriftless, with a joke always on his lips and a sentimental tear always in his eye, was highly successful as a borrower of money from Englishmen—both in Old and New England—who indulged and despised him because he flattered their sense of superiority."[15] Like Boucicault's *The Shaughraun*, *John Bull's Other Island* presents an Englishman in a generic Irish setting, smitten by an Irish maiden, amidst real-estate intrigue. In place of a Shaughraun as center of attention, Shaw puts Larry Doyle, a model young Irish executive and not a lovable rogue at all, a clear-eyed enemy of the Irishman who "cant be intelligently political," an enemy of anyone who "dreams of what the Shan Van Vocht said in ninety-eight. If you want to interest him in Ireland youve got to call the unfortunate island Kathleen ni Hoolihan and pretend she's a little old woman" (81). In contrast, Shaw's Englishman, Tom Broadbent, must then take the role of the dreamer, thus reversing stereotypes central to the whole Victorian, Arnoldian image of Saxon and Celt. The premise, as Shaw describes it in his "Preface for Politicians," is "that the Englishman is wholly at the mercy of his imagination, having no sense of reality to check it. The Irishman, with a far subtler and more fastidious imagination, has one eye always on things as they are" (11-12). Thus it is Broadbent who is most enamored of local antiquities and Doyle who is most impatient with local dignities and dignitaries. Boucicault's Ireland resists all efforts at conquest and absorbs the foreigner. By the end of Shaw's play, Broadbent is engaged to the beautiful Nora Reilly, standing candidate for Rosscullen's MP, and planning to build a golf resort. Shaw's characteristic parable of effectuality and ineffectuality is played against the image of romantic Ireland, against a set much like ones favored by Boucicault, with the generic symbols of moon, dolmens, and round tower.

The notices on Daly's production of *John Bull* initiated a particular charge that would be made about many subsequent Irish plays in New York: it was too literary and consequently not theatrical. To the *New York Post*, Daly's *John Bull* "was not dimly dramatic" and was only "a so-called play, which actually is nothing but an exposition in six divisions of the author's views on things in general, including the Anglo-Saxon and Celtic national character, the true remedy for Irish ills, the secret of agrarian distress, and the ultimate construction of an Hibernian Utopia."[16] Many found the political context too obscure, including the *New York Dramatic Mirror*, which felt that the production "fails to please Americans, partly because they care nothing for the family quarrel between England and Erin, and especially because it is without form and void as regards dramatic structure."[17] The New York audience, however, had been quite delighted by the quarrel between England and Erin as represented earlier by Boucicault, and it will be later by the quarrel as represented by Synge and Lady Gregory. Shaw's polemic failed because his method of attack demanded an audience prepared to dismiss its romantic notion of Ireland for a current political and economic reality. Boucicault's method was to change the audience in increments; Shaw's was to attempt a complete reversal. The reforming influence was totally lost, and this was most conspicuous in the general critical delight over the scenery, especially the full moon behind the round tower and other accoutrements of romantic Ireland that the play was intended to deflate. Coincidentally, the night before *John Bull's Other Island* opened at the Garrick, Boucicault's *Rip Van Winkle*, with Thomas Jefferson, son of the great comedian and legendary performer for whom Boucicault wrote the role, opened at Wallack's, Boucicault's old haunt.

In his correspondence, Shaw noted the failure of *John Bull's Other Island* in New York, though he did not dwell on the more abusive of the printed comments, such as one that called the play "a thick glutinous and imponderable four-act tract."[18] He had his own agenda for theater audiences, one that would not permit boredom or group failure to mind the lesson. The strategy would be altering the audience by escalating rather than changing his own method of attack. By 1898 he had gathered his work into *Plays Pleasant and Unpleasant* with a Preface that recounted his favorite scandals: "I had provoked an uproar; and the sensation was so agreeable that I resolved to try again" (14). The enterprise of his *Plays Unpleasant* was "to force the spectator to face unpleasant facts" (25). Of these three plays, *Mrs Warren's Profession* would prove the most unpleasant, especially in New York, where Daly's 1905 production, in the same month as *John Bull's Other Island,* was the play's world premiere. *Mrs Warren* had been written in 1894, intended for J.T. Grein's Independent Theatre, but it could not gain the approval of the Lord Chamberlain that it was not immoral. There certainly was cause for concern, because even before performance Grein thought the play "unfit for women's ears" and likely to lead men to "insanity and suicide."[19] In London, the Stage Society, technically a private club rather than a public theater, managed, with considerable difficulty, a closed performance for its members in 1902. In 1904, a year before the New

York production and a few months after Daly's visit to Shaw, the playwright gave the producer specific instructions, especially on screening the audience. Shaw told Daly, "Mrs Warren's Profession ought not to be produced without a word of warning to keep the wrong people away from it." Further, he explained to Daly that "the play is simply a study of prostitution; and its aim is to shew that prostitution is not the prostitute's fault but the fault of a society which pays for a poor and pretty woman's prostitution in solid gold and pays for her honesty with starvation, drudgery and pious twaddle." The audience Shaw sought was the audience predisposed to agree with that formulation and already intent on rescuing women from prostitution. The audience he thought "wrong" for the performance consisted of patrons of prostitutes and others likely to profit from exploitation. "Get the rescuers into the theatre and keep the patrons out of it," Shaw told Daly, "and you need have no fear about the reception of the play." The audience, however, would prove to include many who were neither rescuers nor patrons. Shaw closed the letter by writing that the play "was not written to produce enjoyment, nor even the Aristotelian catharsis of pity and terror, but to make people stop knocking women down and then blaming them for being 'fallen.' If I have done this with a brutal hand, I do not feel in the least disposed to apologize."[20]

In his Preface to the play, Shaw was as explicit about his intention as in his letters to Daly. The first sentence declares: "Mrs Warren's Profession was written in 1894 to draw attention to the truth that prostitution is caused, not by female depravity and male licentiousness, but simply by underpaying, undervaluing, and overworking women so shamefully that the poorest of them are forced to resort to prostitution to keep body and soul together" (181). As in the case of *John Bull's Other Island,* Shaw found a literary and a stage convention to exploit for his own purposes: to reverse, in the end, the expected, conventional denouement. Here the sources were Maupassant's *Yvette* and Pinero's *The Second Mrs Tanqueray,* treatments of "notorious" women that fulfilled expectations of melodramatic doom. Mrs Warren takes a far more realistic view of her profession: "It cant be right, Vivie, that there shouldnt be better opportunities for women. I stick to that: it's wrong. But it's so, right or wrong; and a girl must make the best of it" (250). Nor does Vivie have any great difficulty in accepting the revelation of her mother's profession.

Nor, for that matter, did the New York audience of the play. The

Garrick Theatre on West Thirty-fifth Street was in the heart of New York's Tenderloin district along Sixth Avenue. As frequently occurs, brothels were especially active in proximity to theaters, and in New York they were following the movement of theaters uptown from Fourteenth Street, the center in Boucicault's time, toward Times Square, the center in O'Casey's time. By the turn of the century, the middle portion of that stretch of avenue, in the streets numbered in the thirties, was becoming seedier. Timothy Gilfoyle is a historian of Mrs Warren's profession as practiced in New York: "Apart from brothels, prostitutes worked in the many concert saloons that lined Sixth Avenue north of Twenty-third Street. For decades, entertainment entrepreneurs strove for a European cachet and called their places of pleasure the Haymarket, the Strand, the Cremorne, the Cairo, the Star and Garter, and Buckingham Palace. Full of prostitutes, these remained leading institutions of New York's nightlife."[21] It is revealing that Mrs Warren's "profession" is the center of attention only for the first half of the play, which concludes with Vivie's and Mrs Warren's reconciliation at the end of Act II. The second half of the play concerns their separation and requires the subplot omitted from Shaw's public glosses on the play. The subplot concerned a topic more shocking than that of the brothel society outside the doors of the Garrick and one that did not lend itself so well to "the reforming influence."

Contrary to the title, what shocked even Shaw's preferred audience was the possible marriage of Vivie and young Frank Gardner after the suggestion, by innuendo, of a common father. Although absent from the intentions avowed in the preface to the play, the incest theme dominates the second half of the play, including Frank's interest in fulfilling his fantasies of living like "babes in the wood" (259) and his comment on "the imbecility of the little boy's father" (259). When Crofts, Mrs Warren's partner, thwarted in his own pursuit of Vivie, makes Rev. Samuel Gardner's paternity of both young people certain, and Frank repeats his fantasy of "babes in the wood," Vivie tells him, at the end of Act III, "Ah, not that, not that. You make my flesh creep" (267). The element of incest in the plot has always been perceived as a perplexing part of *Mrs Warren's Profession*. Shaw's colleague William Archer had pointed this out before the play had even reached performance; for Archer, the dalliance of Frank and Vivie "cannot possibly be said to present a typical incident in the history of a polyandrous group, and has the air of being dragged in simply for the sake of its unpleasantness."[22] While he did not acknowledge the issue in his preface to the play, Shaw did so in his letters to Arnold Daly in advance of the New York production. Warning about youths in the audience, Shaw adverted to "the problem raised by the relations of Mrs Warren with her old patrons—I mean of course the possibility of close consanguinity between their children—[that] only adds to the charm of the story for children."[23]

The matter was of such importance that the contract for the production Shaw and Daly signed in July 1904 stipulated that "the Manager shall endeavour as far as may be practical to apprise the public of the fact that Play is suitable for representation before serious adult audiences only."[24] The incest motif, perhaps added for "the charm of the story," may satisfy Shaw's own specific criterion for *Plays Unpleasant:* "to force the spectator to face unpleasant facts." But confrontation with a universal taboo cannot possibly result in the kind of reform Shaw intended in his representation of material exploitation. The "charm" functions just as Archer put it: "simply for the sake of unpleasantness."

By the time of Daly's production, Shaw was already well known as an opponent of censorship, and *Plays Unpleasant,* in particular, was part of his campaign against "the obstacle that makes dramatic authorship intolerable in England to writers accustomed to the freedom of the Press. I mean, of course, Censorship" (14). In London, his long battle was against the Lord Chamberlain Examiner of Plays, who had the power to deny license for performance. In New York, his opponent would be Anthony Comstock, secretary of the Society for the Suppression of Vice, who had the power to mobilize protest until the courts issued warrants to halt performance. Simultaneous with rehearsals for Daly's *John Bull's Other Island* and *Mrs Warren's Profession,* Comstock became known to Shaw for an incident in which the New York Public Library removed a copy of *Man and Superman* from the open shelves. Shaw provided Robert Welch of the *New York Times* with a taunting letter for publication: "Nobody outside of America is likely to be in the least surprised. Comstockery is the world's standing joke at the expense of the United States. Europe likes to hear of such things. It confirms the deep-seated conviction of the Old World that America is a provincial place, a second-rate country-town civilization after all." The book was returned to the open shelves. Shaw again wrote to Welch to tell him that "I am sorry to say that every time I scratch an American I *do* find a

Comstocker. Comstock is a thoroughly representative man."[25]

Whether considered a very real menace or a very low comedy, Anthony Comstock was not representative. To St. John Ervine, also an Irish playwright produced in New York, Comstock was Dickensian, "a mixture of Chadband and Stiggins, with a large dose of Pecksniff thrown in."[26] According to the *New York Times* obituary in 1915:

> In 1867 [Comstock] came to New York with $3.50 in his pocket and got a job as porter in a dry goods house. In 1872, after he had risen to be a salesman, the incident occurred which started him on his career. He found two of his fellow employees with indecent books, learned from them that they had obtained them from a sort of circulating library in Centre Street, and on March 2, 1872, arrested the dealer with ample evidence of his guilt.
>
> The ridicule which has followed him began then. Shortly after that he was called the Protector of the Public Morals, the Self-Constituted Censor, and other names.

Comstock's power derived from successfully lobbying for an amendment of postal laws to make it illegal to send obscene materials or even information about them though the mail. Then, in 1873, he secured an appointment by President Grant as a special postal inspector and founded the Society for the Suppression of Vice. By his own count, Comstock arraigned 3,697 people and obtained either guilty pleas or convictions of 2,740 of them. According to the *Times,* he "made a large number of his arrests personally and was frequently in violent fights in which he was well qualified to hold his own, even in later years, by reason of his huge physique and his experience as an arresting officer. Early in his career he was slashed across the face with a bowie knife by one of his prisoners. On a half a dozen occasions he was knocked down and beaten, but more often attempts at force ended badly for his prisoner."[27] The Shaw case arose when Comstock was sixty years of age and well past that frontier charisma, if it ever actually existed. Ten years after the Shaw case, in 1915, he had lost influence and was expected to lose his appointment. In that year he would die ten days after an apoplectic outburst in court seeking fines for distribution of Margaret Sanger's *Family Limitation* by her husband William.

The combative rhetorical style of Comstock's youth can be observed in the conclusion of his essay "Vampire Literature," a warning about the power of obscene material to corrupt youth and so damage the national future, which was published in the *North American Review* in 1891: "Save our youth from this fetid blast of corruption which is being sent out by the fiery greed of thoughtless, reckless, or criminal authors and publishers. Authors and publishers need to call a halt upon themselves, ere they further curse the youth of this free land and undermine our free institutions."[28] Elsewhere, however, and in less florid terms, the article and Comstock's subsequent campaign quite accurately anticipated the Shaw episode on two counts: first, that material alleged to be obscene might be defended by authors, publishers, producers, or others as socially constructed cautionary tales; second, that interested parties might attempt to profit from notoriety by actively seeking official condemnation. Arnold Daly, at least, would do both in New York in 1905. Comstock's anticipation of issues central to the New York production of *Mrs Warren's Profession* is not surprising. He and Shaw were both devoted, in their own ways, to social reform, and both devoted a large part of their energies to the subject of sexual behavior. However, in the face of unpleasantness, Comstock's whole effort was one of suppression, as in the title of his organization. Shaw's, instead, was confrontation, as in "to force the spectator to face unpleasant facts." No one ever accused Comstock of dealing in unpleasantness for its own sake.

Shaw opened his match with Comstock in high style. Told by reporters in London on October 26, or two weeks after the brief run of *John Bull's Other Island* on Broadway, that Comstock had threatened to imprison Arnold Daly for producing *Mrs Warren's Profession,* Shaw responded: "Do you remember the classic telegram sent by Lord Clanricarde to his tenants in Ireland? 'If you think you can intimidate me by shooting my agent you are very much mistaken.'" Just so, Shaw continued, "If Comstock thinks he can intimidate me by imprisoning Daly he does not quite know his man. Let him imprison Daly by all means."[29] In addition, Shaw claimed that he was both elderly and intimidated and that Comstock (twelve years Shaw's senior) was young and bold. Shaw explained once again that the sole unpleasant point of the play was the fact of prostitution, that libertines paid women well to be bad and the pious paid women poorly to be good. At this juncture, the Daly production was in New Haven, where he took a lesson from Shaw in the London opening of *John Bull's Other Island* by selecting a receptive audience. Daly also anticipated Lady Gregory's Irish Players tour of 1911 by seeking that receptive American audience on campuses, in this case Yale University. As was widely reported in the press, Daly took the offense by echoing Shaw's assertion that the play only wished to correct a deplorable social condition. He upped the ante by inviting Comstock to the New Haven tryout. Comstock, familiar with the plea that indecent material was socially constructive and equally familiar with exploitation of notoriety, declined to attend or even to read the play. He told the public that he was acting on alarms sounded by un-named complainants and in an open letter to Daly explained his concern: "If the tendency of your play is to corrupt the minds of the young and inexperienced, or to suggest lewd and libidinous thoughts, then it is forbidden by law, and comes within the [court] decision which I sent you the other night. I leave the matter in your hands, calling especial attention to the law, and decisions of the courts of the State."[30]

The single performance scheduled for New Haven was given at the Hyperion Theatre on Friday, October 27, with the New York open-ing planned for the following Monday evening. When Mary Shaw, who was playing Mrs Warren, wrote her account of the production ten years later, she recalled that in New Haven "there had been a football game between Princeton and Yale that day, and Yale was victorious. There were more than a thousand undergraduates in the galleries. We, in our innocence, assumed that all of these thousand collegians were familiar with a literary play like "Mrs. Warren's Profession." We knew the qual-ity of the audience, which downstairs in the parquet consisted of the faculty of Yale, all the distinguished professors, all the literary people of New Haven." Actually, as she found, the undergraduates were well prepared for the performance and knew in advance what they would find objectionable. It was not Mrs Warren's profession. Rather, it was when Vivie demands that her mother name her father that "pandemo-nium broke loose in the upper galleries": "Knowing something of the methods of controlling mob spirit in audiences, I strode to the head of the table, took on the manner of Lady Macbeth, and played the entire scene in loud, sonorous tones with menace in every one of them. An appalling silence fell upon the theater. There was no more trouble of any kind from the undergraduates, and when the curtain fell upon the second act they paid the tribute that cowards always pay to the coura-geous, and gave us about ten curtain calls."[31] The New York Times cov-ered the first performance as a news story, not a performance for review.

Its correspondent observed some of the town/gown phenomena not unusual in New Haven. New Haven Mayor John P. Studley thought the performance deplorable, while the Yale faculty in the audience felt that attendance was intellectually obligatory. A few spectators walked out, and a few audibly protested passages of the dialogue. As he would later in New York, Daly, whose role was Frank, made a curtain speech at the end of Act III, immediately after Vivie tells Frank, "You make my flesh creep" (267). Before the curtain, Daly, in costume as Frank, told his audience, "I do not think Mr. Shaw's play appeals to the lewd minded, but should be taken as it is—as a strong moral lesson on a phase of society that some might not care to see portrayed, but hidden, but which can with profit be shown in such a play as this."[32] Studley, like Comstock, refused to attend or even to read the play. Also like Comstock, Studley preferred the hidden to the clear portrayal—that which can with profit be shown—and refused license for further performances at the Hyperion.

Back in New York, Daly had already issued from the Garrick box office a memorandum that managed to fulfill both Shaw's contractual stipulations and Comstock's dire warnings about profiting from notoriety: "Mr. Daly, along with Mr. Shaw, believes that the broad and frank manner in which certain uncommendable but undeniably existent social conditions are treated in this drama will make those conditions repugnant to the spectators, and in this way work for the betterment of society—that is, to spectators of mature years and balanced judgments. Young persons still at an impressionable time of life are candidly asked to remain away. Children positively will not be admitted to the Garrick Theatre during this engagement."[33] Daly's next move in public relations, on the eve of opening, was to announce, without Shaw's permission, an expurgation of the prompt book, thus alerting the public to just how salacious the material was. Through his "personal representative," Daly communicated to the press the news that "the changes are purely changes of words, made necessary by the fact that some of the lines, as the play is written, are susceptible of impure constructions which were not at all intended."[34] One cut was Vivie's early reference to liking a good cigar. After the performance, Daly would show the prompt book to city officials to demonstrate his effort to sanitize the text. A final device to focus interest on the production was a promise to follow the critics' verdict on whether to keep the show open.

By all accounts West Thirty-fifth Street was quite a scene on Monday, October 30, 1905, by 6:30 P.M. Extra police had been stationed outside the theatre. The Garrick, seating 963, was sold out, with a long line for standing room, and newspaper reports estimated that from two to three thousand people were turned away. Tickets were sold at scalpers' prices, thirty dollars for two-dollar seats. Most Shaw defenders have deplored the uproar and attributed it to the low, vulgar audience, not at all Shaw's intended one. In this case Archibald Henderson lowered his estimation of the American Shaw audience to "the devotees of the Shaw cult and many disreputable people who came with the expectation of gratifying their depraved tastes."[35] Years later, and at some distance from Broadway, Shaw would claim that because censorship had been threatened "all the worst in the New York population came in enormous crowds."[36] The various press accounts of the evening, however, represent the audience as rather higher on the social scale than usual. On the scene was Police Commissioner William McAdoo. Only two years before he was president-general of the American Irish Historical Society, and in 1911, as chief magistrate, he will feature in an equally contentious premiere in New York of *The Playboy of the Western World*. On the steps of the Garrick in 1905, McAdoo observed that "this is not the usual first night audience at a New York theatre. Most of these people came in their own carriages, and it looks like an opera first night. I don't think that this is a good test of trying it on the dog. The dog in this instance is rather high bred, and the ordinary run of dog may have different ideas."[37] The audience, certainly mixed, was found too low by the Shaw critic and too high by the guardian of public morals. Shaw got at least some of the rescuers of the exploited class of prostitutes, but mixed with the exploiters themselves: the theater held the Shaw cult and the Tenderloin cult. McAdoo would watch the performance from a stage-left box. Comstock, true to his word, would not attend.

Mary Shaw had played Mrs Warren in New Haven with a blonde wig and a flashy dress: "the idea of the management being to emphasize her well-dressed vulgarity," but she entered at the Garrick without the wig, trying to "in every way tone down Mrs. Warren's appearance"[38] and offset expectations raised by Daly's publicity campaign. According to the *Sun,* at the entrance "there was a hush like that which falls on a poolroom at the first whisper of 'police.'" By all accounts, the audience gradually became aware that expectations of high unpleasantness would be disappointed. The *Sun* story reported that the audience—"about equally divided between the Tenderloin and what may be perhaps called

Sir Loin"—calmed because "everybody on the stage wore all the clothes that belonged, and nothing was said that, in Mr. Comstock's legal phrase, could evoke 'lewd and libidinous thoughts.'"[39] There were four curtain calls at the end of the first act. At the end of the second act, after Mrs Warren has justified herself in a speech Daly did not cut and that Mary Shaw recalled delivering directly toward McAdoo's box, there were seven curtain calls. At the end of the third act, after Crofts's revelation about paternity, Daly answered repeated curtain calls with an addition to his prepared speech: "I also believe that a person who attempts to disillusion a child, or to take from them their legends—as of Santa Claus and our revered Washington and his little hatchet—is a brutal and conscienceless destroyer of all that youth owes us. We have many theatres devoted to plays appealing to the romanticist or child. New York has even provided a hippodrome for such. Surely there should be room in New York for at least one theatre devoted to Truth, however disgraceful Truth may appear."[40] This seems to combine in confused form Shaw's suggestion that the incest plot would "add to the charm of the story for children" and Daly's own conviction of the bravery of portraying an important moral lesson. At this moment in the performance, after the prostitution issue is largely resolved, the speech underscored the other truth about to appear. At this juncture, Commissioner McAdoo, who saw the point quite clearly, left. After the final curtain, his assistant, one Inspector Brooks, went over the prompt book with the cast for half an hour.

At the performance the *New York World* polled the audience by distributing cards asking spectators to judge the play "Fit" or "Unfit." Fully 576 spectators complied, with a majority of 304 finding the play "Fit." The critics, however, were uniformly outraged, not at the play's professed subject of prostitution, but at its treatment of incest. The *World* declared that "Bernard Shaw has portrayed with rarest fidelity and minutest detail a form of social ulcer the existence of which is perfectly well known to all persons." The *American* found it "an effort to set before unthinking men and women, by means of the footlights, the putrefaction of social life. It is illuminated gangrene. It is the suppueration of a plague spot." For the *New York Herald*, "the whole story of the play, the atmosphere surrounding it, the incidents, the personalities of the characters are wholly immoral and degenerate. The only way to expurgate 'Mrs Warren's Profession' is to cut the whole play out. You cannot have a clean pig sty."[41] The reviews were quite free with the word "prostitute" in reference to Mrs Warren, but they only alluded to their real objection in the language of pestilence and degeneration. The objections of the press were not, as often is suggested, hypocritical denial of prostitution culture. Rather, the objections were about the additional impropriety smuggled in to sensationalize, not to reform.

Arnold Daly, who had promised to close the show if reviews were negative, and William McAdoo, who did not want his threat to close the show to appear empty, raced each other to see who could close *Mrs Warren's Profession* first. By afternoon on October 31, McAdoo released to the press his notice to Daly: "Sir: This is to notify you that after personal inspection and reports sent to me I have determined that it is my duty to prevent further performance of the play known as 'Mrs. Warren's Profession.' As a further performance will be a violation of the law, I will use the powers vested in me to prevent the same and to arrest those participating therein." McAdoo acted on a part of the penal code concerning public decency. The public he acted to protect were at that time crowding the Garrick Box office, where the offered run of two weeks was nearly sold out, with tickets going in roughly equal proportions to scalpers and to what the *Sun* referred to as examples of the "typical Shawite highbrow." Meanwhile, Daly's notice, which the theater management claimed predated McAdoo's, was posted: "Further productions of 'Mrs. Warren's Profession' will be discontinued owing to the universal condemnation of the press." Daly's spokesman, Winchell Smith, explained: "The action of the police had nothing to do with his closing the run. He intended to take it off as soon as he saw the criticisms. In fact, when he realized last night that most of the audience had come merely to witness a salacious play, he was hardly persuaded to go on with the first performance."[42] This was an outright lie. The action of the moment was maneuvers between the press, the producers, and the police that entirely ignored the audience.

The legal verdict would be decided the following summer by the New York Court of the Special Sessions based on the text. The criterion for criminality, under which Daly and his manager had been arrested, was "whether a production is naturally calculated to excite in the spectator impure imagination," with other elements in the production being accessory to this purpose. The author of the decision, Justice Olmstead, was, as the press reported, "rather hard on Bernard Shaw." Olmstead, having read the play, found that "instead of exciting impure imagination in the mind of the spectator, that which is really excited is disgust." He drew particular attention to "the suggestion that the clergyman in the play is the father of Mrs. Warren's daughter, with the situation which makes the clergyman's acknowledged son a suitor for the daughter's hand, is another of the author's shock producers." Olmstead granted Shaw's attempt to effect "social reforms" concerning prostitution, but, referring to its "other truth," added that "the court cannot refrain from suggesting, however, that the reforming influence of the play in this regard is minimized by the method of attack."[43]

Daly and his manager were acquitted on charges very like those that would end with a conviction in the same court concerning publication in New York of Joyce's *Ulysses*. Shaw, naturally, saluted this outcome, responding by telegram to the New York press that America is a "strange country where the press is blind and the eyes of justice are open," and noting his preference for American censorship law to English.[44] Later, his recollection of the New York production in the "Preface" prepared for *Plays Unpleasant* focused entirely on the abuse of power by critics and the harm done to Daly, who "was morally lynched side by side with me" (207). He protested too much. Even before the verdict was delivered, Daly had expanded his Shaw repertory. In April 1906 he played Bluntschli in an *Arms and the Man* production at the Lyric Theatre in New York, with much of the cast from *Mrs Warren's Profession* joined by Aubrey Boucicault, the playwright's son. According to Goldsmith's 1927 monograph, on this success Daly fully inherited that role in America from Richard Mansfield. In the summer in which the verdict was delivered, Daly was on a national tour with seven plays, four of them by Shaw, and, according to Goldsmith, found "a friendly reception in the various cities which the company visited."[45] *Mrs Warren's Profession,* not in Daly's repertory, would be revived in New York City only five months after the single performance at the Garrick, this time at the Manhattan Theater, without Daly. Neither the audience nor the law conspired with the censors as much as Shaw liked to suggest.

The legal outcome was conclusive and in Shaw's favor. The critical verdict has been more equivocal. Shaw's latest biographer, Michael Holroyd, summarizes the critical case: "The incestuous undercurrents that move mysteriously below the talking surface of the play have been met by two critical objections: the first (voiced by Archer) that they have been dragged in unnecessarily; the second (voiced by Eric Bentley) that, having no idea what to do with the incest theme, Shaw had left the situation doubtful. Shaw, however, insisted that 'the case would be incomplete without it.' For he was taking up incest as an Ibsenite theme and reproducing a structural model without breaking away from it at the end."[46] Nowhere was the Ibsenite influence more marked than in New York, where Mary Shaw's reputation was largely built on her performance in *Ghosts* and where reviewers compared her Mrs Warren to her Mrs Alving. But the model is broken at the end of Shaw's play. The police commissioner, by leaving the theater before the final act, intimated as much. In Act IV, after much titillation, it is revealed that incest is not the central issue after all when Vivie dismisses the matter as making "no real difference" (271). For the denouement, as Frank says of his own interests, "it's not the moral aspect of the case; it's the money aspect" (277). For Frank, that means passing from "love's young dream" (273) to more material prospects. Vivie, too, concludes by ridding herself of her fictitious identity, also ridding herself of any romantic illusions, and, on her successful ascent to partner at the firm of Fraser and Warren, greeting a joyless future. Mrs Warren, shedding her illusions about the rewards of propriety, delivers Shaw's announced message. "From this time forth," she says, "so help me Heaven in my last hour, I'll do wrong and nothing but wrong. And I'll prosper on it" (285). With the incest predicament dismissed, Shaw's play concludes by returning full emphasis to the evils of a social system that rewards "bad" women better than "good" women. His ending provides the Shavian inversion of contemporary theatrical conventions surrounding the fallen woman and the romantic young man. In this Shaw's "structural model" resembles that of *John Bull's Other Island:* the inversion of dramatic types derived from the stage, not the world.

What the New York production of 1905 demonstrates about *Mrs Warren's Profession* is that Shaw's statement on prostitution was neither the principal offense of the play for the local audience nor the principal target of interference by civic (McAdoo), vigilante (Comstock), and cultural (reviewers) opponents of the performance. Instead, the offense was Hsaw's "advance" over Boucicault in evolving a new kind of sensation drama that earned him Comstock's epithet, "Irish Smut Dealer." The epithet could, in 1905, apply to a playwright born in Ireland whether using the stereotypical material of the Irish play, as in John Bull's Other Island, or not, as in Mrs Warren's Other Profession. The "two brilliant Irishmen," Shaw and Daly, understood quite well the shallowness of the local code of propriety and the absurdity of insisting on silence and suppression, as per Comstock, as the means to control social problems. They also saw quite clearly the feebleness of the censorship effort in New York City and the benefits of public notoriety. This advance had the effect of estranging the Irish and the Irish American audience, which were conspicuously not members of the Shaw cult of 1905 and henceforth would congregate for Irish plays, or non-Irish Irish plays, most often to protest them. After 1905, the Shaw play, scarcely as beleaguered in New York as the playwright wished it to appear, prospered. The author did not visit New York until his world tour of 1933, but the production history of his works included a great deal of Broadway, beginning in 1906 with a production of *Caesar and Cleopatra* starring Gertrude Elliott, sister to Maxine Elliott, at whose theater the Irish Players would enrage the Irish audience in New York in 1911.

Shaw plays had off-Broadway careers in New York, notably in the downtown art theaters that would in the 1920s create a Lord Dunsany vogue and give the English-language premiere of Joyce's *Exiles*. But the Shaw audience was largest on Broadway, testimony to the power of success to institutionalize even the most reformist and most abrasive work of art. In addition to the plays, later favored by the Shuberts and other producers for the same "typical Shawite highbrow" appeal they had in 1905, Shaw on Broadway included a dramatization of his novel *Cashel Byron's Profession* with the ex-heavyweight champion James J. Corbett in the title role. Brooks Atkinson reported the prevalent quip on this exercise in commercial exploitation of the once-controversial Shaw allure: "In the last act, Corbett was on his feet, but Shaw was flat on the canvas."[47]

SYNGE'S *Playboy,*
THE IRISH PLAYERS, AND THE
ANTI-IRISH IRISH PLAYERS

Bernard Shaw played a role in the general debate over *The Playboy of the Western World* in New York in 1911. He was called as understudy to the playwright, for J.M. Synge had died in 1909. However, just as Shaw had made an advancement of sorts over Boucicault, he was now surpassed in turn. In his Irish play of 1905, *John Bull's Other Island,* the method of attack had failed to attract attention. In 1911, with Synge's Irish play about a village on the wild Mayo coast, the Irish Players on tour escalated much the same method of attack, as Shaw had before them, and they successfully touched off an uproar. Acclaimed in New York as "one of the healthiest signs of the revival of the ancient Irish spirit" by no less than Theodore Roosevelt, the company, led by Lady Augusta Gregory, was also renamed on the same day "the Anti-Irish Irish Players" by the *Gaelic American.*[1]

The *Playboy* opening was an outstanding instance in the continuing search for the "real" Ireland on stage. Its program for November 27, 1911, a performance of Lady Gregory's *The Rising of the Moon* followed by *The Playboy,* highlighted the company's origin at "the Abbey Theatre, Dublin," documenting its authenticity, and reprinted Synge's note on using "very few words I have not heard among the country people." But in that morning's newspaper, Seamus MacManus, a well-known Irish writer then on his own tour, observed that "I may say without egotism that there are very few people who know our people, our people of the remote mountains and islands, better than I," and then proclaimed the program, including *The Playboy,* as "not Irish at all."[2] With its greater remove from the people of Mayo, *The Playboy* in New York demonstrated even more clearly than in Dublin the gap between artists and audience. It represented a new mark on the course toward what W.B. Yeats would later call "the artist's arrogance": "I was spokesman," Yeats wrote, "because I was born arrogant and had learnt an artist's arrogance—'Not what you want but what we want'—and we were the first modern theatre that said it."[3] In 1911 there would be no indifference like that toward *John Bull's Other Island,* and no "other truth" like that submerged in *Mrs Warren's Profession.* With *The Playboy of the Western World,* the Irish Players on the New York stage offered a view of drama fundamentally antithetical to that of most of the general audience. They offered it bluntly, and surpassed Shaw in the manner of selecting a preferred audience. Appropriately enough for a dispute of polarized sides and adversarial rhetoric, the play at issue was about the power of a lie, a phenomenon familiar to all involved.

Synge provided the ideal text for the efforts of the Irish Players. The power of the play to offend has been generally acknowledged, usually in reference to its premiere in Dublin in 1907. Synge "offended," according to Conor Cruise O'Brien, "because he showed the Catholic people of the country—'peasants'—in what their urbanized children considered to be an unfavorable light. In fact, it was not the peasants, but their urbanized descendants, whom Yeats, Synge, and Lady Gregory disliked."[4] One example that indicates how fundamental this power is to Synge's text is his use of a source for the story. As he recorded it in his prose descriptions in *The Aran Islands,* this source story concerned a man from Western Ireland "who killed his father with the blow of a spade" and fled to the offshore islands, where he was sheltered. Synge wrote: "They hid him in a hole—which the old man has shown me— and kept him safe for weeks, though the police came and searched for him and he could hear their boots grinding on the stones over his head. In spite of a reward which was offered, the island was incorruptible, and after much trouble the man was shipped to America."[5] This leads to Synge's discussion of the adversarial relation of the islanders with the law, then British in jurisdiction, and to Synge's remarkably Arnoldian praise for native wisdom in respecting passion above all possible motives. The incident remains as premise in *The Playboy,* with its only slightly less remote "community" on the Mayo coast. The crime in the anecdote is parricide, as in the play, and the weapon in both is the dread loy. Synge's revision of the outcome, however, is striking. In the source story the people are "incorruptible" in solidarity, in hiding the fugitive from the police, and in rising to the occasion of new and perplexing experience. This was what Synge found in his field work.

However, the success of the community was precisely what he wrote out of the tale in adaptation. Synge revised his source from success to failure, and so reversed the pattern of nationalist, romantic, and melodramatic literature. Like a Shavian inversion of dramatic outcomes, *The Playboy* follows all expectations of comedy until well into the final act. In Synge's treatment of Christy Mahon's "small voice"[6] becoming a powerful voice all out of proportion with deeds, the people of the village are, in comic fashion, as unified and as opposed to Britain as those Synge visited in the Aran Islands. But as the action proceeds, they undo their own harmony. At the outset of the action, Philly Cullen prompts Christy's tall tale of killing his father with a series of rising demands for sensation that culminate in "Were you off east, young fellow, fighting bloody wars for Kruger and the freedom of the Boers?" (71). In the second act, the Widow Quin, too, demands an inflated tale: "Don't be letting on to be shy, a fine, gamey, treacherous lad the like of you. Was it in your house beyond you cracked his skull?" (101). On the brink of the exposure of the tale as a lie, Michael Flaherty, civic center of the village as owner of the pub that is its stage setting, fully certifies Christy by accepting him as son-in-law: "A daring fellow is the jewel of the world, and a man did split his father's middle with a single clout should have the bravery of ten, so may God and Mary and St. Patrick bless you and increase you from this mortal day" (157). Old Mahon's appearance immediately after these words belies the tale with fact, and the group denounces Christy—"You're a liar!" (161)—for what they had asked him to do. Christy's analysis of the moment is delivered as he is captured by the crowd and returned to the status of solitary outsider: "Shut your yelling, for if you're after making a mighty man of me this day by the power of a lie, you're setting me now to think if it's a poor thing to be lonesome, it's worse maybe to go mixing with the fools of the earth" (165). In a draft, Synge made contempt for the people more explicit. There Christy taunts: "You're the mighty moral strong men of a Mayo bog" (164). In the play's treatment of the Mayo characters, a prospect of change and achievement is within their capacity. They have language requisite for action; but when they denounce the action they have bred, their failure is complete. Unlike the people Synge actually visited, the characters of his invention are not incorruptible.

The resulting play did not please, and in a famous uproar it was jeered down in the Abbey Theatre by that audience of urbanized descendants of the peasant. Those offended, however, had more plausible cause than is often allowed. On that evening Maude Gonne, a force both on and off stage in the early Abbey years, proclaimed: "A play which pleases the men and women of Ireland who have sold their country for ease and wealth, who fraternise with their country's oppressors or have taken service with them, a play that will please the host of English functionaries and the English garrison, is a play that can never claim to be a national literature."[7] All plays need not aspire to be a national literature, but Synge's play did by opening at what claimed to be the national theater in Dublin. Gonne's concern was not with whether the play pleased the Irish audience, but only with whether it pleased the enemy. This is not just period sentiment, because it persists, in Ireland, at least. In an influential book in 1931, Daniel Corkery further defined the issue: "A national literature," he wrote in the opening of *Synge and Anglo-Irish Literature,* "is written primarily for its own people: every new book in it—no matter what its theme—foreign or native—is referable to their life, and its literary traits to the traits already established in the literature. The nation's own critical opinion of it is the warrant of life or death for it."[8] Corkery's sense of what will qualify as a national literature is only a degree less reactionary than Gonne's, in part because he wrote from an established Irish state and she did not. But that alertness to the threat of outside judgment remains apparent. What Corkery means by the "life" of the people is much more than anthropological, although doubts about fidelity to actual customs in Mayo would plague *The Playboy* on both sides of the Atlantic. Corkery's point was that the life of the people included what they wanted, not just what they were, and so a national literature is a useful literature because it is compatible with the needs and desires of "the people," because it is part of their collective agenda.

This sense continues to qualify how much *The Playboy* can please in Ireland. Gonne's statement was early twentieth century, and Seamus Deane provides a late-century version of the same case: "In *The Playboy of the Western World* Pegeen Mike's desolate cry of loss brings to an end the prospect of a glorious future with Christy Mahon, one which Christy had invoked by articulating a vision of pastoral romance which properly belongs to the old Gaelic past. The failure of the community to bring the past Eden into a utopian future marks the boundary line of nationalist and romantic desire. The vagrant hero fades into legend or fantasy."[9] The boundary line here is one Synge's play fails to cross and so falls short of the requirements for a literature that will please by corresponding to aspirations, not current conditions. The crucial moment in Synge's text, and its sudden departure from comic expectations, is the broken relationship between Christy and Pegeen Mike Flaherty. In the final act, a comic resolution is proposed:

> PEGEEN [*with real tenderness*]: And what is it I have, Christy Mahon, to make me fitting entertainment for the like of you that has such poet's talking, and such bravery of heart?
> CHRISTY [*in a low voice*]: Isn't there the light of seven heavens in your heart alone, the way you'll be an angel's lamp to me from this out, and I abroad in the darkness spearing salmons in the Owen or the Carrowmore?
> PEGEEN: If I was your wife, I'd be along with you those nights, Christy Mahon, the way you'd see I was a great hand at coaxing bailiffs, or coining funny nicknames for the stars of night. [149]

These familiar lines put full emphasis on speech, articulation, and identity, qualities poised as light against the dark even if associated with fiction or prevarication, as in "coaxing bailiffs" or "coining funny nicknames" (or altering stories from *The Aran Islands*). But comic endings of marriage for local bliss or of flight for married bliss are not delivered, and Pegeen Mike will not be "fitting entertainment" for the like of Christy or the audience. As Michael James is the civic center of the community, so Pegeen is the moral center, the decision maker from the opening lines of the play. Oddly, her decision for the community over Christy Mahon is both its demise and his revival. She says: "It's there your treachery is spurring me, till I'm hard set to think you're the one I'm after lacing in my heart-strings half-an-hour gone by. (*To Mahon.*) Take him on from this, for I think bad the world should see me raging for a Munster liar, and the fool of men" (161). This moment is a quite calculated reversal of the anecdote from which Synge worked. Pegeen, presented with the opportunity to write a future, declines. Synge's taunt to his audience resembles Christy's to the mighty moral Mayo men. The outcome is delivered as bluntly as possible. It could not please the urbanized audience of the Abbey in 1907 because it did not follow their desires and because it might please the enemy. On these grounds, *The Playboy* would fail even more spectacularly in New York with what could be considered the urbanized descendants of the Dublin urbanized descendants of peasants. In New York, however, other grounds would provide the play's greatest victory.

As Conor Cruise O'Brien notes, in 1907 in Dublin *The Playboy* failed with its audience because it failed to flatter, because it presented the origins of the urbanized culture in an unflattering light.[10] This would remain true in New York in 1911, but the distance from Dublin and the proximity of other, non-Irish audiences also focused the issue in new and especially intense ways. Some forceful issues in the Dublin dispute, especially propriety of language and accountability of a national theater, were remote from the New York scene. In fact, some thought the American setting so different from Ireland that the play would succeed in New York despite the uproar it provoked in Dublin. Yeats made this point first, in February 1907, in the midst of nightly protests at the Abbey over *The Playboy*. In a letter to John Quinn, the art collector, lawyer, confidant of Lady Gregory, and general sponsor of the Irish Players tour in 1911, Yeats proposed that the Irish or first-generation Irish Americans would be flattered by Synge's play because "the play means that if Ireland goes on losing her strong men by emigration at the present rate and submitting her will to every kind of political and religious domination, the young men will grow so tame that the young girls will prefer any man of spirit, even though he has killed his father."[11] This proved to be quite wrong because the strong men who emigrated now placed their ambitions much more in New York than in Ireland, though their rhetoric might suggest otherwise. In New York the governing concern was not the marriage prospects in rural Ireland or the absolute priority of Irish national autonomy. It was, instead, local hegemony and ambition. The mighty moral Irishmen of New York were not satisfied by the flattering suggestion that their emigration left Ireland weak. Their interest was in their future, not their past, and this required of immigrants a better pedigree than Synge's characters suggested. Whether the pedigree was fact or fiction was of secondary importance. The image was crucial, and in New York it would be examined by many who had never heard of Mayo.

In New York, self-examination of the Irish, even if by the Irish, amounted to an external rather than internal review. A continuing embarrassment of this sort was the proliferation in New York theaters of the stage Irishman, not the one that Boucicault had created, or even the one Shaw hoped to dismiss, but an American hybridized product in a line descended from Harrigan and Hart. A good example of the stereotype and organized audience protest was *McFadden's Row of Flats,* by E.W. Townsend, which opened to cordial press reviews in 1903, or two years before *John Bull's Other Ireland.* Essentially a musical review, *McFadden's Row of Flats* included many dance numbers on ethnicities including Scottish, English, German, and Cuban. It was held together by that all-purpose Irish American drama plot, local elections, a topic of critical importance for a group focused on local power and how to achieve it. Townsend's play matched an Irish family against a German-Jewish one, and in this respect was scarcely different from any number of the Mulligan Guards episodes in the 1890s or *Abie's Irish Rose* in the 1920s. In between those points of time, at the time of *McFadden's Row* in 1903, the Irish and American Irish audience had reached a point somewhere between threatened and accepted status. From that position they could openly protest what they felt slowed an accelerating rate of assimilation and accomplishment. The *New York Times* recommended *McFadden's Row of Flats* for "laughing purposes only," and praised its "chorus of slender and shapely young women," its "kinetoscope" lighting effects, and the dancing dwarfs Bobby and Jerry. But a week later two hundred Irish and Irish Americans attended the Fourteenth Street Theatre together to protest the portrayal of the McFadden daughter, Mary Ellen, whom the *Times* called "frisky," and that of Weary Willie, a stage drunk with a bright red nose. The protest took the same form as for *The Playboy,* clearing the stage with fruit and eggs, and much more successfully. A protester described as a leader of the group told the *New York Sun:* "It is indecent to depict any race by exaggerating its lowest feature, and to hold up to ridicule an entire people because of any poverty or faults of a small number."[12] The offense in New York, of a sort not suspected by Yeats, was not about origins but about futures, and the familiar stage caricature in *McFadden's Row* and the display of it before a general audience did not serve the collective purpose. This would remain the offense of *The Playboy.*

Another response in New York to exaggerations perceived as insults that might undermine growing local success was counter-exaggeration. This, of course, could be ludicrous. Thomas Flanagan, writing about the founding of the American-Irish Historical Society just before the turn of the century, noted how at that point the Irish and their descendants in America "were a people without a culture, in the honorific rather than neutral anthropological meaning of that term." One reaction was to insist on "a consoling counter-literature which boasted that at some time in the remote and unspecified past, Ireland had possessed not merely a culture but one which surpassed that of Periclean Athens or Florence of the Medicis, with bards loftier than Homer and heroes braver than Ajax."[13] With growing influence and unity, the Irish in New York could counter the image of the Mayo bog with one of their own invention. A notable example was the "Irish Historic Pageant" of 1913, which certainly presented an image that pleased most more than *The Playboy* did in 1911. The pageant at the Sixty-ninth Regiment Armory featured "five hundred participants, recruited from Gaelic societies, the Irish American Athletic League, and the Sixty-ninth Regiment, all in native dress of the period," which was unspecified, and promised to "make the past live again." The performance opened with the High King and Queen on the Hill of Tara watching athletic contests intended to demonstrate "the glories of ancient Irish civilization when the other nations were still submerged in medieval gloom."[14] Whatever the validity of the basic premise of this much-disputed history, the degree in presentation was excessive. This sort of exaggeration of ancient Irish glories in New York would also touch directly on the Irish Players tour. In 1911 the founder of the Gaelic League in Ireland, Douglas Hyde, lacking other representatives to send to New York to raise funds, resorted to Shane Leslie, whom Hyde's biographers describe as "a Cambridge dandy from county Monaghan who wore a saffron kilt," and whom even Hyde acknowledged was "an amateur Irish Irelander." The New York press delighted in Leslie and made a fool of him, which he admitted: "They are out for fun and misrepresentation as surely as I am out for dollars." But what upset Leslie even more was being pushed off the front pages in November 1911: "*The Playboy* has proved a sickening piece of bad luck for me."[15]

The Irish Players performance of *The Playboy* in New York was part of a five-month tour, with a repertory of sixteen plays, through thirty-one cities and small towns from Boston to Chicago and back. Though all involved were associated with the Abbey Theatre, the company was identified as the Irish Players to distinguish it financially and so avoid the charge of diverting the resources of a national theater for the entertainment of other nationals. The purpose of the tour was to raise funds for the Abbey, whose principal benefactor, Miss A.E.F. "Annie" Horniman, had withdrawn her subsidy in 1910. Many predecessors of Shane Leslie proved that America and the Irish in America were an ample resource, and now the Irish Players had an improved market strategy: John Quinn, for one, "admired the players, and Lady Gregory herself, as almost the only Irishmen who came to America not to beg but to trade, to offer their art candidly as value received."[16] The producers of the tour were Arnold Daly's producers, Liebler and Company, which covered expenses and returned 35 percent of profits to the Players. Liebler and Company also added as a condition of contract that *The Playboy of the Western World* must be part of the repertory.[17] Lennox Robinson was with the company for the entire tour. The public persona of the group, however, was W.B. Yeats in advance of their arrival and, after he returned to England, Lady Gregory for most of the tour. The opening in Boston in September met some opposition from Irish American groups unhappy with representation of their origins, but after the local authorities found no legal basis for intervention, the run at the Plymouth Theatre was extended. The company proceeded through New England and Washington, D.C., before arriving in New York in November.

By that time their opposition had organized around the *Gaelic American*. The newspaper had been founded in 1903 by John Devoy, born in Kildare, veteran of the Irish Republican Brotherhood, and paroled from British prisons on the condition that he reside outside the United Kingdom. It was also the mouthpiece of the Clan na Gael, successor to the Fenian Brotherhood in America as organizer of Irish republican sentiment. More than the Fenians, Lawrence J. McCaffrey writes in *Textures of Irish America,* the Clan na Gael "spoke for economically mobile Irish Americans searching for respectability."[18] In response to the Irish Players tour, the *Gaelic American* could already look to its past successes, notably the demonstrations over *McFadden's Row of Flats*. On October 14, 1911, during the tour, the newspaper published a resolution to halt performance in New York, "to make every reasonable effort, through a committee, to induce those responsible for the presentation of *The Playboy* to withdraw it, and failing this we pledge ourselves to drive the vile thing from the stage, as we drove *McFadden's Row of Flats*."[19] In keeping with a general debate almost completely consisting of exaggerations and overstatements, the *Gaelic American's* campaign against *The Playboy* would be guilty of many absurdities, including, because the players were barefoot on stage, hyperbole about the beauty of Irish feet. These are usually repeated in descriptions of these events. But the *Gaelic American*'s campaign also had much more wit than is generally remembered or often granted to any kind of antitheatrical and essentially reactionary effort. Though the newspaper did not ordinarily cover theater, the entire front page of October 21, 1911, was given over to *The Playboy* under a headline on how Yeats "Paints the Playboy in Glowing Colors." The reporters had caught Yeats in a white lie about how in Dublin in 1907 *The Playboy* had met "thunders of applause," and now they delighted in the suggestion "that the thunders of applause which Dublin Loyalists gave to a play that depicts the peasantry of the West of Ireland as barbarians of the lowest type and utterly debased are to be taken by the Irish in America as the emphatic approval of their kith and kin." They also hugely enjoyed the Yeats persona, as in a story on "Ordure and Art in Drama": "We Irish in America are getting a good many lectures on 'art' of late delivered from a lofty pinnacle so far above the understanding of the ordinary man that he has to gaze up into the clouds in vain hope of finding where the voice comes from." Later, when Shaw's essay in defense of the Irish Players was issued from England, the *Gaelic American* reviewed it as a work of fiction, as dramatic monologue by a character. It facetiously concluded that, like other of his most admired works, this one was both ironic and hilarious. The headline announced "Bernard Shaw's Greatest Masterpiece" and the story praised his great humor in apparently insisting that "the only genuine Irish are the O'Shaws, O'Synges, MacYeatses, [and] O'Gregorys."[20]

The opposition to the performances, or the anti-anti-Irish Irish players, formed a position that the touring company represented elitist and aristocratic preoccupations remote from the needs of the working people. Simultaneously, the defenders of the company were shaping up a comparably exaggerated position that their work was not at all "artistic" in the elitist sense and actually was close to the "actual" life of "real" people. Frequently this took the form of distinguishing *The Playboy* and other plays in the repertory from Boucicault for being more "real." The long campaign in support of the Irish Players in *The Outlook,* which later published both Roosevelt's and John Quinn's endorsements, began in July with a piece that told New Yorkers that this new Irish drama would be neither "the rollicking comedies in which Boucicault was so inimitable, nor the conventional Irish farce, which is the broadest and cheapest form of dramatic amusement." Instead, the strength of this new and more real Irish drama would be the "more virile work of Synge."[21] The displacement of Boucicault's cheap Ireland by the real, masculine Ireland would be a continuing theme through the opening nights in New York. On the eve of the first performance of *The Playboy* in New York, the *New York World* told the readers of its Sunday features that "since the time of Dion Boucicault there has also been much sentimental rubbish on the theatrical boards which has been generally accepted as faithful pictures of Irish life." Now, however, that would be corrected when the Irish Players brought the drama of "Irish life and character back to the groove of truth."[22]

It would, of course, require suspension of disbelief on a high order to believe that *The Playboy* or *In the Shadow of the Glen*, which was also in the repertory, were more anthropologically true to Irish life than Boucicault and or that they were totally lacking in qualities of farce. But the claim to realism was the focus of the company's own campaign, especially as led by Yeats. In July, the *New York Times* told the theater audience to prepare for "the poetical, the mystical, the subtly humorous, [and] the obscure." Yeats moved to correct this error in a letter to the *Times*. Writing as managing director of the Abbey, he explained that it was a misunderstanding to "imply that our plays are 'poetic,' 'mystical,' 'subtly humorous,' and 'obscure'": "The artisans, clerks, shopboys, and shopgirls who crowd our pit and gallery, and have been the main support of our movement for years, would not accept your impression. An intellectual movement in Ireland has to begin with the classes or the masses that it may win both in the end, and our work has begun among the masses. We are no dilettante theatre appealing to a few educated and leisured men and women."[23] At the same time, however, Yeats was publishing essays like "The Theatre of Beauty," in *Harper's Weekly* in the month the company from the Abbey played New York, that argued his well-known interests in stylized scenery and ritualistic movement, certainly not where to begin with the masses. The irony of the situation is that in the coming of the Irish Players to New York, the hostile audience, like that represented by the *Gaelic American,* was claiming that the artists were artistic, while the artists themselves denied it in claiming to be soberly documentary and following the kind of priorities that Maude Gonne listed as requisite for a national literature. The claims to realism that would be the source of great dissent were not advanced by the *Gaelic American* but by the Irish Players. On the question of high- or low-class affiliation, an objective judgment was made by Liebler and Company, which was otherwise outside the debate. For the New York appearance, they booked Maxine Elliott's Theatre on West Thirty-ninth Street. It had opened only three years earlier, and in 1911 it was in the center of the theater district gradually moving uptown to Times Square. The interior was designed after Versailles, with a lush treatment of marble proscenium arch, seats framed in ivory, and side walls matted in gold silk. Elliott, a dramatic actress, had banned musicals from the theater, and the venue was distinctly "serious." The site, at least, fulfilled the *Gaelic American*'s claims more than Yeats's.

Yeats was frequently the target of objections to the Irish Players tour. On the eve of the opening in New York, Seamus MacManus argued his case for *The Playboy* being remote from actual Irish life by pointing out to the readers of the *New York Times* that Yeats had just accepted a British pension: "Yeats, a young, strong, healthy man, with his beautiful mind and his genius worth to Ireland ten thousand of us little mortals, was in the past year offered a pension by the British Government, and accepted it. Ireland has lost Yeats; Yeats has lost Ireland."[24] Yeats, however, had by that point sailed from New York (for England). The Irish Players were led into New York by Lady Gregory, who was even more capable than the beautiful Yeats. Guided by Liebler and Company's agent, Mr. Flynn, the company left the brief skirmish in Boston and approached New York via Harvard and Yale. Of New Haven, Lady Gregory wrote in her account of the trip, "Synge's plays and others on our list are being used in the course on English Literature there, and professors and students wanted to see them." The mayor, as in the case of *Mrs Warren's Profession* in New Haven, did not. However, by 1911 declining fortunes of the powers of censorship, like Anthony Comstock's, were evident in New Haven. The guardians of the people announced that they had attended a rehearsal of *The Playboy* and were absolutely shocked by its graphic language; then they were informed in public that in fact they had attended a rehearsal of *The Shewing Up of Blanco Posnet*. Above the fray, Lady Gregory was on that day lecturing at Smith College. The itinerary brought the Irish Players to Washington, D.C., before New York. There, Lady Gregory recorded, "I had to get away early because Mrs. Taft had asked me to the White House to hear the Mormon choir. . . . I was presented to the President—pleasant enough, but one doesn't feel him on the stage like Roosevelt." She and the company arrived in New York on November 18, and she, though not the company, stayed "in a pleasant little set of rooms" at the Algonquin Hotel. On the next day, November 19, the *Gaelic American* was filled with news about anniversary celebrations of the executions of the "Manchester Martyrs," those hanged for the fabled attempt to rescue Fenian prisoners that was used by Boucicault to address his audience on their own terms. Lady Gregory's programs in New York opened on November 20 with her own play about insurrection, *The Rising of the Moon,* along with her comedy *Spreading the News* and T.C. Murray's *Birthright*. These were well received, but problems were expected when *The Playboy* opened later in the week. "The players are convinced they," meaning the troublemakers, "are from some of our non-paying guests," Lady Gregory wrote in her diary. "I think we must revise that list." Far from being put-upon by the threat, she rather welcomed it: "*The Playboy* is to be put on next Monday. I am glad they are not putting off the fight any longer." Advisers including John Quinn suggested means to lessen the direct confrontation, but these Lady Gregory dismissed. The advisers, she wrote, "thought it possible this might be stopped by letting the enemy know we are prepared, but I thought it better to let them show themselves. They have been threatening us so long; we shall see who they are."[25]

"They" were a minority on the night of November 27, and the field of play at the Maxine Elliott gave the advantage to the Irish Players. The *New York Sun* reported that "the audience appeared to be on a par with the first night audience at other plays, and there was almost the usual number of persons in evening dress"; the *World* gave a full list of the occupants of the boxes (two justices of the state supreme court, two retired justices, John Dewey of Columbia University, and so on) and noted that "a majority of the seat holders were in evening dress, quite evidently there for reasons of artistic interest rather than in any expectation of the riotous proceedings that came so speedily."[26] The disturbances came speedily only after an uneventful performance of Lady Gregory's *The Gaol Gate*. The curtain rose on *The Playboy* at nine o'clock. The opening dialogue in which meek Shawn Keogh is chided by Pegeen Mike was played by J.M. Kerrigan, who had played a smaller part in Dublin, and Eithne MaGee, who had not. Trouble began on entrance of Michael James Flaherty, played in New York as in Dublin by Arthur Sinclair, and long before the appearance of the Playboy, played in New York but not in Dublin by Fred O'Donovan. While in Dublin the dispute arose late in the play, on the provocation of villagers worshiping an apparent parricide, in New York the dispute began almost immediately, when Shawn Keogh is asked, at least half in jest, to spend the night protecting his fiancée, and he declines: "I would and welcome," he says to Michael James, "but I'm afeard of Father Reilly; and what at all would the Holy Father and the Cardinals of Rome be saying if they heard I did the like of that?" (63). It was not the parricide or the putative charm of crime to a young lady that ignited the Maxine Elliott. It was this enactment of servility to the church, which in New York was an especially cruel libel on the Irish when played before for a mixed and rather mandarin audience in one of the Shubert houses on Broadway. This moment brought cries of "Put them off!" from the gallery and then a thrown potato that struck Eithne MaGee. That was followed by a barrage of a prepared arsenal of vegetables and stink bombs. The house, however, was as well prepared as the hostile audience, and fifty uniformed policeman entered the theater from the street while fifty plainclothes officers in the audience revealed themselves and rose to eject protesters. With the actors continuing through the first act, through blocking themselves defensively near the wings, the police, almost all Irish and Irish American themselves, began to clear the house of all whose outrage was vocal. The *Sun* reported that the voices of the cast "couldn't be heard, for the angry voices of men and the hysterical cries of women drowned out everything." The shouts included "It's disgraceful! It's vilifying the Irish race." Those escorted out included "four well dressed women who had been sitting in the gallery . . . [who] stopped to shout a half dozen times at the men in the body of the house: 'You cowardly men, you cowardly men, to let a disgraceful thing like this go on!'"[27] The men did not intend to let it go on, and when the curtain fell at the end of the first act, the performance appeared to be halted, as vowed by the *Gaelic American*. The police were not done either, however, and the New York *World* gave an especially entertaining description of the labors of one:

> A gray-haired giant of Traffic Squad B was foremost in this work. He paced the aisles of the first floor like a sentry, and no one sat too far in the row to escape his arm. No one, either, was too strong to resist his yank, and no struggling was able to prevent him from tucking the offender under one arm, while his free hand found its swift way to the hissing mouth. The giant never waited for the opening of a door—his captive went through it as though from a catapult, while the police-

man turned on his heels like a soldier and stalked back for
the next man whose feelings had run away with him.[28]

After a period Fred O'Donovan, in costume as Christy, stepped before
the curtain to announce in a witty speech that the first act would be
repeated because the Irish Players insisted on giving every audience
good value for their money. During the second performance of Act I,
Lady Gregory gave interviews in Maxine Elliott's own dressing room,
"drinking tea and holding in one hand the potato that had struck Miss
McGee [sic]." She happily told the *World* reporter that "we have appeared before an audience that has demanded an encore of us. We had
to play the first act twice. It was a bit tiring, but still it was a compli-
ment."[29]

In the end, ten were arrested and something between fifty and
one hundred ejected from the theater. The performance was completed
at 11:00, the first act twice and the rest of the play in two hours flat. By
the end the house was quieter and many of the seats empty. Those arrested were brought to Night Court at the Thirteenth Street police station for misdemeanor fines of five or ten dollars. In the charge of Captain
McElroy, they were marched before the desk of Magistrate Corrigan,
and there they met their attorneys, Dennis Spellisy and John T. Martin.
The names of the Playboy Ten were O'Callaghan, Cassidy, Casey, Byrne,
Neary, O'Connor, Kelly, O'Coffey, Harford, and Gambler. The principal
complainant was one Rosina Emmet of Washington Square, identified
in the press as an artist and a niece of Robert Emmet. She testified that
she had seen O'Callaghan throw eggs at the stage. The crux of the charges
was premeditation, as evident in the ammunition brought into the theater. Only Lady Gregory, who welcomed the confrontation, told the
World that she was not surprised. Spellisy offered the argument that
the outrage of the ordinary Irishmen was spontaneous, completely un-
planned, and unexpected, but this did not persuade. It was the Shuberts,
owners of the theater, however, who topped everyone in overstatement
and exaggeration. Though they had deployed a hundred policemen inside and outside the theater, they claimed to be completely surprised
by the disturbance. "We did not receive any advance protest of any
kind from the Irish societies, and we had no intimation that it would be
distasteful to the Irish people. . . . we would not voluntarily or intentionally offend the irish societies or the Irish public of this city."[30]

Lady Gregory spoke of the entire affair with much greater clarity and probity than anyone else. As she welcomed direct confrontation with "the enemy," she celebrated triumph. "The whole intellect of America is with us," she told the *Sun*. "We found the most hearty approval of this play at Harvard, Yale, Vassar, Smith, and other colleges." In an adjacent column of the same day's paper, the *Sun* concurred and used the same terms. "Under ordinary circumstances 'The Playboy of the Western World' would probably have met with a triumphant reception by the intelligent part of the audience," the paper editorialized in its review. "The victory had been won by the drama before the curtain fell."[31] This was plainly not the kind of victory imagined in New York by Boucicault or even by Shaw, because it lacked the ingratiating engagement of the first and the reformist intention of the second. When Lady Gregory wrote about these events later in *Our Irish Theatre,* she counted out the Playboy Ten in terms that proved they were not to her mind among the intelligent of New York. "Ten men were arrested," she wrote. "Two of them were bartenders; one a liquor dealer; two clerks; one a harness-maker; one an instructor; one a mason; one a carpenter; and one an electrician." Without indicating the goal of her campaign, and with ample opportunity for revisionary hindsight, she stated again what she had told the *Sun:* "Our victory was complete in the end."[32] She apparently did not know that Yeats had told New York that her work began among the masses.

The victory was an aesthetic one and not without cost. Newspaper reviews were mediocre at best, but an enterprise that was by different perspectives either selective or elitist could count that success rather than failure. All reviewers deplored the behavior of the hostile audience, and, extending a trope already established in newspaper appraisals of Shaw, all used the word "literary" as preface to complaints about lack of dramatic and professional performance qualities. The *Times,* for example, attributed the best of the play to "the art of the poet . . . which helps to make Mr. Synge's play something more than a play in the ordinary sense, and lifts it into the realm of fine art." For the *Times,* however, this same literary quality conspired against performance. Admitting that "nobody doubts that the purpose of the Abbey Theatre and its players is wholly artistic," the *Times* nevertheless grudgingly found that "the skill of the actors is somewhat deficient, but they are at their best in this queer, partly droll, partly pathetic piece by the dead poet."[33] The unqualified aesthetic victory did not come in the press, and the reputation of the Abbey productions for acting style developed in America only during subsequent tours. The unqualified victory came among the artists, and it centered almost entirely on set design, largely ignoring play text and acting style. The immediate influence was exactly what Yeats had been describing until in New York he tried to assume the role of spokesman for shopgirls and shopboys. There are many statements by Eugene O'Neill, Susan Glaspell, and others documenting the influence of the 1911 tour on American drama. The most evocative, however, was by Robert Edmond Jones, writing about "the Abbey theatre on its first visit to America" with its "very simple, far simpler and far less self-conscious" set designs: "Neutral-tinted walls, a fireplace, a door, a window, a table, a few chairs, the red homespun skirts and bare feet of the peasant girls. A fisher's net, perhaps. Nothing more. But through the little window at the back one saw a sky of enchantment. All the poetry of Ireland shone in that little square of light, moody, haunting, full of dreams."[34] None of this charmed the less intelligent audience in New York. Nor did any of it pertain to the putative mission to eschew the mystical for the real.

The loss of a popular audience was immediately apparent. On the night after Lady Gregory's victory, the readers of the *Gaelic American* effectively conceded defeat by leaving the field. At the second performance, their places were taken by Theodore Roosevelt, who sat in a box with Lady Gregory and John Quinn and applauded mightily. With them was Chief of Police McAdoo, who found little conflict and so no cause to prosecute *The Playboy* as he had prosecuted *Mrs Warren's Profession*. Roosevelt asked Quinn to write about the Irish Players for his journal *Outlook,* which was devoted to national uniqueness, Irish, American, and other. The piece appeared in December 1911, prefaced with introductory notes by Roosevelt and followed by Lady Gregory's play *MacDaragh's Wife*. Quinn gave a credible account of the Irish Literary Renaissance and its inspiration in Celtic culture, all leading to an exposition on the Abbey's valuable lesson in "how to make the theatres a success and yet give nothing that is not good art."[35] The success, even without a popular audience, was financial, which, after all, was the pragmatic purpose of the Irish Players tour. Ironically, this victory was at the expense of another Irish fund-raising expedition in America, Shane Leslie's. In the midst of Clan-na-Gael protests about *The Playboy,* Douglas Hyde of the Gaelic League, Leslie's director in Ireland, attempted by public telegrams to John Devoy of the *Gaelic American* to divorce himself from Lady Gregory's productions. The result was a rift with

Lady Gregory and consequently with that consummate fund-raiser John Quinn. Another effect was a backlash in that class that included the Playboy Ten because of the hint of association, even if denied, between Hyde and Gregory. In January, while the company headed toward further protests in Philadelphia, Shaw resumed making his contributions to the public rhetoric of accusation and overstatement. "I warned the Irish Players that America, being governed by a mysterious race—probably one of the lost tribes of Israel—calling themselves American Gaels, is a dangerous country for genuine Irishmen and Irishwomen," Shaw wrote in an English journal. "The American Gaels are the real Playboys of the Western World." Of course, a year later Shaw could, on another occasion, and also in an English journal, revise himself by writing that "The Playboy's real name was Synge."[36]

Shaw's sense of the Playboy on both occasions was of a figure capable of a powerful lie; on the first occasion, Shaw associates this with danger and on the second with benefits. In the play itself, Synge put this dilemma in explicitly theatrical terms. Christy's fiction of parricide is exposed by the entrance of the father, who carries with him all the associations in the play of "the naked truth" (135). Near the end of the play, father and son confront one another before the "crowd" of villagers, and Christy addresses his on-stage audience with the lines quoted earlier: "Shut yer yelling, for if you're after making a mighty man of me this day by the power of a lie, you're setting me now to think if it's a poor thing to be lonesome, it's worse maybe to go mixing with the fools of earth" (165). This fits the position taken by Lady Gregory and the Irish Players: it may be a poor thing to lose the popular audience, but it is worse to pander to its demands. The position of the Mayo villagers, who withdraw into mediocrity, and of Pegeen Mike, whose recognition of loss provides the final line of the play, parallels that of the 1911 audience in New York: chastened, they withdrew. It was their lies and exaggerations, not those of the Irish Players, that were subsequently ridiculed. Another loss in this outcome, however, was the opportunity to bring a wide audience to art that tested its expectations and challenged its collective agenda. This was the kind of opportunity always seen by Boucicault, and his results were not always losses. The decision to cultivate a select audience aided the immediate cause of raising funds for the Abbey, but it ignored the greater one of fulfilling the role of a national theater. Even Yeats admitted that fulfilling such a role would require some qualification of the "artist's arrogance—'Not what you want but what we want.'" On this occasion in 1911, Lady Gregory would not qualify that arrogance. The only gesture toward the audience was a posthumous one by Synge included in the program at the Maxine Elliott: "In all the healthy movements of art, variations from the ordinary types of manhood are made interesting for the ordinary man, and in this way only the higher arts are universal."[36] His admonition was ignored.

However, on subsequent tours in America the Abbey company would recognize the interests of the ordinary man, with disappointing results, and so prove the benefits of Lady Gregory's resolve in 1911. The company returned for a second tour in 1913, getting generally positive receptions with *The Playboy* and the rest of the repertory, and then again for a third tour in 1914. But then there was a long absence, during which their own example of a repertory company devoted to art before audience inspired the growth of "art theater" in New York. In the 1920s the Provincetown Players, the Washington Square Players, and the Neighborhood Playhouse all became places where Abbey principles were followed, often in productions in New York of Irish playwrights such as Lord Dunsany, St. John Ervine, and, in a striking example in 1925, James Joyce. But by the time an Abbey company finally returned in 1931, it chose a safer repertory, including *The Playboy,* which by that time had been wholly assimilated into audience expectations in New York and elsewhere. Adele M. Dalsimer has analyzed the American programs of the Abbey in the 1930s and found them "unwilling to take any chances" and organized mostly by the strategy of avoiding political confrontation and following "the safe middle road."[37] The result served the purpose of raising funds for enterprises in Dublin, but it also created a stereotypical view of an Irish play, which was invariably rural and rich in brogues and trademark antics. It was a neutered version of Synge's "virile" subject matter known to its detractors in Dublin as PQ, or Peasant Quality. In New York, with its greater distance from any rural Irish culture, the image was especially artificial. It was distinctive, however, and a known quality. Though peasant drama was in the minority of works by Irish playwrights produced in New York in this period, it became more closely associated with the Irish play as a genre than Joyce's *Exiles,* for example. The resulting clash between the Irish play of a known quality and a play by an Irish playwright outside formula, non-Irish Irish play, would be especially apparent in 1934, when O'Casey's non-Irish play *Within the Gates* played New York at the same time as an Abbey production of his Irish play *Juno and the Paycock*.

Lady Gregory's victory in New York in 1911 was the victory of artists over audience, an outcome that is almost always the case in theater history in the twentieth century. Like Shaw, she chose an adversarial relation with her audience, and she improved on his example by posturing in public with her most elite supporters. The crucial play, *The Playboy*, tested the audience's ability to see in art something close to its own life. The audience represented by the *Gaelic American* failed the test, insisting in calculated lies and exaggerations that no play about lies and exaggerations could possibly address their own condition. In 1911 Lady Gregory and Yeats were stern tutors. They did not help their tutees and in fact misled them by insisting, in their own hyperbolic terms, that their work did not challenge because it came directly from the lives of the audience. This loss was like the loss in the lives of the villagers in the play: a failure of the community to achieve a utopian future of their desire. The principal reason in New York, as in the Mayo on stage, was fear of public exposure, of outside judgment. Lady Gregory, however, was fearless, and the potential benefits of the confrontation she staged were the benefits of the power of a lie to provoke, of a work of art to examine collective desire. *The Playboy* was later assimilated into audience expectations, and in fact became as much a favorite of the Irish American audience as the Irish audience. The assimilation was not aided by any new capacity for self-examination. Instead, it was aided by a shift in audience identification: a shift from identification with the chastened villagers in 1911 to identification with Christy, with his individualism and creativity, in subsequent productions. The 1911 production was confrontational because the audience enjoyed no easy power of disaffiliation from group identity. Then the power of the play to offend rested on its unvarnished contempt for the audience addressed by Christy on stage and for the audience off stage. This was a power impossible to retain in a public art, and subsequent artists and audiences found a means to domesticate it. As in the case of Shaw in New York, *The Playboy* in New York was an example of a method of attack whose initial success was inevitably qualified by the honor of being institutionalized.

4

JAMES JOYCE DOWNTOWN

The Abbey Theatre of Dublin contributed to New York theater history by rejecting Shaw's *John Bull's Other Island* for pragmatic reasons, and Ireland's national theater, once more in the person of W.B. Yeats, contributed again by rejecting James Joyce's play *Exiles* for aesthetic reasons. As Yeats wrote to Joyce in 1915, the play "is a type of work we have never played well." He could not have said the same to Shaw a decade earlier because exactly what the Abbey did play well was not evident before the J.M. Synge years. After Synge, Yeats could be quite specific about what the Abbey did, which Joyce's play was not: "It is too far from the folk drama."[1] Shaw found producers for his play, which was also very far from the folk drama, in London, but by 1919 the Stage Society there, including Shaw, had twice decided against producing *Exiles*. Sylvia Beach gives a humorous account in *Shakespeare and Company* of the various confusions that thwarted attempts to produce Joyce's play in Paris. In the end *Exiles* opened in German translation in Munich in 1919. Six years later the play had its first production in the language in which it was written, and it was, much to Joyce's surprise, in New York.

In 1925 Joyce was scarcely unknown, in New York or elsewhere. As reactions to *Exiles* will make clear, the New York audience at that point had a quite precise image of Joyce the artist, and it was quite familiar with works of his in addition to the notorious blue-bound edition of *Ulysses* published by Shakespeare and Company in 1922. However, New York was also a place where Irish drama had its own small place in the theater world, and, consequently, artists and audiences were presented with a choice between repeating success and risking innovation. Innovations are surpassed in time, and in New York by 1920 the drama of Yeats, Synge, and Gregory that had entranced artists had become cliché. In fact, it had produced its own counterreaction: interest in Irish playwrights not known for the folk "realism" that the Irish Players insisted informed their work. One example of this position is the influential critic Ludwig Lewisohn's *The Modern Drama: An Essay in Interpretation,* which was published in 1916 by B.W. Huebsch, also publisher two years later of *Exiles.* Lewisohn was plainly impatient with the amount of attention paid to Irish drama: "So much has been written of the Irish movement by people who understand it well, that I shall let my own account of it be quite brief." With few exceptions, Lewisohn dismissed all works by "the chief representatives" of the movement, whom he numbered Yeats, Synge, and Gregory. His principle complaint was that "these plays are not symbolical. They are 'folk and history' plays, and are supposed to move us by their humanity. . . . It hurts the eyes of the mind as unendurably as the eyes of the body would be hurt if you passed in front of them thousands of yards of Irish lace of the same pattern." This seems unfair to the work of Yeats, Synge, and Gregory, but it is the response of the time to the plays included in the American tour repertories and to their staying by the Abbey Company. Lewisohn suspected that there was a problem singular to the export product, that "the unsophisticated and sensible Irish people" saw through this ruse and that the American audience would realize that "the Irish movement, indeed, [has] lost all vision of reality."[2] The confusing demand here for the symbolic and the real is made clearer when the emphasis in the last passage is put on "vision" and not on reality. In this episode of the continuing debate over "real" and "unreal," the Lewisohn position is that what is most unreal is consequently most real in a visionary and a theatrical sense. This resembles the position of those "unsophisticated and sensible Irish people" of 1911, the readers of the *Gaelic American,* who attributed vision to Yeats, who denied it. By 1916 the general backlash against folk drama made conditions in New York ideal for plays apart from established Irish formulas—ideal for non-Irish Irish plays. While Ludwig Lewisohn wrote, two Lewisohns of no relation, Alice and Irene, were founding the Neighborhood Playhouse on the lower East Side, where they would present Joyce's departure from Irish formulas.

However, the first Irish playwright to benefit from the counterreaction to the Abbey and demand for the symbolical was Lord Dunsany, who enjoyed a great vogue in New York from 1916 to 1920. *Vogue* was the word chosen by Alice Lewisohn, and Dunsany's sudden popularity in New York surpassed that of the earlier "Shaw cult" developed by

Arnold Daly. In 1916 Clayton Hamilton told readers of the American *Bookman* that Dunsany was "more talked about than any other playwright in commercialized New York"; in the same year Lynde Denig reported in *Theatre* that Dunsany's "A Night at the Inn" was "the most talked of one-act thriller of the year"; a year later, *Theatre* reported that Dunsany was "as much talked about among the theatrical people who frequent Broadway as George M. Cohan or G.B. Shaw"; and in 1917 the first monograph on Dunsany, by Edward Hale Bierstadt, was published to explain why "all New York was Dunsany mad."[3] As the gushy quality of these commendations suggest, there was a significant personality cult at work in the Dunsany vogue. By 1919, introductory notes for a published interview with Dunsany described him as follows: "Not only is he a poet of unique originality, creating new realms and peoples, strange cities and stranger gods. He is a soldier, veteran of two wars, and bears a bullet scar on his cheek. He is a keen cricketer and huntsman and the best pistol shot in Ireland."[4] The marksmanship became legendary, as did his wound in the 1916 "Dublin riots." His title was dutifully explained for American readers, as was his ardent desire that "if he happened to emerge from the present war alive, his first act, after peace had been reconquered, would be to visit the United States, for a physical and spiritual renovation."[5] The image in New York of Dunsany the Irish playwright was unusual in its emphasis on patrician accomplishment. The more frequent image of the Irish playwright was either of humble origins, as in Boucicault and O'Casey, or as the victim of philistines, as in Shaw, and, in 1925, Joyce.

The production history of Dunsany in New York begins in 1915, when *The Glittering Gate,* which was written for the Abbey Theatre and performed there in 1909, opened at the Neighborhood Playhouse in the company's first season in its new quarters on Grand Street. A model of the rather expressionist set was sent to Dunsany, who reciprocated with rights to "A Night at the Inn." As part of a bill of one-act plays, "A Night at the Inn" had its world premiere at the Neighborhood Playhouse in spring 1916, before the play text was published. In the next season, 1916-17, the Neighborhood Playhouse productions had new competition in Stuart Walker's Portmanteau Theater, where three Dunsany plays were in repertory in New York in December. But in the same season, the Neighborhood Playhouse linked a Dunsany with a Shaw to great success. For Shaw's *Great Catherine,* the company had recruited Gertrude Kingston, founder of the Little Theatre in London,

for credentials, in Alice Lewisohn's words, in "the theatre of sophistication and intellectuality." For Dunsany's *The Queen's Enemies,* Lewisohn
herself took the lead and shared directing credit with Agnes Morgan,
sole director of all other Dunsany productions at the Neighborhood Playhouse and also director of the 1925 Joyce production. The company had
the further advantage of hosting Dunsany during the production.
Lewisohn breathlessly reports: "The first meeting with the soldier-poet
was at our home the afternoon of the performance; whatever anticipation I had harbored was held in check by the perpendicularity of
Dunsany's form." Dunsany's interest was in hearing Lewisohn as the
Queen read the climactic speech on the Nile after the river had risen to
drown her enemies. Apparently, he was disappointed. Lewisohn had
edited the speech, and this, she admits, "proved to be a stab in the back
to Dunsany's Celtic imagery."[6] The program, though, was successful
enough to be moved uptown in December 1916, to the Maxine Elliott,
where Lady Gregory had staged Synge, Yeats, and her own work. The
only change in the Dunsany production was that, in the role of the
Queen, Alice Lewisohn had been replaced by Cathleen Nesbit.

   The appearance at the Maxine Elliott underscored the comparison of Dunsany with Synge and other "realists" whose earlier achievement he was seen to have surpassed, and this comparison encouraged
statements of the evolving expectations in the New York audience of
the Irish playwright. For Harry Esty Dounce, writing in the *New York
Sun,* it was imperative to correct "the curious notion that [Dunsany] is
one of the Irish revivalists."[7] By 1919, general sentiment agreed that he
was not, because his work was romanticist rather than realist. This was
the quality that most satisfied commentators like Clayton Hamilton:
"Lord Dunsany is one of the most original dramatists of modern times.
In an age of realism, he has dared to blow a brazen trumpet in celebration of the ceaseless triumph of romance."[8] Unlike the one-act plays
performed by the Irish Players, Dunsany's short dramas, all allegorical
vignettes, were so extreme in their fables about heaven's gates, Egyp-
tian queens, and oriental gods that they offered no opportunity for
debate over whether they were realist or romanticist, much less whether
they maligned the Irish people. Joyce's play would open in New York as
a drama somewhere between these extremes: neither realist, as Irish
folk drama was perceived, nor fabulist, that style epitomized by Dunsany.
In only nine years, from the Irish Players tour in 1911 to the Dunsany
vogue, New York notions of the superior Irish play had swung from

"folk and history" to romance. Either characterization was reductive, but productions in New York encouraged these broad judgments on Irish drama, simplified but not inaccurate, that were not possible closer to the complications of proximity in Dublin.

In her own florid way, Alice Lewisohn described the Neighborhood Playhouse expedition uptown with the Lord Dunsany production in 1916 as "a timely reminder that our way was not along the thoroughfares, but in lonely bypaths."[9] But soon there were many on that lonely bypath, and one comparable expedition illustrates both the success of small theater companies with Irish playwrights and the demand for Irish drama between the established extremes. At the end of 1918, the Theatre Guild was founded by Lawrence Langner, along with members of Washington Square Players and others, including the former Abbey Theatre actor Dudley Digges. The premises of the new group included both greater professionalism and greater attention to a broader audience. Thanks to the owner, Otto Kahn, the Theatre Guild was able to take up residence on reduced terms at the Garrick Theatre, built by Harrigan, renamed by Mansfield, and always remembered for Arnold Daly's *Mrs Warren's Profession*. There the Guild opened with a very disappointing production of Benavente's *Bonds of Interest,* including Edna St. Vincent Millay in a supporting role.

Though folding the enterprise was considered, the decision was made to complete the theater lease by opening on May 12, 1919, a production of St. John Ervine's *John Ferguson*. Ervine was younger than either Dunsany or Joyce. A veteran of the Great War, he was left with a more conspicuous wound than Dunsany, but he never cultivated a similar personality cult around it. A frequent critic of Irish Drama, Ervine, in terms of previous Irish productions in New York, was closer in intentions to Shaw than to the Irish players. He thought that "Yeats, to whom laughter was positively painful, had little or no critical judgment," and he praised *John Bull's Other Island* for having "infuriated routine-minded Irish."[10] In 1919 Ervine was already ex-manager of the Abbey Theatre; his brief tenure there was undone as much by his abrasive personality as by his antipathy to folk drama. *John Ferguson* was about a rape case, which it treated without the softening humor associated, in New York at least, with the Irish play, whether derived from Synge or from Dunsany. John Corbin, reviewer of the *New York Times,* welcomed *John Ferguson* precisely because it differed from the previous Abbey fare of Yeats, Synge, and Gregory. "The Theatre Guild explored a new region of the literary map of Ireland last night at the Garrick," he wrote. "Instead of the whimsical comedy and the eerie, imaginative tragedy of the Irish players from Dublin, we had a bit of dour, upstanding realism from the north." After that praise for departing from the Irish Players's precedent, Corbin then praised the production for not emulating the Dunsany fashion. "It is perhaps because of the richer humanity, the sterner passions, of 'John Ferguson' that the performance of the Theatre Guild players seemed to reach a new level in our experience of drama from Ireland."[11] Aided in part by a labor strike that shut other theaters, *John Ferguson* continued for sixty-six performances at the Garrick. This success surprised even those artists of the company prepared to coexist with commerce. Since Arnold Daly's time, however, the theater's capacity had been reduced by closing the second balcony. The members debated the relative merits of artistic purity and financial security before opting for the latter by moving *John Ferguson* to the larger Fulton Theatre, which had opened only eight years earlier as the extravagant Folies Bergere. There it played an additional sixty-five performances through the end of the summer of 1919.[12]

By 1918 the "little theater" movement in New York City acknowledged its debt to the past Abbey example at the same time as it planned advancement. In 1925, the year of the Neighborhood Playhouse production of *Exiles,* Montrose J. Moses took up the topic of the one-act play in *The American Dramatist* by acknowledging that "the Abbey Theatre gave us the Irish one-act plays, and they went consciously to work to create a dramatic literature." Like Archibald Henderson introducing Shaw in 1904, Moses introduced the "little theater" movement in 1925 by reference to the "fervor of Yeats" and his essays on the national drama of Ireland.[13] At the time and immediately after the tour of the Irish Players in 1911, there was widespread ambition to escape the commercialism of mainstream theater. Major theater producers could be involved, though the results were likely to be disappointing. In 1913 Broadway producer F. Ray Comstock opened the Princess Theatre on Thirty-ninth Street, near the Maxine Elliott and the Metropolitan Opera. Designed specifically for programs of one-act plays before a capacity audience of 299, the Princess gradually drifted toward musicals and proved most successful as a venue for Jerome Kern's work. Something of the "fervor" of alternative theater groups in downtown New York, Greenwich Village, can be inferred from the opposition, including David Belasco. Though later a sponsor of "little theater" events, in 1915 Belasco could declaim that "this so-called art of the theater is but a flash in the pan of inexperience. It is the cubism of the theater—the wail of the incompetent and degenerate."[14] The emerging degenerate of 1915 included the Provincetown Players and the Washington Square Players. The designer Lee Simonson, originally with Washington Square and then with Theatre Guild, gives an idea of the inspiration of at least some of the participants: he recalls how in college he collected the works of Synge, "read Yeats aloud, [and] argued the world significance of the Abbey Theatre and the Celtic revival."[15]

Nineteen fifteen was also the opening season of the Neighborhood Playhouse, which was more devoted to foreign works than its counterparts, and so produced more Irish plays than Provincetown or Washington Square. The project had, in fact, begun earlier, when Alice and Irene Lewisohn were introduced by their industrialist and philanthropist father Leonard to Lillian Wald at the Henry Street Settlement. The Lewisohns' direction, though, would be much less activist than Wald's, especially after coming into their family inheritance. Alice recalled this event as follows: "Like children in a mythical tale we were sent into the stormy world with a heavy bundle to seek our fortunes. Free in a sense, because that bundle contained among other things nuggets of gold, yet they added considerably to its weight. For freedom cannot be purchased ready made." Elmer Rice was less starry-eyed. According to him the Neighborhood Playhouse was different because it "was endowed by two wealthy young women" and consequently was "far better equipped than almost any theatre on Broadway."[16] Alice's heavy nuggets certainly did help construct an entirely new theater, a luxury not enjoyed by many other companies. The location was on Grand Street, on the lower East Side, in part tribute to their inspiration in the Henry Street Settlement and in part testimony to their commitment to innovation, social and aesthetic. Then as now, bohemian/beat/beatnik Greenwich Village was downtown, geographically south and culturally *outre* relative to bourgeois midtown, and the lower east side was further downtown than that. All this was cause of much merriment when *Exiles* opened. Arthur Pollack in the *Brooklyn Eagle* called the Neighborhood Playhouse "one of those products of the Little Theatre Movement that justifies the use of the word movement by the simple process of occasionally moving," and Gilbert W. Gabriel, in the *Telegram*, explained "Irish genius entering via Grand Street" by reference to the play's double romantic triangle, "which was, after all, the Star of

David."[17] The Lewisohn image was also evident in the design and construction of their lonely outpost, with apparent austerity in what was actually a very expensive theater interior and stage installation. The latter disappointed Dunsany. He did not expect to see his "Prayer to the Nile" in *The Queen's Enemies* delivered in darkness, but he was told by the Queen, Alice, that the theater had copied a very up-to-date European system that gave little real variation between full light and blackout. The Lewisohn sisters also acknowledged the ethnic character of the theater location by opening it in 1915 with an Old Testament "dance drama," *Jephthah's Daughter*. The production was poorly received, especially by the lower East Side Jewish neighbors of the playhouse, who responded with cartoon caricatures of "Miss Neighborhood Playhouse." Dunsany's *Glittering Gate* set the Neighborhood Playhouse on its course to later successes. There were lapses, of course, even with Irish authors. After closing for a year of intense exercises with Moscow Art Theatre director Richard Boleslavsky, the company reopened in 1923-24 with a double bill of Shaw's *The Shewing Up of Blanco Posnet* and Yeats's *The Player Queen*. Even Alice Lewisohn acknowledged that "the plays selected were an unfortunate choice for a Russian director" and that Yeats's play "would have exacted far more finished and subtle playing by actors versed in the Celtic idiom to give it stature."[18]

All "little theaters" took from the Abbey example programs of mixed one-act and full-length plays produced and performed by a company. They also all shared great artistic ambition and equally great impatience with formulas, even those of the Abbey. There was an unusually beneficial, mutually supportive relation between the Neighborhood Playhouse and the Irish playwright. The playwright, including Joyce, enjoyed what Shaw, Dunsany, and Ervine enjoyed in New York: greater acceptance—always critical and sometimes popular—than in London or Dublin. The playwright also benefitted from the presentation of Irish plays in culturally prestigious settings, even if distinctly "downtown." The Playhouse, in turn, benefitted from the "discovery" of art and originality. This was a frequent source of self-congratulation in the New York press. For example, in 1919 Frank Wright Tuttle wrote in *Vanity Fair* that "it is somewhat remarkable that Americans should have found Dunsany, but after all they did the same thing with Bernard Shaw while London managers were so doubtful of his worth that Granville-Barker had to bribe one of them."[19] By the time of the production of *Exiles*, the Neighborhood Playhouse could unequivocally announce its mission of discovery in the program: "The Neighborhood Playhouse is particularly interested in presenting its permanent company of actors and dancers in bills as varied and unusual as possible. It welcomes every opportunity to try new experiments in drama, music, color, and movement." This mission fit the specifications of both "downtown" and "little theater": experiments as unusual as possible. According to the program, this mission led directly to Joyce as innovator and author of an "essentially modern psychological drama."[20]

The name James Joyce was certainly familiar in the 1920s, and associations with it in New York had been evolving over several years. The American edition of *A Portrait of the Artist as a Young Man* had been generally well received, with caveats about "realistic" language. For example, while welcoming "a perfect picture of genius in the making that has just come over from Ireland," the *Nation* warned against a "free use of privy-language and a minute study of the sex-torments of adolescence."[21] In 1917, in the midst of the Dunsany vogue, John Quinn, the lawyer and supporter of Lady Gregory and the Irish Players in 1911, used *Portrait* as an occasion to introduce readers of *Vanity Fair* to the author. "He writes with frankness and freedom that is not uncommon in Ireland," wrote Quinn, who already knew something about *Ulysses*. "That Irish frankness surprised and shocked a few in Synge's plays, notably in *The Playboy of the Western World*. But Synge's writings have now taken their place as classics. If James Joyce can keep up the pace that this book sets, he is assured of an equally high place. . . . He has written a play which may be as great a success as *The Portrait* [sic] and *Dubliners,* and one can never tell how far a first-rate man will go."[22] The American edition of *Exiles* was published in 1918, and its reception continued to give notice of vulgar language. However, these reviews focused much more specifically on his treatment of sexual matters with "Irish frankness." Padraic Colum, with his wife Mary a principal Joyce emissary in America, gently tried to prepare readers for the triangular relations in *Exiles* of Richard Rowan, his wife Bertha, and their old acquaintance Robert Hand. "The play is a triangle, but we forget to name it so because of the oddness of the trio's relations," Colum wrote in the *Nation* in 1918.[23]

Even more telling were the commentaries offered in a printed symposium on the play, long in advance of any production, that was published in the January 1919 issue of the *Little Review*. The assembled panel of experts detected triangles unmentioned by Colum. Israel Solon, described as "an American writer," stated that "Joyce in 'Exiles' has taken for his dramatic vehicle the fate of two men who are in love with each other and who are at the same time bound by the letter of conventional morality more completely than most men." That literary opinion was supported by a medical one from Dr. Samuel A. Tannenbaum: "To the psychologist trained in psychoanalysis the book will be welcome as an inspired contribution from the depths of an artist's soul to one of the most tabooed and falsified motives of human conduct—we mean homosexuality." When she republished this exchange, Margaret Anderson, editor of the *Little Review,* added notes of her own: "To which I can only say 'Bosh' for Solon, and, for Tannenbaum, 'Ditto,' as above." She much preferred and often repeated the remarkable opinion of her colleague Jane Heap:

> There are people, a few, always the artist I should say, who inspire such strong love in all who know them that these in turn become inspired by love for one another. The truth of the matter is that such a person is neither loved nor lover but in some way seems to be an incarnation of love, possessing an eternal element and because of it a languor, a brooding, a clairvoyance of life and a disdain. In other people he breeds a longing akin to the longing for immortality. They do not love him: they become him. Richard is one of these.[24]

This libidinal quality was the attraction for Heap and other proponents of "little theater" in an Irish play that spurned the realism of the inaugural Abbey tour and the fabulist style of Lord Dunsany. It was an attraction throughout New York in the 1920s. Ann Douglas's study *Terrible Honesty* describes the vogue in Greenwich Village, especially, for "*mania psychologica,*" "Freuding parties," and "psyching" entertainments with one another's motives and desires.[25] Irish drama had no monopoly on this particular attraction: Douglas notes, just in reference to Oedipal representations, John Barrymore's 1922 *Hamlet* derived from Ernest Jones, O'Neill's *Desire under the Elms* in 1924, and even Ludwig Lewisohn's celebrated divorce on the grounds that his wife was too old for him, which was the premise of his 1926 novel *The Case of Mr. Crump.* In the 1920s "Irish frankness" was a frankness among others in New York. But for a brief interval this was a principal association with Irish drama in the public mind. Later, Irish drama would be welcomed in

America as a rather safe product, unlikely to offend. At this moment, however, the Joyce play was produced in New York and not elsewhere because sexual content was valued in lower Manhattan. This kind of "Irish frankness" was an important part of the playwright's reputation. The place and the reputation, however, may have conspired against the play.

Jane Heap's statement is a striking description of the character Richard Rowan and the personal relations in the *Exiles,* which fully deserve the word William Archer used to describe *Mrs Warren's Profession:* "polyandrous." Joyce's notes when composing the play describe the action as "three cat and mouse acts,"[26] and the principal act is the writer-artist Richard's encouragement for his wife Bertha to meet Robert Hand in the cottage that was once site for the young men's "wild nights, talking, drinking, planning" (50). The *coup de théâtre* at the opening of the second act is Robert opening the door of the cottage to discover Richard not Bertha. After Bertha's arrival, Richard leaves them. At the final curtain, after all attempts to resolve the subsequent events at the cottage have failed, Richard, having attempted complete honesty, is left in doubt about Bertha's love of him and his of her. Heap's interest in the play, however, was in an entirely beneficial relation of artist to less-than-artist, though that was not at all true to the play text. Oddly, in this case it was a downtown artist who constructed a positive simplification of an ambivalent work. That role is usually counted the bourgeoisie's. Previous Irish plays in New York, including *Mrs Warren's Profession* and *The Playboy of the Western World,* demonstrated audience construction of less than beneficial transactions between artists and less-than-artists. In 1925, the staging of *Exiles* gave art and the artist a sanctified, privileged status: for Heap, "neither loved nor lover but in some way . . . an incarnation of love." New York, the 1920s, Joyce, *Exiles,* New York publishers, and New York producers all combined to assert a special privilege of art over audience, and no resistance could be found.

While it was publicizing *Exiles,* the *Little Review* was also publishing, in New York, the first excerpts from *Ulysses.* After beginning the journal in Chicago in 1914, Anderson moved it to New York, where it coexisted downtown with the Washington Square Bookshop on Eighth Street, and where she was joined by Heap in 1916. They were aided in this endeavor by John Quinn, who arranged an endowment of $1,600 and provided legal assistance without charge. In her autobiography, Anderson recounts being advised about Quinn in a letter from Ezra

Pound: "Don't go wrong about Quinn. He made me mad the first time I saw him (1910). I came back to him four years later, and since then I have spent a good deal of his money. His name does not spell Tight-Wad." She also recalls receiving the Joyce manuscript from Pound: "This is the most beautiful thing we'll ever have, I cried. We'll print it if it's the last effort of our lives."[27] Though the money was in place and the art object was at hand, Quinn warned about possible prosecution under obscenity laws. That became fact when the United States Post Office confiscated and burned four issues of the *Little Review* containing excerpts of *Ulysses*. Joyce was concerned about implications for book publication but amused by the medievalism of book burning. He wrote to his sponsor Harriet Shaw Weaver that "this is the second time I have had the pleasure of being burned while on earth," the first having been part of the long publication problems with *Dubliners,* and so "I hope I shall pass through the fires of purgatory as quickly as my patron S. Aloysius." He also hoped that the notoriety of litigation would help publicize *Ulysses.*[28] However, the *Little Review* publication stopped entirely with the July-August 1920 issue containing an excerpt from the "Nausicaa" chapter that records the sexual fantasies of Leopold Bloom triggered by Gerty MacDowell. Anderson, in her autobiography, recalls Quinn at that moment and adds a parenthetical note: "What did I tell you? raged Quinn. You're damned fools trying to get away with such a thing as 'Ulysses' in this puritan-ridden country. (His sixteen-hundred-dollar endowment had been primarily to assure our published 'Ulysses.') I don't think anything can be done. I'd fight it for you, but it's a lost cause. You're idiots, both of you."[29] B.L. Reid, Quinn's biographer, reports his subject's exasperation, expressed in letters to Ezra Pound intended to be handed on to Joyce, when Anderson and Heap staged "'defiant' speeches, refused to express any regret for their actions, 'gloried' in what they had done, vowed to do it again, and hoped the provocation would continue: it 'would be the making' of their magazine." Reid also reports Anderson's stance, which was worthy of Shaw in cultivation of notoriety by apparent aloofness to its pettiness. "I know practically everything that will be said in court," she said, dismissing all arguments. "I do not admit that the issue is debatable."[30]

Thus James Joyce's work came to be in the same New York Court of Special Sessions that had heard arguments on *Mrs Warren's Profession.* Joyce's prosecution occurred when Anthony Comstock's successor as director of the Society for the Suppression of Vice, John Sumner, pursued a complaint from an unnamed correspondent who received an unsolicited copy of the *Little Review* and discovered his daughter reading it. Even Quinn felt this was "not a case where Sumner, or Comstockery, or the Society can be honestly knocked."[31] The relationship between Sumner and Anderson was an improvement over that of Comstock and Arnold Daly. "Before the trial we had a skirmish or two," Anderson, otherwise aloof to debate, recalled. "One in the Jefferson Street Police Court and one walking along Eighth Street where he and I engaged in such a passionate exchange of ideas that we had to go into the Washington Square Bookshop to finish. . . . He was the perfect enemy—I won every point and he seemed to like it."[32]

Sumner won in court. The test for obscenity, as in the Shaw case, was whether the material would deprave and corrupt. Quinn's plan for defense was to keep Anderson and Heap silent, to call expert witnesses, including Philip Moeller of the Theatre Guild, and to argue, as Daly had, that the material in question was too disgusting to encourage immoral behavior. Quinn demonstrated this by pointing to the prosecuting attorney: "There is my best exhibit. There is proof that *Ulysses* does not corrupt or fill people full of lascivious thought. Look at him! He is mad all over. He wants to hit somebody. He doesn't want to love anybody."[33] On February 21, 1921, the three judges found for the prosecution argument on the corrupting influence of the text, ordered a halt to publication of excerpts from *Ulysses,* and fined Anderson and Heap fifty dollars each. The subsequent decision on *Ulysses* by Judge John Woolsey in 1933 essentially reversed this verdict, finding *Ulysses* too "emetic" to be an "aphrodisiac."[34] However, the 1921 decision was largely based on the unsolicited circulation of the text and not on a more repressive code of acceptability in art. As Quinn put it (and he paid the fine), it was not a case of Comstockery bullying a luminous art world. It was, rather, a case of artistic vanity. The unfortunate immediate effect was that in 1921 Joyce was left without publishing options other than Sylvia Beach's 1922 edition, which while illegal was ordered and circulated by the Washington Square Bookshop. But the distance between guardians of art and guardians of the public in New York had not widened since the parallel Shaw episode. Indeed, public tolerance had risen but so had expectations from artists for special privilege. The uptown *New York Times* predicted this in its editorial on the verdict, which foresaw "the usual outcry from circles self-styled artistic and literary over the fining of the two women who edit and publish *The Little Re-*

view." Downtown, Jane Heap saw only the perversion of repression: "It was the poet, the artist, who discovered love, created the lover, made sex everything that it is beyond a function. It was the Mr. Sumners who have made it an obscenity."[35]

These events all contributed to the image of James Joyce in New York at the time of the premiere of *Exiles*. Though the play was composed before *Ulysses* and so is frequently discussed as anticipating the novel, in New York the trial publicity preceded the production and created the local image of James Joyce the playwright. That image in 1925 was not so fixed as it would be once the canonization of Joyce, especially in the United States, got fully under way in the 1950s. The image was also a superb complement to the play, which put the artist figure, Jane Heap's poet and discoverer of love, at center stage in the figure of Richard Rowan. The poet/lover, in both Richard Rowan and James Joyce, is identified closely with transgressions against sexual codes of behavior. In the publicity surrounding *Ulysses,* the American public learned that Joyce, like Richard Rowan, had expatriated himself from Ireland with a woman who loved him but not his work. Rowan is a portrait of the artist as combatant. In the time of the action of the play, Bertha is a fully developed character and Rowan's equal. But their elopement nine years before was not driven by love. It was at least in part manipulative and staged to scandalize. Bertha establishes this in conversation with Richard: "You take advantage of my simplicity as you did—the first time" (52). Robert Hand, far less bold, introduces this matter in the first act: "Everyone knows that you ran away years ago with a young girl. . . . How shall I put it? . . . With a young girl not exactly your equal. *Kindly.* Excuse me, Richard, that is not my opinion nor my language. I am simply using the language of people whose opinions I don't share" (39). The intent to scandalize has been so successful that Robert advises Richard against correcting it because that will revive the scandal: "Refrain from contradicting any rumours you may hear concerning what happened . . . or did not happen after you went away" (39). The text of *Exiles* presents the artist as transgressor motivated at least as much by desire to shock as by sexual desire. This is as well understood by Rowan, who has no delusions of purity, as by the audience. In the code of New York in the 1920s, however, the axiom of artistic privilege means that any criticism of the transgression transforms the artist into a victim.

Though it was communicated without trademark cottage or round-

Left, caricature of Dion Boucicault transforming a "real" Irishman into a stage Irishman using a meat grinder (1880). Author's collection.

Below, Boucicault as Conn the Shaughraun early in what would prove to be a long series of revivals, wearing what he called his Tony Lumpkin's hunting hat, named after an early ne'er-do-well in Irish drama, the character in Oliver Goldsmith's *She Stoops to Conquer.*

Right, Boucicault as Conn in a studio photo. Courtesy Hampden-Booth Theatre Library at The Players, New York City.

Below, Boucicault as Conn, apparently shot in his rescue of Robert Ffolliott. Courtesy New York Public Library for the Performing Arts. The two photos are from different photographic studios, each with its own version of the generic Irish scenery that would outrage Shaw.

Above, Arnold Daly (left) as Marchbanks in the production of *Candida* that created the Shaw cult in New York City. Author's collection. *Below,* Mary Shaw in an American revival of *Mrs Warren's Profession* some time after the premiere of the play in New York in 1905. Courtesy New York Public Library for the Performing Arts

Above left, Mary Shaw in another, evidently later, American revival of *Mrs. Warren's Profession*. *Above right*, program cover for the American opening of *The Playboy of the Western World* at Maxine Elliott's Theatre in New York City in 1911. *Below,* The interior of the Maxine Elliott Theatre and the box where John Dewey sat on the American opening night of *Playboy* and Theodore Roosevelt sat for the second performance of the play in New York City. All Courtesy New York Public Library for the Performing Arts

MAXINE ELLIOTT'S THEATRE

WEEK BEGINNING MONDAY EVENING, DECEMBER 4, 1911.
Matinees Wednesday and Saturday.

First Appearance in New York of the

IRISH PLAYERS

FROM THE ABBEY THEATRE, Dublin.

(American Tour Under the Direction of Liebler & Co.)

Thursday, Friday and Saturday Evenings and Saturday Matinee

THE RISING OF THE MOON
A Play, in One Act, by Lady Gregory.

The Characters.

A sergeant .... Arthur Sinclair
Policeman X .... J. A. O'Rourke
Policeman B .... U. Wright
A ballad singer .... J. M. Kerrigan
Scene—Side of a Quay in a Seaport Town.

THE PLAYBOY OF THE WESTERN WORLD
A Comedy, in Three Acts, by J. M. Synge.

Margaret Flaherty, called "Pegeen Mike" .... Eithne MaGee
Shawn Keogh, her second cousin, a young farmer .. J. M. Kerrigan
Michael James Flaherty, called "Michael James," a publican,
                                                Arthur Sinclair
Philly Cullen.... }   } .... U. Wright
Jimmy Farrell .. } small farmers } .... J. A. O'Rourke
Christopher Mahon .... Fred. O'Donovan
Widow Quin .... Sara Allgood
Sara Tansey .... Eileen O'Doherty
Susan Brady .... Maire ni Shiubhlaigh
Honor Brady .... Cathleen Nesbitt
Old Mahon, a squatter .... Sydney J. Morgan
Scene—Flaherty's Publichouse.

The action takes place on a dark autumn evening and the following day, on the coast of Mayo.

PROGRAM CONTINUED ON SECOND PAGE FOLLOWING

Program for the "first appearance in New York of the Irish Players," with casts of the opening one-act and *The Playboy of the Western World.*

Above, Stuart Davies portrait of James Joyce that appeared in the program of the English-language premiere of his play *Exiles* in New York City in 1925. *Below left,* Phyllis Joyce as Bertha and Malcolm Fasset as Robert Hand in the Neighborhood Playhouse production of Joyce's *Exiles. Below right,* Joyce as Bertha with Ian Maclaren as Richard Rowan in New York the same year

Above, Ian Maclaren as Rowan and Malcolm Fasset as Hand in *Exiles.*
Left, Lillian Gish (center) before the war memorial on the stage set of Sean O'Casey's *Within the Gates* at the National Theatre in New York in 1934.
Below, the Young Whore (Gish) confronting the Bishop (Moffat Johnston) expires in the arms of the Dreamer (Bramwell Fletcher) in *Within the Gates*

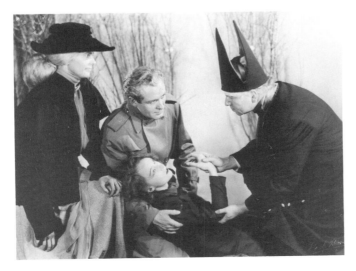

Above, Waiting for Godot as tried out at the Coconut Grove in Miami in 1956. Tom Ewell (center), Charles Weidman as Lucky, the tree, the mound, and almost everything but Bert Lahr (right) would be dropped before the play opened in New York. *Right,* the cast of *Godot* (Lahr, E.G. Marshall, Alvin Epstein, and Kurt Kasznar) as directed by Herbert Berghof at the John Golden Theatre in 1956. *Below,* Donal Donnelly (front) and Brian Bedford in the American premiere of Brian Friel's *Philadelphia, Here I Come!* in New York City in 1966. Courtesy Sam Siegel

tower settings, an important component of the image of the playwright and the artist on the stage is his Irishness. Later in the first act, Robert Hand tells Richard that "if Ireland is to become a new Ireland she must first become European," a point that does not impress Richard, whom Robert then links to "that fierce indignation which lacerated the heart of Swift" (42). Interestingly enough, in New York the question of whether James Joyce was "really" Irish or more generally European was at issue at the time of the production. In this case the Irish-Irish Joyce's local emissary was Ernest Boyd, who would write explanatory notes for the Neighborhood Playhouse production. Boyd had mounted a long campaign against Valery Larbaud's statement that with *Ulysses* "Ireland is making a sensational re-entrance into high European culture." Boyd, in part embarrassed because the 1916 first edition of his *Ireland's Literary Renaissance* had failed to mention Joyce, labored to prevent "the logical outcome of this doctrinaire zeal of the coterie," which was, he warned in the 1923 revised edition, "to leave this profoundly Irish genius in the possession of a prematurely cosmopolitan reputation."[36] Boyd brought his case to the readers of the *New York Times Book Review* two months before the Neighborhood Playhouse production of *Exiles*. There he warned against "the mystic hierophants" who would obscure the fact that Joyce's work is quite specifically "the revolt of an Irish Catholic Puritan against the peculiar conditions of Irish prudery."[37] Joyce himself was unhappy with this, writing to Larbaud: "Did Miss Beach send you the N.Y. Times? I think it [Boyd's piece] ought to be answered."[38] But he could scarcely control his image in New York. It had been set, and in 1924 Malcolm Cowley reiterated most of it in a profile in the *Bookman:* "During the silence you observe him more closely, noting his abnormally high forehead and silky beard, but especially the gestures of these long, soft, white hands, these cold and astonishing hands. There is little else remarkable about the person of this outcast and expatriate against whom all the forces of custom and decorum and propriety thunder daily. He is a slim, bearded Irishman of forty."[39] Joyce provided both a play and an image of the Irish playwright that was beyond Abbey precedent. No product of the "folk," James Joyce, like his character Richard Rowan, was perceived by the theater audience of 1925 as aloof, intellectual, and sexual. The play, equally distant from "folk," presented a suburban Ireland, neither the rural image of Synge's plays already familiar in New York nor the gritty slum image about to travel from Dublin to New York in the first plays of O'Casey. Between the realist and the fabulist, and also between the stage images of cottage and tenement, *Exiles* offered on stage a real Ireland outside formulas. It also tested the question of whether "real" Ireland, not familiar images of it, could be presented without dissolving into a generalized European identity. It could. Evidently, Joyce thought so. Interestingly, his surrogate on stage, Rowan, does not.

The New York production of *Exiles* began to take shape in 1923, aided immensely by the sculptor Jo Davidson. "I telephoned to Mrs Davidson," Joyce wrote to Harriet Shaw Weaver, "who told me that her husband got a wireless message from Miss Lewisohn who is the proprietress of a New York theatre asking him to telegraph to me and then to her as they want to put the play into rehearsal." But the contract was not signed until July 1924. Again, Joyce to Weaver: "The Neighbourhood Playhouse of New York sent me a contract agreeing to all my terms of last year: advance of $250, limit of 1 year or retainer of $500 for another, accounts weekly and stipulations as to production. I have signed and am returning it."[40] Jane Heap recalled how, after the *Ulysses* courtroom case, several "intellectual theatres" in New York and elsewhere in America became interested in producing *Exiles,* drawn, certainly, by both the notoriety of the author and the safety of presenting a work other than the one prosecuted. In New York, the Theatre Guild was frequently suggested, and the Provincetown Playhouse was considered, but, according to Heap, "John Quinn, who represented Mr. Joyce, was afraid of the Provincetown properties and wanted a decently furnished living-room, guaranteed, before he would talk rights."[41] Alice Lewisohn, in Europe during the winter of the production, visited Joyce in Paris. In addition to inquiring about his homesickness for Ireland, "I confided my reactions to the play and asked him if he had intended to indicate the two men as different aspects of one man. He admitted that the idea had never occurred to him, but it was quite possible and an interesting angle. 'But,' he continued, 'the artist is not concerned with the interpretation of his work.'"[42]

When the play opened on February 19, 1925, playgoers first met, on the opening page of the program, Ernest Boyd's continuing concern with "the clutches of aesthetic hierophants" and "devotees of the cult" who "are in charge of the funeral arrangements for burying the author in esoteric ground." Boyd, instead, introduced the play to the playgoers as an intense confrontation of artist with those spectators "with the courage of one's convictions." As would several reviewers, Boyd introduced Joyce the playwright by reference to his broadside of 1901, "The Day of the Rabblement," in which Joyce attacked the Irish National Theatre for stooping to the level of its audience. "It is strange to see the artist," wrote Joyce, then nineteen years old, "making terms with the rabblement."[43] Elsewhere, the playbill printed poem XXXII from Joyce's *Chamber Music* and a portrait sketch by Stuart Davies of Joyce glaring at the viewer from a tawdry Irish pub. However, in *Exiles* the image of the artist in Richard Rowan is more complicated. Robert Hand says to Richard of the elopement, "You are not so young a man as you were then" (39). Nor was James Joyce the playwright as young as James Joyce the author of "Day of the Rabblement."

The cast of the production was largely recruited from the Neighborhood Playhouse regular company and instructional staff in its school. The director, Agnes Morgan, was director of thirty-five Neighborhood Playhouse productions from 1915 until its close in 1927, including plays as different as Dunsany's and five editions of the Neighborhood Playhouse's celebrated annual *Grand Street Follies*. She was also a graduate of George Pierce Baker's famous drama workshop at Harvard. Her governing concept for *Exiles* was debate, and there was general dismay that the pace of the dialogue was both slow and unvaried. Ian Maclaren, as Rowan, was especially criticized for revealing in three full acts only a single tone of voice. Phyllis Joyce, whose name pleased the playwright, received praise for her Bertha because, as the actress was undertrained, the character was not wholly indoctrinated into the Neighborhood Playhouse style of momentous revelation. By simplifying the text, the production managed to produce what Jane Heap called "a languor, a brooding," without the "clairvoyance" she thought would necessarily follow.

In press reviews of *Exiles,* comparisons were made with Shaw and Ibsen, not Synge or Lady Gregory. The contemporary suburban setting of Merrion and Ranelagh did not feature a pub. The sole gesture toward the predictable "stage Ireland" is an offstage fishwoman, a dissonant note in any production. Still, as George Jean Nathan put it, "One can tell with one ear plugged up that the author is an Irishman." In fact, Robert Benchley's negative notice was reserved for a month so it could appear in the Saint Patrick's Day issue of *Life,* an early magazine of wit and sophistication in the mode of the *New Yorker,* along with cartoon caricatures of drunken, fighting Irishmen. Despite Boyd's efforts, the reception demonstrated that neither a play nor a playwright need adhere to recognizable formulas to be considered Irish: that at this point expectations allowed for a non-Irish Irish play, as they had for Shaw and as they will for O'Casey. *Exiles* also established expectations for the Irish playwright to be distinctly intellectual, rather more in the mode of Shaw than Boucicault or Synge. In the *New Republic,* Robert Littell described the text as "brain spun heaviness" and the production as adding "ludicrous sagginess of its own." The *New York Graphic* assigned an amateur "Critic for a Night," who allowed that "for the ultra intellectual the drama, *Exiles,* presented at the Neighborhood Playhouse, will prove exceedingly interesting."[44] In this respect *Exiles* in the 1920s established an identity for the Irish play that would be reclaimed by *Waiting for Godot* in the 1950s.

The first English-language performance of *Exiles* communicated the privileged status and special prerogatives of the artist in the unilateral terms one might expect from the sponsorship by Anderson, Heap, and Lewisohn. Only Joseph Wood Krutch, then at Columbia and a distinctly uptown rather than downtown voice, saw the outcome as more than a predictable homage to the artist. Whether from the text or from the performance, he alone was most precise on the predicament of the artist at the end of the play. "The play ends in complete despair," he wrote in the *Nation.* "Alienated from his wife and from his friend, doubtful of his own motives, the hero stands sure of only two things: the intensity of his own suffering and the fact that he has never bowed to any convention or accepted any compromise."[45] The more general reception welcomed without qualification the special prerogatives of the artist, Richard Rowan's superiority to the social conventions controlling less-than-artists, and his right to manipulate others in service to his solitary and noble goals. In general, response resisted the text's presentation of this prerogative as a bleak prospect. Richard Rowan at the end of *Exiles* concedes the liability of principle: "I have wounded my soul for you—a deep wound of doubt which can never be healed. I can never know, never in this world. I do not wish to know or to believe. I do not care. It is not in the darkness of belief that I desire you. But in restless living wounding doubt" (112). This was a final uncertainty that George Jean Nathan could not accept. He did not fault Joyce's dramatic "materials," mainly the triangular relationships. But he reported that in failing to resolve these relationships, most conspicuously the unresolved questions of Bertha's faithfulness to Richard, Joyce "lacked clear analysis of this theme and dramatic materials" and so fell prey to "the typical

Irish vagueness": "This Irish vagueness—in many cases it is described as mysticism (for what reason, God knows!)—is not so often the appealing merit that some find it as an irritating fault. It is merely the result of a befuddlement of mind which produces either fine poets like Synge or bad playwrights like Joyce."[46] For clear analysis of the theme, Nathan meant certainty in conclusion. In a few years he would sponsor unshakable certainty in the face of contrary reality in Sean O'Casey's *Within the Gates* in New York. In 1925, Nathan restricted *Exiles* to hagiography of the artist figure, and he reprimanded the production for any departure from that resolution. Joyce's downtown sponsors in New York in 1925 were not exploring a lonely bypath at all; they were satisfying a general expectation. Stark Young of the *New York Times,* uptown paper of record, thought the evening "one of the events of the theatrical year."[47]

Joyce put uncertainty on New York stage long before Samuel Beckett, but *Exiles* closed without any publicity or influence comparable to *Waiting for Godot* in 1956. This disappointed Joyce, who on the evidence of his letters had hoped for a *"succes d'estime"* and then resigned himself to less: "I don't think *Exiles* was a great success," he wrote to Harriet Shaw Weaver, to whom he later sent the program and some notices. "There is neither a motor car nor a telephone in it."[48] Joyce apparently was unaware of it, but considerable attention had focused instead on Eugene O'Neill's play of triangular relations, *Desire under the Elms.* It had opened at the Greenwich Village Theatre, colleague of the Neighborhood Playhouse, in the fall of 1924, and by the time *Exiles* opened, *Desire* had moved uptown to the Earl Carroll Theatre. It was, in fact, advertised in the Neighborhood Playhouse program for *Exiles.* In February, when Joyce's play opened, *Desire* attracted attention as the target of a censorship program to "clean up" the Broadway stage. The author of *Exiles* did not attract the attention of the vigilant censors as had the author of *Ulysses.* O'Neill, who had three productions on stage in February 1925, certainly knew of Joyce's play. His biographer Louis Shaeffer reports that, in 1924, "O'Neill met Padraic and Mary Colum, a young literary couple from Ireland who knew all the big guns at home—Yeats, Joyce, Lady Gregory, Synge, Lennox Robinson—and played host to them one weekend. O'Neill was particularly interested in Joyce and asked so many questions about his play *Exiles,* which he had not heard of before, that Colum afterward sent him a copy."[49] Of course, O'Neill's play did not have a motorcar or a telephone either. Joyce's version of the familiar playwright's complaint about expectations for the momentarily chic certainly misses the point of the New York production. The point was not that the production of *Exiles* had too little to please the audience. It was that it had too much.

The subsequent history of *Exiles* helps account for why a play by a figure such as Joyce could fail to please or to outrage a 1925 audience. Explanations were proposed immediately by Joyce's American publisher, Ben W. Huebsch, in a letter to the Neighborhood Playhouse producer, Helen Arthur, and copied to Sylvia Beach. "The difficulty becomes complex," he wrote, "in that each character must be realized from the point of view of what he permits the audience to hear and from what he permits the audience to infer." Huebsch's point was about the need for the staging to work with inferences and silences to complement the action's inconclusiveness and doubt. "The audience must get a notion of what the characters think of each other without depending entirely upon what they say to each other," he wrote to Arthur after seeing Maclaren and the rest of the cast on opening night.[50] Joyce's intention to work with inferences and silences has been analyzed by John MacNicholas, who has shown how silences dominate the third act and how Joyce in manuscript was as exacting in stage directions as to correct "a long painful silence" to "a long silence." "It is an interesting irony," according to MacNicholas, "that two Irishmen, Joyce and Beckett, should have been the first to exploit silence in an art defined by human speech."[51] More of Joyce's intentions became known when his composition notes became available, and these notes help explain the limitations of the Neighborhood Playhouse production and strengths of later successful productions. In 1940, the year before his death, Joyce had left his personal papers with Paul Léon, who died in a concentration camp during the war. Eventually the notes passed in ownership from the National Library in Dublin to the University of Buffalo. Published in 1951 in an edition of the play with an introduction by Padraic Colum, the notes reveal a number of biographical details in the play's action at a time after his death when Joyce's entire biography was becoming better known. The influence of the biography was clear in the Renata Theatre revival in New York in 1957, which largely repeated the Neighborhood Playhouse conception of the courageous artist. Brooks Atkinson of the *Times* greeted this enthusiastically: "In 1957, when most of the facts about him are on the record, it is a sobering thing to hear the voice of a writer who made a complete break with the world for intellectual freedom."[52] Taking as its premise, like the first production in New York, the unquestioned virtue of artistic freedom, this production aroused less interest and no resistance. Early in the century, the Irish play in the hands of Shaw and Lady Gregory had introduced New York to the idea of selecting an audience, which contained but did not eliminate opposition. Later in the century, and Joyce's *Exiles* in the 1950s is just one example, the Irish play, like others in New York, resorted to selecting acceptable statements, which made opposition unlikely.

Joyce's notes also indicate intentions that escaped the production in the 1920s and that, once heeded, make the work powerful and influential on the stage. The greatest interest of the notes, and an additional link between Joyce and Beckett, is the design for a more metaphysical than psychological statement. This is apparent in the degree to which Joyce hoped to avoid emotion in performance. "The greatest danger in the writing of this play," he wrote," is tenderness of speech or of mood" (126). The metaphysical interest is also apparent in what Joyce wanted to present as subject in place of emotion: "Robert is convinced of the non-existence, of the unreality of the spiritual facts which exist and are real for Richard, the action of the piece should however convince Robert of the existence and reality of Richard's mystical defence of his wife. If this defence be a reality how can those facts on which it is based be then unreal?" (116). Marvin Magalaner and Richard M. Kain, who published an early history of the reception of Joyce, recognized in 1956 that already there were two well-defined approaches to *Exiles*: "the naturalistic and the metaphysical, the first centering on psychological problems, the latter dealing with ultimate contradictions in existence."[53] The Neighborhood Playhouse production, like the Renata one, used as a point of departure the psychological conception of the play. The most acclaimed productions of the play, however, were those directed by Harold Pinter in London, first at the Mermaid Theatre in 1970 and then, with some cast changes, as a Royal Shakespeare Company production at the Aldwych in 1971. Pinter's interest in inferences and silences like those in Beckett's plays was well known, and he had no interest in contributing to Joyce's evolving biography. Instead, it was the metaphysical conception of the action that made the production so successful. In his laudatory review, Martin Esslin demonstrated the kind of provocation Pinter designed:

> Have Bertha and Robert made love in the cottage after Richard left? The next morning Robert talks about his having *dreamt*

of possessing her. And she agrees that it was no more than a dream. Yet—does that mean that he did consummate the affair but realised that she would never leave her husband, hence this one consummation was no more than an imitation, a dream of what might have been? Or does it mean that the *intention,* her willingness in principle was all that remains to him? And in that case: does it matter whether the affair ever took physical forms? The thought being more important than the deed?[54]

The 1925 production in New York produced no similar interrogation. Its statement on the privilege of the artist, and the easy reception of that by mainstream critics, gave the performance a satisfying resolution, which is a simplification of Joyce's text. Focused on the psychological, specifically the libidinal, the Neighborhood Playhouse production did not provoke the broader kind of reflections that Pinter's did. For all the rhetoric about purity of art, the 1925 production bent the play to local interest, the kind of thing that even Boucicault considered an error fatal to art.

Beckett's influence, in general and as channeled through Harold Pinter, had its retroactive effect on *Exiles,* just as, later in time, Beckett's influence will rejuvenate Sean O'Casey's work. The historical example of the Neighborhood Playhouse production shows how Joyce's play, like any play, can be undone by enthusiasts. By its limitations, this production also indicates something of the potential power of *Exiles,* which is more than the work of the novelist on his day off. There are many elements that control the attention any theatrical performance attracts. Because of the prominence of Joyce at this time, the Neighborhood Playhouse production had some important elements in place, as the number of front-line reviewers lured as far downtown as Grand Street proves. The general lack of reaction to the production is a useful example of art theater's capacity to shroud in iconoclastic rhetoric a very facile capitulation to local expectations: the work of art rendered innocuous, not by civic officials, but by artists, or, as the *Times* put it in its editorial on the *Ulysses* decision, "circles self-styled artistic and literary." That characteristic of the 1925 *Exiles* production has contemporary parallels at a time when "downtown" feels itself beleaguered less by opposition than by lack of support. In terms of the Irish playwrights produced in New York, the Neighborhood Playhouse *Exiles* suggests something of the merits of Shaw's or Lady Gregory's choice of direct confrontation as a "method of attack" and of the benefits in theater of real opposition. These playwrights illustrate how for a brief period in New York, roughly from the time of Boucicault to the time of the Joyce production, theatrical productions could flourish because of opposition, and how subsequently productions would not suffer from opposition but from lack of interest. This history in New York from Shaw to Joyce to O'Casey and then to Beckett demonstrates a very ready reception for Irish plays that did not conform to formulas set in a very brief period of influential Abbey tours. The conventions include the rural setting, the Catholic church as oppressive authority, and the puritanical bias on sexual matters, all associated with the well-known PQ, or Peasant Quality, genre play. In New York in 1925 it was not considered at all odd that an Irish play would be a "modern psychological drama" informed by "Irish frankness." Because of its distance from Ireland, which between the Irish Players tour and the opening of *Exiles* had become the Irish Free State, New York provides a valuable perspective on modern Irish drama that reveals the real achievement and ready reception of Irish dramas more diverse than those that would in the future travel across the Atlantic from Free State and then Republic culture.

5

SEAN O'CASEY AND
Within the Gates:
THE IRISH PLAYWRIGHT
COMES TO NEW YORK

The image of James Joyce that informed the Neighborhood Play-house production of *Exiles* was, appropriately enough, remote, pro-jected from afar, a telecommunication from Europe through the New York agents. In late 1934, in support of his non-Irish Irish play, Sean O'Casey came to New York to supervise personally the image of the playwright. He had no shortage of local agents for his play *Within the Gates,* notably George Jean Nathan and Eugene O'Neill. He was, of course, interested in preparing a new production, for in early 1934 the play had been assailed in London. But the effect of his visit was to project a quite specific image of the Irish playwright on both the dra-matic press and the society pages of New York. The timing, in fact, insured that he would be in New York with a non-Irish Irish play like *Windfalls* while the Abbey Players were in New York performing his earlier more Irish Irish plays like *Juno and the Paycock.* The result was a revealing juncture in both play and playwright that bears comparison back, in time, to Boucicault and forward to Beckett.

By 1934 O'Casey was established as a regular presence on the New York stage. *Juno and the Paycock* was staged in New York by Augustin Duncan, director of the Theatre Guild's production of St. John Ervine's *John Ferguson,* in 1926, or two years after its Dublin opening. *The Plough and the Stars* took only one year to travel from Dublin to New York, where it opened in 1927. After its rejection by the Abbey, *The Silver*

Tassie opened in London in 1929 and took only two weeks to open in New York. In 1927, sixteen years after the Abbey Theatre's first American tour and *The Playboy of the Western World* protests, Abbey Theatre personnel under the name Irish Players staged their own production of *Juno* in New York. That production took as home the distinctly opulent Gallo Opera House, which had opened only a month before. Having failed as an opera house with *La Bohème* and failed as a legitimate theater with a production of *Electra,* the Gallo—in later lives the New Yorker, Studio 52, and the Ritz—found its first audience in the five-week run of *Juno* with Arthur Sinclair, veteran of the first *Playboy* in New York, and Sara Allgood. Both received especially high praise. *Juno* would become a mainstay of subsequent tours of companies under the names "Abbey Theatre Irish Players" and "Abbey Theatre Players from Dublin," which was the name when it performed both *Juno* and *Plough* opposite O'Casey's *Within the Gates* in 1934.

At that time Abbey Theatre tours, by whatever name, were also a regular presence on the American stage, where particular Irish Irish plays were especially popular. After a lapse of twenty years, the official "Abbey" companies resumed touring America in the 1930s. By the time it produced *Playboy* in 1932, it was the fifth New York revival of the play. The repertory became rather rigid, with *Juno* in it: Arthur Shields, who played Johnny to Barry Fitzgerald's Captain Boyle in 1932 had grown up enough to play Joxer to Fitzgerald's Captain when the play was offered up again in 1940. There were exceptions, usually one-act openers, to the usual Abbey fare, and these were critical if not popular successes. When W.B. Yeats appeared after a performance of his play *Words upon the Window Pane* as opener to *Playboy* in 1932, Brooks Atkinson of the *New York Times* evidently was grateful: "After the play Mr. Yeats, who arrived on the Europa two evenings ago, appeared on the stage to make a brief acknowledgment. He is a solid man with straight white hair; he wears bone glasses, and when he speaks about Swift and Ireland he is very much in earnest. To a prosaic New York audience he comes like a man filled with the fire of the heavens."[1] More often, however, the opener was more in the "folk" mode—especially Lady Gregory's *Rising of the Moon* and *Spreading the News*—and the critical reception of the entire program more respectful than ecstatic. The general trend of critical impatience with "Irish realism," evident soon after its initial success, continued through the 1920s.

By the 1930s the context of a New York performance of an Abbey production differed from that of 1911, when Synge's *Playboy* caused such a row, in that the Irish Free State had been created, thus removing the most nationalistic grounds for categorical positions: either objections to portrayals on stage of Irish life or to demands for unqualified support for a cultural agenda. A further difference was the Abbey Theatre's need, despite the status as national theater, for financial support. The American tours were especially remunerative, drawing an audience cultivated over time. It was, ironically, precisely the audience shunned in 1911 by Lady Gregory, the audience of the Playboy Ten and the *Gaelic American*. By fall 1934, the time of the opening of *Within the Gates,* the *Gaelic American* was writing about "the simplicity and the rich, sparkling wit for which the Abbey Players have been acclaimed both here and abroad."[2] Having dismissed the popular Irish and Irish American audience cultivated by Boucicault for a higher-class one, and having lost that replacement audience by its own repetitive repertory, the representatives of the Abbey Theatre in New York set about recapturing the original audience rather than addressing the element of repetition. In doing so, of course, they sacrificed artistic edge.

By the 1930s the Abbey group had grown very cautious and most unlike Lady Gregory's unshakable resolve of 1911. In her study of the Abbey Theatre's American tours, Adele Dalsimer found that in the 1930s the repertory emphasized "carefree pieces of make-believe that had none of the satiric or somber overtones characteristic of the earlier comedies. . . . Designed to amuse, [the repertory plays] said nothing profound, but they would not offend." In essence, she continues, "the American idea of what constituted an interesting Irish play was limited, but, then, the Abbey agreed to these limitations in the majority of its offerings."[3] The American idea of an interesting Irish play followed particular formulas, including cottage setting, folk decor, and high Kiltartan dialect, all sometimes muted but requisite form, and this idea was reinforced by the Irish tours. It was this sense of the "Irish play" as a limited and known quality that O'Casey evoked on arrival in America in 1934. Asked by A.J. Liebling whether he was troubled by *Within the Gates* competing with "the Abbey Theatre Company of Dublin, the organization with which he won fame and which will also play in New York this season," O'Casey replied that he was not: "I don't write Irish plays, or English plays, or Dutch plays, but Sean O'Casey plays."[4] At this point, he was committed to a play that was not Irish Irish formulas, but he also planned to capitalize on the playwright's persona established with his earlier success. In short, a non-Irish Irish play, or, a non-Irish play with a conspicuously Irish playwright. This was the image of the Irish playwright Joyce had resisted and, after O'Casey, Beckett would resist.

In 1934, O'Casey was at this important juncture in his own work. As is well known, the Abbey Theatre profited immensely—due to both acclaim and controversy—in the 1920s from his realistic "Dublin trilogy": *The Shadow of a Gunman, Juno and the Paycock,* and *The Plough and the Stars.* In a famous episode in 1928, W.B. Yeats, speaking for Ireland's national theater, contributed once again to the New York and London theatrical world by rejecting, as he had plays by Shaw and Joyce, O'Casey's next, *The Silver Tassie,* for its expressionist departure from the trilogy. The result was a rift between Yeats and O'Casey that was only slightly mediated years later when O'Casey visited Ireland and Yeats "on money gained out of New York's production of *Within the Gates.*" The result was also alliance of O'Casey with Shaw, who would offer advice on negotiating with the American stage. As O'Casey put the matter in his autobiographies, where he refers to himself in the third person: "While clenching his spirit into the fight against the Abbey Theatre's determination to stereotype a writer's manner and style, and, through them, to fight the wider literary influence of those who believed that at the name of Yeats every knee should bow, Sean received unexpected reinforcement from the mind of Bernard Shaw." Shaw offered momentary solace by explaining that Yeats's opinion of *The Silver Tassie* could not possibly matter because Yeats "is not a man of this world."[5]

Nor was O'Casey, if "a man of this world" implied a working relationship with the artistic marketplace. As the passage from the autobiography makes clear, O'Casey, whose work had long challenged national and religious causes, saw artistic integrity as a cause to defend: his problem was not that knees should bow, but whose knees to whom. O'Casey's plays would continue—with obstinacy proportionate to negative criticism—along the direction of *The Silver Tassie,* and *Within the Gates,* subtitled "A Play of Four Scenes in a London Park," was the next departure from the "Dublin trilogy." Eileen O'Casey even described her husband's sequence of works as if the dispute of the first play propelled the second. "The rejection of *The Silver Tassie,*" she wrote in her memoir *Sean,* "the ensuing arguments, and the effort to get the play into London production, had not distracted Sean from other work. He wrote on steadily at the final version of *Within the Gates,* his symbolic play about Hyde Park from the opening of the gates in the morning until their closing at night."[6] In a later memoir, *Cheerio, Titan,* about O'Casey and Shaw, Eileen O'Casey expanded on this factor. She recalled luncheons with Bernard and Charlotte Shaw and the "polite manner" of Charlotte's charge that O'Casey was a "quarrelsome" man:

> "Why do you do it?" [Charlotte] said.
> "Why do I do it?" echoed Sean. "Somehow or other I am made to do it. Your husband did it, and still does!"
> "There you go again. You quarrelled with Yeats, you quarrelled with George Russell [AE], and now you are quarreling with James Agate."
> "I didn't quarrel with Yeats," said Sean quietly, "I differed with him on the question of drama, and I differed with Agate on his opinions."
> "You see, you stay obstinate. Why do you do it?"
> "I don't know," said Sean, "something within me speaks before I am aware of it." Sean was trying very hard to be good humoured, "maybe it is the promptings of what they call the Holy Ghost!"
> G.B.S. was trying very hard to ease the tension. There was a slight feeling of discomfort, and he said, in a calm, humourous voice, sitting upright in his chair, "He simply means, Charlotte, that he has got something and I have got something which you have not got."
> Then [Eileen] said, "Actually Sean is too honest; he says things in a blunt way. He doesn't mean to be unpleasant, he is merely truthful. I think he is right!"[7]

This was the reinforcement from the mind of Shaw, who by his own terms certainly meant to be unpleasant and perhaps untruthful. The suggestion of unqualified benefits to be derived from artists by less-than-artists resembles the version of *Exiles* constructed by Jane Heap and Margaret Anderson, and not by Joyce.

The question of how well this new O'Casey product compared with his proven successes became central to discussions of O'Casey's work thereafter. He frequently referred to this with some exasperation and some humor. For example, "they want him to go back to the writing of another *Juno and the Paycock,*" he later wrote about Irish critics.

"Because, so far, he has declined, they are about the build a wailing wall in Dublin to commemorate the poor playwright who took the wrong turning."[8] In 1934, this question of the old versus the new O'Casey was essential to reception of the new play, *Within the Gates.* In New York at this moment the question was especially pointed because O'Casey's old, "successful" work was playing at the same time as the new "experimental" work. Reviewing *The Plough and the Stars* in New York in November 1934, two weeks after he reviewed *Within the Gates,* Brooks Atkinson posed this question directly: "Since the time when he was writing 'Juno and the Paycock' and 'The Plough and the Stars,' Mr. O'Casey has turned his back on realism and written 'Within the Gates.' The comparison is vivid, now that the two of his plays are simultaneously visible representing two kinds of craftsmanship." Atkinson preferred the new work while allowing the "firm, muscular, overpowering drama" of the old work. Robert Garland of the *New York World Telegram* preferred the old work and posed the question more wittily: "Once you are in the presence of a B.T.S.T. drama by Mr. O'Casey— B.T.S.T. stands for 'Before the Silver Tassie'—you see quite plainly why he is the most popular dramatist on the Abbey Players' list." Garland thought the new work "hot and bothered over questions every schoolboy has answered to his own satisfaction" and preferred the old work for "guts."[9] What he failed to understand was that O'Casey did not want to be "the most popular dramatist" on any list. O'Casey believed that guts meant refusing that role.

O'Casey had replaced gritty Dublin dialogue with antiphonal chanting in *The Silver Tassie,* and in *Within the Gates,* his next production after an interval of six years, he invested as heavily in antirealism as Lord Dunsany. An initial impulse was to design the script as film because, as O'Casey wrote of himself, "he thought of film as geometrical and emotional, the emotion of the living characters to be shown against their own patterns and the patterns of the park." That project went so far as dinner with Alfred Hitchcock, whom O'Casey later rather cruelly described as "like an over-blown seal, sidling from place to place, as if the hard earth beneath couldn't give him a grip."[10] A later account of the project and the meeting indicates that this hostility again derived from the artist's contempt for the mercenary. The film could make "all its patterns to form a unity—its footballs, displays, speakers, evangelists, idlers, summer community singers; its swans, birds, dogs, traffic, and trees were to mingle together forming a changing and varied pattern around the life of a few people." But this was not to be because of philistine movie producers: "The things that didn't happen in Saragossa and Honolulu were more important to the film magnates than those which happened under their noses in Hyde Park. . . . So I turned the idea for a film into the idea for a play, and it appeared under the name of *Within the Gates*."[11] Coincidentally, in the same week O'Casey's new play opened at the National Theatre on Forty-first Street and the same month as the Irish company appeared in New York, the Abbey Players also began the world premiere run of its first film, *Norah O'Neale*, one block away on Forty-second Street.

O'Casey transferred much of the idea of patterns and geometry to the play text. As he recalled its genesis in his autobiographies:

> Sean worked off and on at a new play, *The Green Gates*, a title he afterwards changed to *Within the Gates*. He had written a lot of dialogue and rough drafts of themes, and now he was trying to knit the wild themes and wandering dialogue into a design of Morning, Noon, Evening, and Night, blending these in with the seasons, changing the outlook of the scenes by changing the color of flower and tree, blending these again with the moods of the scenes. The dominant colour of Morning and Spring was to be a light, sparkling green, that of Noon crimson and gold; Autumn's crimson was to tinge itself with violet, and Winter and Night were to be violet, turning to purple, and black.[12]

The play text that resulted insisted on stylized representations, very different from the carefully decorated interior sets of *Juno* or *Plough*. The printed text directed that "the scenic effects should be as simple as possible, suggesting, rather than emphasizing, the features of the Park."[13] O'Casey was also quite specific about a stage curtain, carrying the image of the park gates, opening and closing as gates between the scenes, a design he acknowledged as having derived from Eugene O'Neill's *Mourning Becomes Electra*. O'Casey filled this set with a series of characters identified only by their type: the Dreamer, the Bishop, the Atheist, and so forth. The critical role is that of the Young Whore, who, oppressed by poverty and disease, is shown the various available life routes of optimism, repression, and cynicism presented in palpable form by the other characters. Passing through this allegorical scene is a rather large Group of Down-and-Outs, embittered social victims and social outcasts, and a smaller chorus of Young Men and Girls. Both choruses sing songs based on traditional airs, many of them Irish, like "The Foggy Dew," or simple folk melodies, such as the "Spring Chorus," sung at the first curtain opening by the Young Men and Girls to the melody of "Haste to the Wedding":

> Our mother, the earth, is maiden again, young, fair, and a
>   maiden again.
> Her thoughts are a dance as she seeks out her Bridegroom,
>   the Sun, through the lovely confusion of singing birds,
>   and of blossom and bud.
> She feels the touch of his hand on her hair, on her cheeks,
>   in the budding of trees,
> She feels the warm kiss of his love on her mouth, on her
>   breast, as she dances along. [3-4]

The intention certainly was to revolutionize mainstream drama; the B.T.S.T. O'Casey had a regional base at the Abbey Theatre, and the new O'Casey, given the rift with the Abbey, would attempt to storm the strongholds of commercialism in the West End and Broadway. *Within the Gates* would succeed, according to O'Casey, sounding the defiant note, when "it broke out into an unsteady but glowing cascade of speech, movement, colour, and song. . . . the play would justify its full and defiant appearance."[14]

It did not justify itself when it opened in London, and the ensuing debate set terms that would be played out in New York in a more balanced exchange. In London, O'Casey had many disputes with the director, Norman MacDermott. As he later wrote to George Jean Nathan, who was instrumental in getting the play produced in New York, MacDermott "began to get frightened, and cut out almost all the symbolism, and adapted the play 'to the human needs of the audience.' The result was a production from which the guts and soul were gone."[15] After it opened at the Royalty Theatre on February 7, 1934, with O'Casey and Shaw sitting in a box beside each other, O'Casey in angry correspondence with the newspapers defended the play, scarcely mentioned the production, and attacked the critics. Among them was Gordon Beckles, whose *Daily Express* review had appeared under the headline "What Is His New Play Really About?" His chief complaint was that he did not know the answer, and his review described O'Casey at the premiere as sitting "with a twisted smile, listening to his own ranting denunciations of the world's hypocrisy." O'Casey's reply was to remind readers of the *Daily Express* that Beckles "challenges me to tell him what the play really means" and then to refuse to do so.[16] However, O'Casey's chief antagonist on this and other occasions was James Agate of the *Sunday Times*. Agate was unwilling to accept the allegorical function of characters, especially the Young Whore, a title he did not like: "The young street-walker is the idealized harlot that intellectual Bloomsbury is always running after. She prates rather than prattles, uses words like 'oblate,' and talks about 'composing hymns to intellectual beauty.'" A particular difficulty for Agate was accepting a non-Irish play from an Irish playwright who, Agate found, was more Irish when trying to be less so: "Mr. O'Casey is essentially an Irishman who, while labelling his characters English and dropping the accent, still retains the Irish idiom." This was also Agate's final word on O'Casey's point-by-point rebuttal, which was too long for the *Times* to print in full. "The difficulty," Agate wrote in summing up the disagreement, "is that I write in English and Mr. O'Casey thinks in Irish. This being so, I suggest that if Mr. O'Casey will get some Anglo-Hibernian to explain my article to him, he will realise that his letter was unnecessary."[17] Some London critics did welcome *Within the Gates,* but the production closed after twenty-eight performances.

All this was part of a longer dispute between artists and critics over the direction of drama. O'Casey, committed to his "defiant appearance" with or without success, was an important spokesman for revolutionary change, and Agate, with the influence of the *Times,* was an important spokesman for maintaining standards. A particular focus was Nöel Coward, who to Agate epitomized the best of the stage and to O'Casey the worst. Coward's popular play *Cavalcade,* celebrated by Agate, and also by St. John Ervine, especially galled O'Casey: "*Cavalcade* is a tawdry piece of work, a halfpennyworth of bread to an intolerable deal of sack." For O'Casey, "Coward's Codology" demonstrated particularly well that "commercial success carries the banner of pleasure, but there is no symbol of honor on that flag. It can add nothing to, as it can take nothing from, the intrinsic value of any work of art."[18] Thus the artist dismisses commercial success in the theater as dishonor while negotiating runs of *Within the Gates* on the West End as well as on Broadway. For a playwright very defiantly carrying the banner of a new and presumably more artistic kind of work, the importance of reception could not be negligible, but there could be honor in denying it.

When Henry James measured the worth of Boucicault's work, it was in reference to his audience. By the 1930s debate over O'Casey's work was about its two types, Irish and non-Irish, and between critics, both journalistic and academic. The critical debate that continues over O'Casey's work is about intrinsic artistic merit: whether O'Casey's defiance of the status quo of theater constituted an artistic breakthrough, or, alternatively, whether his insistence on novelty scarcely disguised a failure of imagination.[19] With particular reference to Coward, Agate, and the London production of *Within the Gates,* David Krause presents the first position:

> Perhaps Nöel Coward did not entirely earn the swatting he received through three chapters of *The Flying Wasp,* but it should be remembered that O'Casey was using the 'Coward Codology' to attack the concept of featherweight drama prevalent in London at the time. Just as he had fought the Abbey directors, he was once again defending the dramatist's need to explore new forms and provocative themes. . . . He was pointing out the direction that the drama should take at a time when the universal 'ache of disorder' was impelling most of the significant dramatists and leading figures in the allied arts to turn away from safe subjects and stock realism.[20]

All this O'Casey certainly intended to demonstrate in New York, where he expected a fairer hearing, and Krause goes on with some justice to compare "lightweight" English drama between the wars unfavorably with the accomplishments of American drama. O'Casey had long associated New York with dramatic integrity, particularly in comparison with London and Dublin. As early as 1928, on signing his contract with C.B. Cochrane to produce *The Silver Tassie,* he wrote to his sponsor Lady Londonderry that Cochrane "thinks that it may be best to have the play first performed in New York. Play production in America is nearer to courage & original effort than production here [London], & I think he is right." In the same letter O'Casey told Lady Londonderry: "England is fifty years or more behind the present power in Drama & limping badly too. And Ireland has had to abandon Dramatic effort to allow her to concentrate all her energies toward the creation of her Peg o' my Heart Pound notes."[21] New York became a more promising venue as O'Casey's resolve to surpass and not to repeat his dramatic work grew stronger. By 1932, after losses on *The Silver Tassie,* Cochrane had to decline the chance to produce *Within the Gates.* His advice to O'Casey was, "You can't go on writing fine things, Sean, unless they bring some material reward. I suppose you are tired of people advising you to get back to the method of *Juno.* I wish you would." O'Casey's reply was: "Your advice to go back to the genius of 'Juno' might be good for me, but bad for my conception of drama."[22]

When *Within the Gates* opened on Broadway, some innovation had already prepared the way there, and O'Casey could expect to enjoy some slightly greater degree of interest in his conception of drama in New York than in London. In November 1934, there were two Elmer Rice productions playing on Broadway, *Between Two Worlds* and *Judgment Day,* as well as Sinclair Lewis's *Dodsworth* and, entering its second year, *Tobacco Road.* But Anglophilia—linked to "safe subjects and stock realism"—was also evident when *Within the Gates* opened: Coward's *Conversation Piece* was playing alongside the D'Oyly Carte *H.M.S. Pinafore* and Sybil Thorndike in a vehicle called *The Distaff Side.* Thus while the American stage in the 1930s can be considered more venturesome than the English stage, and so compatible with O'Casey's ideas, *Within the Gates,* by appearing on Broadway, would compete with some of the same safe and commercial vehicles as in London. The "social drama" provoked by the Depression was a presence on Broadway, not a monopoly. Off-Broadway and downtown, there was a groundswell of work closer to the kind of defiance O'Casey planned. Good examples from the 1933-34 season, before *Within the Gates,* were the Theatre Guild production of John Wexley's *They Shall Not Die,* about the prosecutions of the Scotsboro Boys for rape, and the Theatre Union production of *Stevedore,* by Paul Peters and George Sklar, about race relations and the dispossessed. Soon after *Within the Gates,* in January 1935, Odets's *Waiting for Lefty* was first performed at the Civic Repertory Theatre on Fourteenth Street. Hence O'Casey would find in New York a degree of interest in a social drama about down-and-outs with, by contemporary standards, procommunist sympathies and a portion of agitprop. He would also find quite stiff competition from successful productions of just that sort of drama and an audience—general and socialist as well as critical—well trained to locate and denounce vacuous political statements. While in 1934 O'Casey thought New York a promising venue for his work, he would find there an audience in part disdainful of the dramatic harangue, however aesthetically arranged by colors, and in part too well prepared for the theater of "what really happened" in Hyde Park or elsewhere to accept less than completely successful exposure of hitherto invisible exploitation. Of course, he also faced the competition of B.T.S.T. while *Juno* and *Plough* were in town.

O'Casey had personal reasons to seek support in America. His conception of drama had long owed a great deal to the American critic George Jean Nathan, whom O'Casey had been reading with admiration since the Dublin protests over nationalistic and religious blasphemies in *The Plough and the Stars*. In his autobiographies, O'Casey recounts how in the late 1920s, "Nathan's *The Critic and the Drama* was a book of revelations to Sean. He was becoming less of the innocent gaum every page he passed."[23] In 1932, O'Casey met Nathan in London and began, at Nathan's invitation, to publish short articles in *The American Spectator,* a journal to advance social and artistic reform launched by Nathan in 1932 with a board of editors that included Ernest Boyd, New York authority on Irish artistic matters, and James Joyce. In 1933, after reading a manuscript copy of *Within the Gates* provided by O'Casey, Nathan declared it "one of the most beautiful plays I have read in a very long, long time" and suggested as American agent Richard Madden, who also represented O'Neill.[24] By late 1933, the Theatre Guild had decided against a production, which was the kind of rejection that in Nathan as in O'Casey only strengthened resolve. He wrote to O'Casey "I still believe that your play is one of the true masterpieces of the modern theatre. . . . I shall leave no stone unturned to get it the best hearing here possible." In addition, Nathan had secured O'Neill's enthusiasm for a New York production. A day after the letter above, O'Neill wrote to O'Casey thanking him for the stage direction reference to *Mourning Becomes Electra* and hoping that *Within the Gates* would get "the New York production it deserves," which had to include O'Casey on hand to oversee it.[25] In January 1934, before any contract had been signed, and before the London opening, Nathan began New York preproduction publicity with a piece declaring *Within the Gates* "a damned fine play" and the playwright "one of the outstanding geniuses among the younger dramatists of Europe." In March, after the London production had closed, Madden had struck a deal with John Tuerk and George Bushar Markell, who committed themselves to staging the play at a mainstream Broadway house. The agreement included a $1,500 advance for O'Casey, which

Nathan called "a record advance, I believe, for New York," and passage to America so that the playwright could insure there would be no repetition of the London decisions he thought gutless and soulless.[26]

The outstanding genius of the younger dramatists was age fifty-four when he arrived in New York City on September 19, 1934, aboard the *Majestic*. He was not a man of means, wearing a suit made from cloth given him by Lady Astor and bearing a letter of guarantee of £200 from Lady Londonderry. But he was a man of some importance, and the arrival was noted in the press. The Joseph Alsop account for the *Herald Tribune* even evoked Oscar Wilde's famous quip at American customs of having nothing to declare but his own genius: "Sean O'Casey, playwright and poet, landed in America yesterday for the first time in his fifty years with a prophesy of a better and revitalized drama as his most important baggage. His arrival in New York was the signal for the first rehearsal of a specimen of the new drama, his own 'Within the Gates,' which George Jean Nathan has described as the 'greatest play of the last twenty years.'"[27] O'Casey was met at customs by Madden and Nathan, in "a greatcoat," O'Casey wrote in retrospect, "so full in the shoulders that it fell round him capewise down below his knees, a curving wrinkle of humour, now in repose, trimming the corners of a full, sensuous, handsome mouth."[28]

Guided by Nathan, in his sophisticated wardrobe, O'Casey, in plainly cut suit and sweater, toured New York from his base in Nathan's hotel, the Royalton. O'Casey's immediate reaction to New York was recorded in letters to Eileen: "I am in New York at last, and my first impression is as usual a feeling of resentment; it goes its way too quick and I have to try to keep up with it."[29] The retrospective impression he chose to create for his autobiography was rather different: "The streets were deep and Dantesque, dizzying the mind when one looked up to the tops of the buildings towering up as if they sought a way to the blue sky and the sun ashine therein; and the whole city in its aspect and its agitated life grew into a rosy, comfortable, and majestic inferno; life so busy and stimulating that all but the sick in soul and very sick in body forgot the time they would come to dust in the cool of the tombs."[30] The autobiographical persona and the description of New York's vitality and timelessness closely resemble those of an earlier Irish playwright in New York, Dion Boucicault. Boucicault came to New York, like O'Casey, because he was dissatisfied with the lot of the dramatist in London. Like O'Casey, he also claimed to have found in the New World metropolis a sensation of rejuvenation. Like O'Casey, Boucicault was enthusiastic about American theater, which he too compared favorably to British theater, and about the opportunities the New York dramatic world offered the playwright. Both claimed that high artistic intentions were more likely to be welcomed in New York audiences than in London. Eighty years in advance of O'Casey, Boucicault was more candid about material gain as adjunct to artistic merit. "Mr. Boucicault was an author," he wrote of his own arrival in New York more than forty years after the fact. "His object was to benefit his craft—to obtain for the dramatist not only the place of honor at the entertainment, but the largest share of the loaves and the fishes."[31] O'Casey was publicly silent on this part of his mission, though his personal lack of means was well known and his play was about material inequity. His silence was not because a share of the loaves and fishes was out of his mind, but because in the 1930s, unlike the 1850s, it was inappropriate for an artist prophesying a new drama to admit that it was on his mind.

When Boucicault came to New York, he was best known for *London Assurance,* a success he hoped to repeat. Only later would he turn to the Irish Irish play, which then constituted a novelty and an innovation. When O'Casey came to New York, he was best known for the Dublin plays he was determined not to repeat. Newspapers gave regular dispatches on his activities: "Sean O'Casey will lecture tomorrow afternoon at Harvard on 'The Old and the New Drama'"; "Sean O'Casey will speak at a meeting of the Drama Study Club at the Waldorf-Astoria tomorrow afternoon."[32] The message O'Casey delivered on these occasions at Harvard or the Waldorf reiterated what O'Casey had told A.J. Liebling on arrival: he didn't write Irish plays, he wrote O'Casey plays. But the messenger made it difficult to forget the B.T.S.T. author. O'Casey and Nathan's preproduction publicity machine exploited the "innocent gaum" Nathan's own criticism was supposed to have eradicated. Above all, there was the peasant wardrobe, in even sharper contrast against Nathan's outfits. By October Joseph Alsop could open his regular O'Casey story by noting that: "As usual, he was wearing the turtle-neck sweater which has so fascinated Johnnie, the bootblack on Forty-first Street outside the National, and an expert in dramatic authors, that he has made O'Casey known to the whole floating population of the neighborhood as the 'writing guy in the joisey.'"[33] The costume fascinated more than Johnnie, apparently, and the effect pleased O'Casey. After the opening he wrote to Eileen: "A strange thing has happened here. Lots of young men are beginning to wear turtle-necked jerseys, and I am told it is hard to find one now in any New York shop, so I have set a fashion anyway."[34] He set it with some calculation; the November issue of Nathan's *American Spectator* included an O'Casey piece called "Why I Don't Wear Evening Dress" that he had written five months before his arrival in New York.[35] It is true, of course, that O'Casey did not wear evening dress, that his choice had more to do with socialist sympathy than with fashion, and that his theatrical and literary successes had not brought material return beyond minimal financial security. However, the profile of the playwright linked to *Within the Gates* in New York had very theatrical qualities. One week before the opening, Bosley Crowther gathered up most parts of the O'Casey character for readers of the Sunday *New York Times*. After difficulties locating O'Casey in the National during rehearsals, because "he had apparently impelled himself by some Celtic charm to vanish," Crowther described the dress:

> Then, from the wings of the stage and as casual as one might please, there strolled a lean, raw-boned man of more than medium height. It was, of course, Mr. O'Casey. He wore a shaggy, russet-colored tweed suit, with a brown turtle-neck sweater under the jacket, and a cap of the same material pulled down at a haphazard angle over the left eye. . . . It was easy to perceive why this man, when he first went to London from Ireland's Abbey Theatre as a new dramatic "lion," had refused to array himself in dress clothes for formal dinner parties. He was too obviously comfortable in the ones he was wearing. And when he did speak the richness of his Irish brogue and the low modulation of his voice were as warm as a Dublin snug.

The character was not entirely Crowther's creation. O'Casey contributed too. Though he didn't write Irish plays, his most frequent topic in interviews was Ireland. "There's no more sincere people in the world than the Irish," he told Crowther. "Why, an Irishman would murder his own father or brother over a difference in creed or politics. If you want more evidence of sincerity than that, I don't know where you can find it." After that gesture to *The Playboy of the Western World*, O'Casey evoked the world of B.T.S.T: "Never in my life did I feel better than when I did physical labor. . . . My chest measured 46, my arms were as big as tree limbs and I had a great ball of muscle here on my hand where I gripped the pickhandle. I weighed twelve stone twelve, and I worked all day and was ready to live joyously through the night."[36]

The Irish playwright of 1934 had the advantage of being able to combine the Boucicault and Synge man-of-the-people precedents with the more arrogant and dangerous models of the artist established by Shaw and Joyce. O'Casey's meeting in New York with Eugene O'Neill is an excellent example of this juncture of the humble Irish artist with high art. In October, Nathan brought O'Casey to O'Neill's room in the Madison Hotel. The O'Casey who didn't write Irish plays told O'Neill that he, the American, did: "You write like an Irishman, not like an American." O'Casey would repeat this, insisting that with O'Neill "you have to remember that he's Irish, particularly in his humor," and that he and O'Neill told jokes that "only two Irishmen can share." The Irish quality of O'Neill's work was something O'Casey would wax eloquent about much later, on the occasion of the naming of the Broadway theater after O'Neill: "Our Shamrock twines a leaf or two around every flower symbolizing each State of O'Neill's great and urgent country." But O'Casey would not accept the label himself. "Celtic this and Celtic that! . . . Who ever heard of anything being Celtic?"[37] What he added to the role associated with Boucicault and Synge was an aloofness derived from Shaw and Joyce. This, too, was evident in the meeting with O'Neill. In a frequently told tale, Nathan and O'Casey planned to taunt O'Neill by pretending to subscribe to the outlandish proposition that the artist should work in contact with the audience's life. In Nathan's words, he and O'Casey feigned to believe the "lush arguments as to the necessity of an artist's—and particularly a dramatist's—mingling with the stream of life if he is to comprehend it and interpret its depths and mutations." After a time of this sort of mugging, O'Neill, "jumping out of his chair," "exploded": "That mingling with people and life that you talk about, far from giving anything to an artist, simply takes things away from him, damned valuable things. If he hasn't everything in himself, he is no good. The life outside him can steal from him but it can't contribute a thing to him, unless he is a rank second-rater."[38] When Nathan and O'Casey revealed the joke, they all laughed heartily.

This combination of aloofness to audience indicates some of the difference between the 1934 Irish playwright in New York and the earlier role, humble servant of the audience, played by Boucicault. One casualty of this new dynamic, scarcely noticed after the explicit contempt for it of Shaw and Joyce, was the Irish American audience. Richard Watt, writing for the *Herald Tribune,* noted this at the time of the *Within the Gates* opening. He recorded the large number of recent Irish products in the New York "dramatic annals," including Stuart Gilbert's *Anna Livia Plurabelle* film treatment, the film *Norah O'Neale,* Robert Flaherty's *Man of Aran,* and, especially, *Within the Gates.* "My regretful suspicion," he reported "incidentally," "is that news of the current Celtic renaissance will prove of less concern to local Irish-Americans, who should be proud of it, than to other racial groups in the vicinity."[39] Ironically, that Irish American audience, which had protested *The Playboy of the Western World* so vehemently in 1911, was the audience cultivated by the Abbey Theatre touring company and its hopelessly B.T.S.T. repertory, including *Playboy.* While the *Gaelic American* waxed eloquent over *Norah O'Neale,* it never even mentioned *Within the Gates.*

Lack of attention would be a problem, because O'Casey, drawing from Shaw's example, intended to offend. As he told Cecelia Ager of *Variety,* the mainstream entertainment journal, "a good play arouses dissension, attacks, praise. It has vitality, it penetrates." He would, in many minds, succeed. John Anderson, the *New York Evening Journal* reviewer, would report, under the headline "O'Casey Drama Scales Peak of Greatness; Audience Awestruck," "you may not like it, and that won't matter, either."[40] But unlike Shaw, O'Casey did not supply offensive unpleasantness. Instead, he would offend by loftiness. Like Beckett twenty years later during the first productions of *Waiting for Godot,* O'Casey cultivated the qualities of enigma and evasion. Perhaps borrowing from his enemy the London critic Gordon Beckles, he professed not to know what his play was about and maintained this inscrutable quality even before the cast. Lillian Gish would play the Young Whore in New York, and O'Casey spent a great deal of time in her dressing room, fleeing, as he told her, the audience: "They keep asking me what my play is about, and I don't know what to tell them." So that was what he told them. *Variety* reported that O'Casey "has contributed two plays to the Abbey Players of Dublin, but his latest work is not Irish. It's quite British, but what he is driving at he himself is not certain, judging from his quoted remarks." Anderson later reported that *Within the Gates* "worried the playgoers over the meaning of it all," and that when he asked O'Casey what it was about he got the reply: "I am simply trying something new, for I don't believe we'll ever get anywhere by standing still talking about it. I am out on the road, working toward an unknown destination."[41]

O'Casey did know what his destination was not, and he explained that for the readers of the Sunday *New York Times* on the day before the opening. This piece, called "From 'Within the Gates,'" was approved by Nathan before publication.[42] It opened with a review of O'Casey's well-known conflict with the London reviewers of the play. "It was over their heads," he told the New York audience, "and they immediately began to try to trample it under their feet. They were perplexed, and then they were frightened." After dismissing the English critics, "old and doddering minds," O'Casey dismissed most British and American playwrights, and in the course of doing so resurrected the terminology of honor previously used to dismiss Coward's Codology: "Nine-tenths of those who write for the theatre are gigolo dramatists in whom [there] is no vestige of honor and scarcely a vestige of life." Their failure was quite precisely diagnosed:

> The pomp and circumstance of life have been degraded down
> to the pomp and circumstance of a bed. Imagination has been
> lavished on the sheen of silk stockings and short chemises,
> and very short chemises, too. There is a place, of course, for
> a pretty woman in a chemise and silk stockings in a play, but
> that place is not an important one, and a woman is something
> above and beyond a camisole. And the cult of these things
> has banished power and fantasy, music and song and great-
> ness far from the drama, so that she is no longer a matron or
> maid, but a cheap, aging and bedizened harlot.[43]

In response to this trend, O'Casey assigned to himself a role rather like that of the Dreamer in the play. In the catalogue of the various "symbols" who constitute the cast of the play, O'Casey explained in the *Times,* the Dreamer was "symbol of a noble restlessness and discontent; of the stir in life that brings to birth new things and greater things than those that were before; of the power realizing that the urge of life is above the level of conventional morality." The outcome, in the play through the Dreamer and in theatre through O'Casey, would be "a new form of acting, a new form of production, a new response in the audience; author, actors and audience will be in communion with each other— three in one and one in three."[44] The last phrase is taken from Keegan's hapless notion of a new Ireland expressed at the end of *John Bull's Other Island*.

The production of *Within the Gates* that opened on October 22, 1934, certainly promised something significant. By October the book edition of *Within the Gates* was in its third printing. Advertisements for the opening at the National Theatre boasted "a cast of seventy." Lillian Gish had returned to Broadway after her long term with D.W. Griffith's Biograph film company; the O'Casey role came between her successes in *Uncle Vanya* in 1930 and Ophelia to John Gielgud's Hamlet in 1936. Melvyn Douglas, the director, had also returned to Broadway after working in films, and he had a major success on Broadway the season before as a philandering husband in *No More Ladies*. Mary Morris, playing the role of the Old Woman, mother to the Young Whore of *Within the Gates,* was a distinguished New York actress who had begun with the Washington Square Players and then moved uptown to a long series of Broadway productions. In the Dreamer and the Bishop, who vie for the allegiance of the Young Whore, the production used two distinguished British actors, Bramwell Fletcher and Moffat Johnston. But only the name of the playwright appeared above the title on advertisements. There were highly publicized complications with the set, the costume designer, and the music, but no more than ordinary in such a large production and a bonus in visibility. The importance of the work was underscored by printing the lyrics to the songs in the program, which also included an insert reiterating O'Casey's explanation of the play's symbolism. The author, on the evidence of his letters to Eileen, was pleased with the production. His only disappointment was the opening night performance: "The company gave on my first night a dead performance," he wrote her a week after the opening. "The play didn't come over at all, though happily the audience thought it did, and I, Melvyn, and John Tuerk were miserable. The company were too afraid of the dialogue and the new form and went through the play in a dream. It was terrible, but now they are used to the swing of it and one wouldn't know the play. It is very moving."[45]

O'Casey's treatment of his material—a cross-section of the demoralized in a park—was striking and successful. O'Casey's boast was that his play, planned as patterns and geometries, "would justify its full and defiant appearance." However, it would be more accurate to say that the appearance was the sole justification for the play. The series of scenes and tableaux, with different lighting for different seasons, is vivid, es-

pecially with the War Memorial, a public sculpture of a defeated soldier, as a central silhouette. The play text has a number of moments
more visually interesting than textually provocative, especially the late
entrance of the large chanting chorus of Down and Outs. Among the
stylized visual elements was the costuming of the Scarlet Woman,
"dressed in red, with a crescent in black on her right hip" (20), and
that of the Young Whore, dressed in black with a red crescent. It was
the staging that was most praised by Brooks Atkinson in a review
celebratory of the play, the author, and the general theatrical significance. "Being the theatre of spiritual magnificence," he wrote, "it needs
all the glories of stage art, and it has them in this superb production."
For Atkinson, "nothing so grand has risen in our impoverished theatre
since this reporter first began writing of plays." Even Stark Young of
the *New Republic,* who was much cooler to the play, allowed that "Good
or bad, his play is theatre. It returns to the Gothic barbarism that the
Elizabethans followed; it has the confusions of turbulence, the clipped
transitions of heated themes, the will to sonority in the ear."[46] All this
represents a departure from realism, from Coward's society plays and
from O'Casey's own Dublin trilogy. It also permitted some operatic qualities, such as of Lillian Gish in the role of wan beauty proclaiming "Give
us a song, for God's sake! Heart ready to stop beating any second, but
game for anything. If I die, I'll go game, and die dancing" (116). The
audience, the press, and the production personnel all welcomed the
departure from realism and fully accepted the melodramatic qualities
that resulted. *Variety,* though, did note that "it isn't easy to believe that
Lillian Gish is a prostie, despite the frequency of her declarations."[47]

There was critical resistance to O'Casey's claim to be offering "a
new drama," however, and it was based on the playwright's failure to
fulfill the terms set in his own manifesto "From 'Within the Gates.'"
Though stylized, his play scarcely offered any more than "the pomp
and circumstance of the bed" that he attributed to "gigolo dramatists."
In addition to the frequent lascivious entrances and exits of the Young
Whore and the Scarlet Woman, *Within the Gates* includes scenes of
Young Guardsmen ogling nursemaids, the Bishop fondling the Young
Whore's stockinged knee, and general gossip about kept women: "Must
'ave nerve, I will sy. Fancy just for a fur coat, or a bricelet 'ot with
jewels, to stand in a man's room, 'is 'ands 'urrying off your silken flimsies
till you stand cool en nyked in from of 'is nibs!" (52). The only difference between most offers to the Young Whore and those made by the

Dreamer, "symbol of noble restlessness," is that he offers to pay in song. O'Casey's play certainly insists on something new. For example, there is the refrain from a chorus of the crowd:

> Bellow good-bye to the buggerin' lot 'n come out
> To bow down the head 'n bend down the knee
>   to the bee, the bird, 'n the blossom,
> Bann'ring the breast of the earth with a wonder-
>   ful beauty! [48]

But in the end the life force seems to take only a single and familiar form. In the words of the Old Woman, "The birds'll be busy at buildin' small worlds of their own in the safe an' snug breast of the hedges; the girls will go ramblin' around, all big with the thought of the life in the loins of the young men" (142-43). Though innovative in style, *Within the Gates* was unable to present "a woman [as] more than a camisole." After the Young Whore has a tryst with the Dreamer, she falls mortally ill with heart disease and at curtain has a deathbed conversion to the church aided by the Bishop, who is revealed to be her father. In regard to sexual stereotypes, prostitution, paternity, male messianism, and sexual liaison, the text of *Within the Gates* is much more simplistic and so much less provocative than the precedents on these topics already provided on the New York stage by the Irish playwrights Shaw, Synge, and Joyce, as well as a wealth of treatments by others. O'Casey as much as conceded the point later, in his autobiography: "It was a beautiful production in every way, and any fault shown on the stage was in the play itself."[48]

The production of *Within the Gates* at least satisfied the O'Casey criterion for success of divided opinion. In addition to Brooks Atkinson of the *Times*, Robert Garland of the *World-Telegram* thought the production historic: "The theatre, as far as America is concerned, is richer today than it was twenty four-hours ago." There were also those of the B.T.S.T. persuasion who remained unconverted. Gilbert Gabriel of the *New York America* thought that the play proved "O'Casey [is] in dire need of another Irish revolution."[49] Much more interesting, however, was the unusual diffidence of influential reviewers working on longer deadlines than the newspaper reviewers. Because of the reputation of the playwright, the preproduction machinery launched by George Jean Nathan, and the avowed reverence, at least among critics, for aesthetic innovation over commercial repetition, Stark Young of the *New Repub-lic* and Joseph Wood Krutch of the *Nation* apologized for their dissatis-faction and used the unusual trope of citing other reviews. Stark Young prefaced his review with an elaborated exposition on his enthusiasm for a kind of total theater, "all elements of living: speech, gesture, ap-pearance, the words, the music, the actor, the movement, the scene." He also appreciated O'Casey's effort in this direction: "Good or bad, his play is theatre." Ultimately, however, he found the result disappoint-ing: "What this Irish play lacks and Shakespeare had is air, light, basic relevance; its comic talent is almost as good as Shakespeare's, its final sum, taken seriously, is likely to be adolescent where Shakespeare is ripe, solid, and significant." Young then apologized to John Anderson of the *Evening Journal* and to Atkinson: "I respect and record their reactions."[50] In the same fashion, Krutch recorded the publicity sur-rounding O'Casey's visit to New York and the verdicts of reviews pub-lished before his own: "'Within the Gates' was received with more wholehearted salvos of critical approval than have fallen to the lot of any very pretentious play seen here in years." Then he too apologized: "Any tendency on my part to moderate my transports will be taken, I fear, as sheer perversity": "Either some Message to which I am unfortu-nately not attuned is cunningly hidden beneath a mass of conventional, rather adolescent verbiage or the author is merely saying at great length and with the intense air of a discoverer what we have all said about Life when the mood was upon us."[51] Soon after, George Jean Nathan pub-lished a long piece in *Vanity Fair* that summarized and quoted five positive and negative reviews of *Within the Gates*, including Young and Krutch, to demonstrate the sorry state of dramatic criticism.[52] But the critics' reaction was not philistine. Enormously tolerant of any effort to bring "new things" to the stage, the reaction respectfully insisted only that the new thing proclaimed be, in fact, new.

Within the Gates was a reasonably popular success in New York. It ran for a hundred performances while plans were made for touring other cities. A week after the New York opening, O'Casey, sounding rather different from his Dreamer, could write to Eileen: "We took in the first week nearly 14,000 dollars, but this included £60 for the first night. This week Monday was £360 and Tuesday £240, which would be mag-nificent in London, but the running costs here are high. However, all seems almost certain of a success, and the company is on its toes, cer-tain of a success, too."[53] Tuerk and Bushar wanted to send O'Casey to

Boston and Philadelphia to create interest in the play, but O'Casey sailed from New York on December 12 to rejoin Eileen before the birth of their son Niall. The play needed no playwright to create interest in Boston, where it was banned after intense lobbying by clergymen upset with the role of the Bishop and the general prurient interest. This tour did not follow the precedent of the Irish Players' *Playboy of the Western World* by simultaneously challenging and capitalizing on protests. Instead, *Within the Gates,* for all its defiance, ceded the field and retreated to New York, where it reopened on Broadway for an extended run of four months. In the new year, 1935, Nathan could write to O'Casey in England that "the whole enterprise remains, in my mind, the one completely distinguished thing of the New York theatrical year."[54]

Nathan was alone in that judgment, and in a letter to a colleague and friend one is not under oath. But the 1934 *Within the Gates* in New York can be claimed to be a distinguished illustration, at a particular point in time, of the Irish play in New York. In his search for a "new drama" and in his resistance to realism, the Dublin style or other, O'Casey embraced the style of Dion Boucicault, his predecessor in arrival in New York as Irish celebrity playwright. At the time, this was noted rather glumly by St. John Ervine, who criticized O'Casey's work as "superb music-hall." In more recent times it has been noted by Katharine Worth, who has praised O'Casey's work for going "back to the tradition rejected by realism, the music style of Boucicault's type of melodrama."[55] In the grand tableau of the Salvation Army Officer and the Young Whore at the end of Act III of *Within the Gates,* for example, O'Casey created a visual moment equal to Boucicault's highest melodrama and also equal to O'Casey's own extravagant *dicta* on theater while on tour in New York. But this kind of example is Boucicault's style without the embrace of audience and artistic marketplace. By the time of *The Shaughraun,* Boucicault had captured the popular audience and sought the intelligentsia; by the time of *Within the Gates,* O'Casey had captured the intelligentsia and sought no more. The melodramatic and music-hall style was certainly one way to proceed when Abbey Theatre folk drama had become an extremely limiting formula. But the old style could not succeed as delivered by a defiant celebrant of high art, which was the persona cultivated by O'Casey. The Boucicault style could not succeed without the meeting of artist and audience so merrily ridiculed by O'Casey and Nathan in O'Neill's hotel room. *Within the Gates,* in the terms of debate over the new versus the old O'Casey work, proved that novelty alone was not provocative and that some increment of provocation was required to create active response. *Within the Gates* as staged in New York in 1934 proved to be, to rephrase David Krause's verdict, the direction drama should take without being the new drama. O'Casey's unknown destination remained unknown.

This production in this place, *Within the Gates* in New York, does help answer that vexed question for O'Casey personally and the Abbey tours collectively of whither next? B.T.S.T. O'Casey in New York, *Juno and the Paycock,* for example, would from this point go into a long period of dispirited revivals, including a privately produced reunion in New York of Barry Fitzgerald and Sara Allgood in 1940, sixteen years after they originated the lead roles in Dublin. This period included early O'Casey as a Broadway musical, *Juno,* in 1959, with Melvyn Douglas, director of *Within the Gates,* in the role of Captain Boyle. However, the play would be rejuvenated in the late 1980s, when *Juno and the Paycock* was staged to great effect in New York in a Gate Theatre of Dublin production, rather than an Abbey production, and with a strong influence from the work of Samuel Beckett. The record is that O'Casey's Dublin plays survive in subsequent reinterpretations and that his "new" drama does not. In the retroactive influence of Beckett on O'Casey, Irish Irish drama was revitalized by non-Irish Irish drama, and the result of cross-fertilization was a localized drama that was not parochial. In 1934 O'Casey personally came to New York to perform a role of enigma and evasion much like Beckett's public image later, but he had neglected to provide a play as innovative as *Waiting for Godot.* In his non-Irish Irish play of 1934, O'Casey created stage business, especially the routines of the Chair Attendants of *Within the Gates,* or the codology of its Arguing Group, that anticipated Beckett's non-Irish Irish play *Waiting for Godot.* New York, more than London, was receptive. In fact, the *Within the Gates* episode demonstrated a susceptibility always strong in New York to relish the spectacle of the artist in action and to tolerate weaknesses in the work of art as interesting products of personality. Despite that susceptibility, New York could and did refuse to award all accolades for innovation in the absence of a genuine newness. *Within the Gates* had not, as its chorus memorably put it, bellowed good-by to the buggering lot and come out with a wonderful beauty. The difficulty of accomplishing that adds magnitude to O'Casey's effort in New York in 1934 and to Beckett's success there in 1956.

6

Waiting for Godot
IN NEW YORK

A very broad trajectory of the playwright's imagination of audience in the twentieth century can be traced from a beginning point with Dion Boucicault and an ending point with Samuel Beckett. In 1875, at the closing of his successful production of *The Shaughraun,* Boucicault stood on the stage before his audience and told them: "You offer me the most honorable distinction to which any artist can aspire, and that is the assurance of his fellow citizens that they perceive in his works, together with something that is sweet, something that is good."[1] About seventy-five years later, when *Waiting for Godot* was in a disintegrating production in Miami, the author wrote sympathetically to the director, Alan Schneider: "Success and failure on the public level never mattered much to me, in fact I feel much more at home with the latter, having breathed deep of its vivifying air all my writing life up to the last couple of years. . . . When in London the question arose of a new production [of Beckett's *Waiting for Godot*] I told the [producers] that if they did it my way they would empty the theatre."[2] Schneider already knew this to be true. Elsewhere he describes Beckett at the English-language premiere of *Waiting for Godot* in London in 1955, and how when a portion of the audience walked out during the performance, he, Schneider, "always felt that Sam would have been disappointed if at least a few hadn't."[3] Beckett did not, like O'Casey, travel to New York for his Broadway debut. "They want me to go to New York," he wrote to his friend the Irish writer Thomas MacGreevey, "but they won't pay my fare, so there is no question of that."[4] Beckett had been in close contact with the Paris premiere of *En attendant Godot* in 1953, and later visited the London production with Schneider. However, in New York, Beckett's

absence, much like the absence in the play of Godot, fueled specula-
tion. It opened an opportunity for the audience's imagination of the
playwright, which had also been transformed over the course of the
twentieth century. A widely shared suspicion was that both play and
playwright were frauds. *Variety,* in its fashion, announced it as such:
"a theatrical whatsit, written by an Irish-born, Paris resident and former
secretary to doubletalk genius James Joyce."[5]

Despite the artist's general disdain for public approval, however,
there was in the case of *Godot* in New York a general recognition of the
quality and importance of the art work. The audience was not given
Boucicault's humble offering of "something that is sweet, something
that is good." But that was not the only possible attraction. The comparison of *Godot* and *The Shaughraun* in New York illustrates how over
seventy-five years in theater culture the role of the playwright changed
from public affection to public disdain verging on contempt, how the
role of the audience transformed from celebration to suspicion, and
how the expectations of the art work shifted from local and provisional
to universal and monumental. When *Godot* first played New York, the
press and the public were asked to accept a work packaged in disdain
for their own concerns, but they welcomed the challenge. Brooks
Atkinson's *New York Times* review of the 1956 New York production
gestured toward the more ordinary Broadway fare then playing by noting, "Although 'Waiting for Godot' is a 'puzzlement,' as the King of Siam
would express it, Mr. Beckett is no charlatan." There was a subsequent
piece in the *Times* during the production, a much-quoted interview
called "Moody Man of Letters," where Beckett memorably accounted
for his French residence: "I preferred France in war to Ireland in peace."
Israel Shenker reiterated Atkinson's (or perhaps the *Times*' house) vo-
cabulary: "There is pretty general agreement that he is no charlatan,
but hardly more than enlightened puzzlement about his message."[6]

Beckett's posture as playwright took to a new level the playwright's
aloofness to audience evolving since Boucicault. After Boucicault, the
persona of the playwright evolved from Shaw's barely patient explanations of his work through O'Casey's inability or unwillingness to explain his work. In turn, Beckett surpassed his predecessors as authors
of non-Irish Irish plays in New York. His statements were better re-
hearsed than O'Casey's: "If I knew [who Godot was], I would have said
so in the play"; "My work is a matter of fundamental sounds (no joke
intended) made as fully as possible, and I accept responsibility for noth-

ing else. If people want to have headaches among the overtones, let them. And provide their own aspirin."[7] The public role of the playwright had not diminished since Boucicault. It had changed in nature from the helpful and even obsequious to the imperious. In the case of the figure of Beckett in New York, the effect was to move him beyond the recognizable image of the Irish playwright, which was a loss to the national drama and its international audience. In the case of the play, the production history in New York is a good example of the rising authority of the artist and its corollary restriction of the art work. *Godot's* impact was so great, and the figure of the playwright so impressive, that all other participants in the theatrical transaction—the casts, the directors, the designers, and so forth—were reduced to subordinate roles. That, as *Godot* demonstrates, especially in its history in New York, narrowed the possibilities of the play and raised the issue of whether restriction of the work to authorial intention was protection of it or reduction of it.

Waiting for Godot was a very well known product by the time it reached New York in 1956. It had been written as part of Beckett's post–World War II burst of productivity. During his earlier relocations from Dublin to England and the continent, he had written plays, including an early exercise on Dr. Johnson and Mrs. Thrale written in 1937, and he had also published novels to little or no notice, such as *Murphy* in 1938. After his wartime experience, when he lived quietly near Rousillon and aided the Resistance effort, Beckett returned to his flat in Paris and began to write, now in French rather than English. In retrospect, much has been made of this, particularly the idea, suggested by Beckett to Nicholas Gessner, that in French it is "easier to write without style." *En attendant Godot* is inimitable in style, of course, and a surer sense of the advantage of French is given by Beckett's comments to Laurence Harvey, one of the first American commentators: "For him, an Irishman, French represented a form of weakness by comparison with his mother tongue."[8] That is, Beckett writing in French, rather than the French language itself, was compatible with the particular vein of obstacles, compulsive effort, and futility he would explore in *Godot* and the novels written at the same time, *Molloy, Malone Dies,* and *The Unnameable.* The first two novels were published in Paris in 1951, and *En attendant Godot* was published there in 1952, early enough so that the printed volume served as the prompt script in the first production.

That production was due in large part to Suzanne Deschevaux-

Dumesnil, whom Beckett lived with then and later married. She circulated two play texts, *Godot* and also *Eleuthéria,* written in 1946, which was a rather conventional staging of the kind of predicament central to the later play. A production became fact when she contacted Roger Blin, who was then widely known as an innovative director and at that moment for a production of *The Ghost Sonata* that Beckett was happy to find playing to half-empty houses. Blin was also known to Beckett as a director in France of *The Playboy of the Western World.* Of Beckett's two plays, Blin chose *Godot:* "There were only four actors and they were bums. They could wear their own clothing if it came to that."[9] Financing was improvised, including use of a government grant, and Beckett helped with staging. For reasons of economy and the spatial limitations of the tiny Théâtre de Babylone, the costuming was ordinary and the set a skeletal tree before a drapery backdrop, as required for the direction "A country road. A tree."[10] Beckett did insist at this early point on bowler hats all round, and that late specification survives as a lone footnote to the American edition. He also revised in prompt book a famous exchange of insults so that the ultimate expression of abuse escalated from "architect" to "critic." A decade later, Blin would remark that for the opening Beckett "did not yet have the fussy desire for precision he has acquired since and while following the rehearsals actively, he left the director his share of freedom."[11]

If freedom was allowed, the text offered ample opportunity for directoral creativity. Many years later, Beckett himself directed an influential production of *Warten auf Godot* at the Schiller Theater in Berlin. There his notebooks, described in detail in Dougald McMillan's and Martha Fehsenfeld's *Beckett in the Theatre,* reduced the play to three parallel actions in each act: Vladimir and Estragon wait for Godot, they meet with Pozzo and Lucky, and they receive news from the boy that Godot isn't coming.[12] This structure left a great deal of stage business undetermined. The relevance of the kind of business suggested by popular entertainment is immediately apparent from the text. Vladimir and Estragon establish character in a familiar kind of dialogue:

VLADIMIR: It hurts?
ESTRAGON (*angrily*): Hurts! He wants to know if it hurts!
VLADIMIR (*angrily*): No one ever suffers but you. I don't count. I'd like to hear what you'd say if you had what I have.

ESTRAGON: It hurts?

VLADIMIR (*angrily*): Hurts! He wants to know if it hurts! [7R]

Later, the dialogue refers to pantomime, circus, music hall, and the business includes bathroom humor, pointing off, addressing the audience, and, at final curtain, dropped trousers. The power of the play is its mixture of the familiar and the cosmic. In *Within the Gates,* O'Casey, in his initial elaboration of abstract patterns of colors, essentially began with the cosmic. Beckett begins with the familiar and raises it to metaphysical analogies:

> ESTRAGON (*chews, swallows*): I'm asking you if we're tied.
> VLADIMIR: Tied?
> ESTRAGON: Ti-ed.
> VLADIMIR: How do you mean tied?
> ESTRAGON: Down.
> VLADIMIR: But to whom? By whom?
> ESTRAGON: To your man.
> VLADIMIR: To Godot? Tied to Godot! What an idea! No question of it. (*Pause.*) For the moment.
> ESTRAGON: His name is Godot?
> VLADIMIR: I think so.
> ESTRAGON: Fancy that. (*He raises what remains of the carrot by the stub of leaf, twirls it before his eyes.*) Funny, the more you eat the worse it gets.
> VLADIMIR: With me it's just the opposite.
> ESTRAGON: In other words?
> VLADIMIR: I get used to the muck as I go along.
> ESTRAGON (*after prolonged reflection*): Is that the opposite? [14R]

In *Godot* the mundane provokes the metaphysical. In this quality the play counters charlatanism and "doubletalk genius." Without the mundane, and the business it requires, the play would be a "theatrical whatsit."

Godot was not an overnight success, but interest grew steadily after its opening on January 5, 1953. In Paris, attention was paid after high praise from Jean Anouilh, for being a theatrical breakthrough, and from Alain Robbe-Grillet, for finding pure expression of the existentialist sense of the predicament of being. Both of these kinds of praise helped shape the resistance to *Godot* across the channel, where Beckett's own translation of the play was published in 1954 with the new subtitle "a tragicomedy in two acts." The first London proposal was for a major production with Alec Guinness and Ralph Richardson, actors whose training did not suit *Godot* and whose temperaments did not suit philosophical pretensions. The final straw was Beckett's already studied pose as enigma. Richardson recalled meeting Beckett, "wearing a knapsack, which was very mysterious," and presenting the playwright with a "laundry list of things I didn't quite understand." Richardson pleaded bewilderment at the cosmic magnitude without a familiar anchor. "But Beckett just looked at me and said, 'I'm awfully sorry, but I can't answer any of your questions.' He wouldn't explain. Didn't lend me a hand. And then another job came up and I turned down the greatest play of my lifetime."[13]

Due to objections on counts of unacceptable language from Shaw's old nemesis, the Lord Chamberlain, the first London staging was at the Arts Theatre Club, outside the censor's jurisdiction, in August 1955. An altered production directed by Peter Hall did succeed in opening with required license in September at the Criterion Theatre. Peter Bull, playing Pozzo, recalled that "waves of hostility came whirling over the footlights, and the mass exodus, which was to form such a feature of the run of the piece, started soon after the curtain had risen."[14] Though not involved in the production, Beckett visited, with Alan Schneider, who described the playwright "clutching my arm from time to time and, in a clearly heard stage whisper, saying, 'It's ahl wrahng! He's doing it ahl wrahng!"[15] Beckett was particularly unhappy with the London set, because "the text asks for a bare stage—except for the tree, and there the stage was so cluttered the actors could hardly move."[16] As in Paris, the London production benefitted immensely from praise by the influential, in this case Harold Hobson and Kenneth Tynan. The result was a general debate, one that was carried out with particular energy by both the enthused and the unenthused in the pages of the *Times Literary Supplement*. A long anonymous piece, whose author was later revealed to be G.S. Fraser, insisted on the Christian meanings of the play: "It is also a play by an Irishman, by a friend and disciple of James Joyce: a play, therefore, by a man whose imagination (in the sense in which Mr. Eliot used this phrase of Joyce himself) is orthodox." Subsequent responses included a letter lamenting Christian overtures by

William Empson: the Christian "attitude seems to be more frequent in Irish than either English or French writers, perhaps because in Ireland the religious training of children is particularly fierce." By April 1956, *TLS* had to take the unusual step of banning any further debate from its pages. The editors summed up the situation: many suspected Christian allegory, many suspected a hoax, and, finally, "it would have helped greatly if at some stage in this correspondence Mr. Beckett had himself intervened with an authoritative statement of what he was after, but no close student of the play can have expected this to happen."[17] By the time *TLS*, rather in the fashion of Vladimir and Estragon in Beckett's play, abandoned discussion, an American production, after a less than encouraging trial in Miami and the departure of Alan Schneider as director, was about to open at the Golden Theatre on Broadway.

The American premiere of *Waiting for Godot* at the Coconut Grove Playhouse on January 3, 1956, is generally portrayed as a disaster of legendary proportions and is mostly remembered for its self-advertisement as "the laugh sensation of two continents" (a ploy that would be tried again in England in 1962). A more accurate account of the production would be of a promising assemblage that failed to mesh and so was altered for New York. The assets of the Miami production were many. The producer, as so often, has been portrayed as greedy and philistine. In Schneider's account, Michael Myerberg "lived up to his reputation for being devious and unreliable."[18] But Myerberg's experience, at least, was well suited to a work that combines high intellectual ambitions with low comic routines. He had begun as a professional musician and then as a producer of vaudeville musical acts. His first Broadway production was *Candide* in 1933. A number of fairly commercial shows followed, including a road company of *Star Dust* by Walter Kerr, who would later warn Schneider about Myerberg and who, as the *Herald Tribune* critic, would deplore *Godot*. But Myerberg was also the producer in 1938 of the Orson Welles–Marc Blitzstein *The Cradle Will Rock* and in 1942 of Thornton Wilder's *The Skin of Our Teeth*. In addition to Broadway shows, he produced concerts for Leopold Stowkowski and engagements for the Philadelphia Ballet. Myerberg was disappointed in the London production of *Godot* but quite resolved to do the play in America: "*Waiting for Godot* was a revolutionary play that had never been done here. Beckett had not really been introduced to the public." Myerberg chose Broadway because only with that ultimate destination could he attract the cast of his choice. He also knew the obstacles he faced: "Let's face it, *Waiting for Godot* is not everybody's cup of tea. It's a theatrical property; it might be called a great play. I call it a theater piece. I don't know what a play is myself. Everybody else seems to know, but I don't."[19]

Alan Schneider did, and his unhappiness with what happened at the Coconut Grove focused on the unwillingness of others to subordinate their own contributions to the text. He had the great disadvantages of being hired as director after Myerberg's first choice, Garson Kanin, declined, and after Myerberg had hired leads of his own choice, Bert Lahr and Tom Ewell. Schneider had the benefit of having met the playwright, but the others, who with the exception of Lahr had all traveled to see the London production, seemed to feel that he was not sharing it. Recommended to Myerberg by Wilder for a revival of *The Skin of Our Teeth,* Schneider, by his own account, was experiencing a minor professional recession: "During 1953 I had directed ten productions, starting with the Arena's *All Summer Long* and culminating with my first Broadway venture, *The Remarkable Mr. Pennypacker.* In 1954 I wound up with three, the Arena *Summer and Smoke,* and *All Summer Long* as well as *Anastasia* on Broadway. The year 1955 had witnessed only two, *Samarkand* and *Skin,* neither one exactly pleasant; I had actually started on *Godot* in December." Though Schneider was later Beckett's most important American director, he counted the Coconut Grove experience "my most disastrous failure." The whole experience would include having to go to salary arbitration to claim his due after Myerberg dismissed him. Even much earlier, during rehearsal, Schneider regretted joining the project. "We were starting off on this difficult play with all the wrong ingredients. The setting was wrong. We had two stars who were probably more concerned with themselves than with the play, and two other actors who were almost certainly miscast. And we had a producer who not only did not understand but did not want to understand the problems and confusions I already saw looming. Only my memories of that great gaunt figure of Samuel Barclay Beckett kept me going. I couldn't bear the thought of walking out on him."[20] The actors playing Pozzo and Lucky, Jack Smart and Charles Weidman, respectively, were most certainly miscast and never succeeded in the roles, even in their own estimation. Tom Ewell, best known at the time for *The Seven Year Itch* with Marilyn Monroe, would withdraw, even though he maintained the importance of the play. After Miami, he refused to compete on stage with Bert Lahr, the sole member of Myer-

berg's cast to continue in New York. Perhaps the only person ever associated with *Godot* to have real roots in vaudeville and burlesque, Lahr's
most recent Broadway show had been *Two on the Aisle,* a successful
revue that opened in 1951 and included a sketch called "Schneider's
Miracle." As in Paris, the published text existed before a local production, and Myerberg recruited Lahr by sending him the Grove Press edition. In the account of his son, John Lahr, Bert Lahr "felt unsure of the
play's complexities and of his ability to stamp it with his own personality," precisely the ability Schneider thought conspired against the play.
Lahr told his son, "When I first read it, I realized that this was not stark
tragedy. Beneath it was tremendous humor, two men trying to amuse
themselves on earth by playing jokes and little games. And that was my
conception."[21] By bringing Lahr and Schneider together, Myerberg had
successfully staged a conflict between the sanctity of the play text and
the power of performance, between what Blin called that "fuzzy desire
for precision" and chewing the scenery. In rehearsal in Manhattan, the
conflict developed. For example, an early disagreement was over the
reading of Vladimir and Estragon's early statement about their predicament:

> ESTRAGON: Let's go.
> VLADIMIR: We can't.
> ESTRAGON: Why not?
> VLADIMIR: We're waiting for Godot.
> ESTRAGON (*despairingly*): Ah! (*Pause.*) You're sure it was here?
> [10R]

According to Schneider, this piece of dialogue typified the problems in
rehearsal with Lahr as Estragon. "Every two minutes Bert would smile
and say, 'It's all opening up, kid. It's opening up!' I would feel good for
a couple of minutes, until Bert would come up with the idea of replac-
ing the end of the 'Let's go. / We can't. / Why not? / We're waiting for
Godot' sequence with his old vaudeville 'Ohnnnnggggg' instead of
Beckett's 'Ah.'" According to John Lahr, in rehearsal "Lahr originally
wanted to substitute 'gnong, gnong, gnong,' for Beckett's pointed and
pathetic 'Ah!' He argued, but Schneider prevailed."[22]

Schneider prevailed on the sublime "Ah!" which would later re-
doubt to Lahr's credit, but the star would have his compensating victory. According to John Lahr: "Comedy without movement was

impossible for Lahr. He balked at Schneider's dicta, at being asked to harness his energy. Lahr was suspicious and ignorant of the allegorical reasons at the basis of Schneider's demands. When the director would go on stage with masking tape and place strips where he was to stand, Lahr was shocked. 'I began to think to myself—this is all wrong. It's stark. This is the wrong approach to the play. It's dire; it's slow. There isn't any movement.'" According to Schneider, "Bert never came back to the same location twice, even though the stage manager had marked the location of the mound with a taped X on the floor. (Years later, critic John Lahr accused me of tying down his father's freedom of movement to a mark on the floor.)"[23] Schneider didn't tie Lahr down, but only because Lahr wouldn't comply. The conflict was fundamental: Schneider's adherence to the author's intentions, which he had on personal authority, and Bert Lahr's adherence to audience response. However, Lahr's position, if not his specific desires, can find some support in Beckett lore. Beckett would himself alter dialogue when he came to direct *Godot* at the Schiller Theater in Germany, though not to insert vaudeville mugging. In 1962 Beckett would also tell Jean Reavey that for *Godot* "he had just written dialogue without seeing the stage movement in strict detail," thus leaving the question of movement open. The Lahrs, father and son, would also have been heartened to know that some time later Beckett would tell Schneider that "all my plays should be played light and fast. I don't want to dwell upon their seriousness. . . . my plays shouldn't be ponderous."[24]

Having built a fundamental conflict into the production, Myerberg added the worst possible scene for the production. Disappointed by ticket sales in the more usual tryout cities, Washington and Philadelphia, he accepted a two-week guarantee not only to play at the Coconut Grove Playhouse near Miami but to open the theater of a new leisure complex at the height of the vacation season, January. The vacation audience had every reason to expect a "laugh sensation of two continents," particularly after advertising that additionally billed Lahr as "Star of *Harvey* and *Burlesque*" and Ewell as "Star of *The Seven Year Itch*."[25] After a last six o'clock rehearsal for a nine o'clock opening, the cast waited until ten for the audience to move from the dining room and bar to the theater. The director's estimate was that one-third left before intermission and another third did not return from it. There were curtain calls, led by Tennessee Williams, Joseph Cotton, and William Saroyan, but, according to the *Miami Herald* headline the next day,

"Mink Clad Audience Disappointed in *Waiting for Godot.*" There was a ranting denunciation by Walter Winchell about the profanity of the play, but in general the reception, certainly disappointing, was respectable. The production completed the two-week run, developing an audience other than the vacation one, but Myerberg, later taking full blame himself, closed the show. Lahr's famous explanation, "Playing *Waiting for Godot* in Miami was like doing *Giselle* in Roseland,"[26] attributed the failure to the setting not to the play. Schneider thought the cast failed by its unfaithfulness to the play, and dismissed the suggestion by the subsequent New York director, Herbert Berghof, that it failed because "I had directed it 'for style and crucifixion,' whatever that meant."[27]

Even before reaching Broadway, the American *Godot* established, even in Schneider's mind, that there were different ways to do the play. By the second wave of productions in the 1970s, that sense of flexibility would be replaced by "style and crucifixion," by absolute solemnity. Berghof's feeling would be echoed by Roger Blin when he recounted his own experience with the original *Godot* in Paris: "There is a great deal of Irish sense of humour in [Beckett's] theatre. For that reason it is a mistake to play it as a tragedy, Godot must not end on an impression of crucifixion, it must not be interpreted tearfully."[28] Without a long history on stage, and without intervention by the playwright, the American *Godot* enjoyed the publicity benefits of a notorious product and the artistic benefits of great latitude in production. Beckett's first biographer, Deirdre Bair, reports that "the American production had been through more upheavals than either of its European counterparts and was probably the most original of the three because Beckett had no direct connection with it. However, every one of the major participants, except Lahr, made a special effort to see and study the London production . . . and based what they did and didn't do on what they had seen."[29]

What they did do on Broadway was the conception of Berghof, approved by Lahr, who only agreed to join a new Myerberg production if he had veto power on director. "The play in Miami was directed for significances, meanings," Berghof later told John Lahr. "My understanding of Beckett was different, more affirmative. Only somebody who loves life strongly could see all the flaws and weaknesses in an attempt to find out what it was all about. The exploration of existence becomes a sublime clown's act."[30] This was a conception rather closer to that of the author, one of whose memorable glosses on the play explained it as an effort "to give artistic expression to something hitherto almost ignored—the irrational state of unknowingness where we exist, this mental weightlessness which is beyond reason."[31] Berghof had developed his conception of *Godot* during multiple stagings in his actor's studio. His casting also brought the production closer to Beckett's text, not further from it. E.G. Marshall provided an intellectual counterpoint to Lahr's clownishness. Kurt Kasznar as Pozzo studied Peter Bull's famous performance in London and constructed his own role, which the actor in Miami was unable to do. The Lucky who could not go on in Miami was replaced by Alvin Epstein, who would go on to a distinguished career in Beckett productions. The Broadway enterprise was a balance between the play's highbrow reputation and Lahr's lowbrow one, a balance not possible a decade later, when the sublime had totally evicted the clown's act. Later productions, as Derek Mandel would say after directing *Godot* in Berlin in 1965, were "all doing A BECKETT PLAY in capital letters."[32]

Perhaps lest the effort seem too solemn, Michael Myerberg made a dramatic entrance of his own in a preproduction publicity interview with Arthur Gelb, later biographer of O'Neill, in the Sunday *New York Times* the weekend before the opening. "Wanted: Intellects," the headline read, and beneath it: "Producer Myerberg Seeks 70,000 of Them to Support Plotless Play." Often erroneously described as an advertisement, the piece's most outrageous claims, particularly the call for "70,000 bona fide intellectuals in New York," were Gelb's words, not Myerberg's. Gelb further explained that Myerberg, hoping in Miami to make an intellectual play accessible, slightly overshot the mark by pairing Lahr with Ewell. Myerberg did in all modesty allow that in Miami "I went too far in my effort to give the play a base for popular acceptance." In New York, Gelb wrote, Myerberg "is taking the precaution of publicly warning theatregoers in search of casual entertainment not to buy tickets to 'Waiting for Godot.'" Gelb also added the news that Tennessee Williams, then represented on Broadway by *Cat on a Hot Tin Roof,* thought that *Godot* is "one of the greatest plays of modern times and has invested his own money in it." Further, Thornton Wilder, then on Broadway with *The Matchmaker,* "has seen it five times in Europe and has spent many impassioned hours explaining, discussing and illuminating various aspects of it." The third Pulitzer playwright to be brought forth was William Saroyan, who "all but weeps with emotion when he speaks of it" and who believes "it will make it easier for me and everyone else to write freely in the theater."[33] Myerberg had adjusted his market target without altering the means. "The laugh sensation of two continents" advertisement was replaced with one that emended Beckett's English-language edition subtitle to: "Waiting for Godot: The International Tragicomedy Hit." Production publicity posed as the outstanding question whether or not America was culturally and intellectually developed enough to welcome *Godot.*

On April 19, 1956, *Waiting for Godot,* by the playwright invariably referred to as "Joyce's secretary," opened at the John Golden Theatre. The site for the new play was a distinguished Broadway house, previously known as the Royale, that was established by the success of Mae West's *Diamond Lil* in 1928. A small Broadway theatre, with a capacity of eight hundred, or no more than the Coconut Grove Playhouse, it perfectly suited Beckett's own preference for a formal proscenium stage. Advising Schneider on a subsequent production, Beckett told him that "I don't in all my ignorance agree with the round and feel *Godot* needs a very closed box."[34] The Miami set, built around a large, stylized mound in center stage, had been abandoned, and the New York designer, Louis Kennel, provided an open space before a drapery backdrop much like the set approved by Beckett at the Théâtre de Babylone. Like Beckett's favored contrast between the formal proscenium and his "formless" drama, the set usefully represented the opposed motives of Berghof, philosophical, and Lahr, pragmatic. As Berghof later said of the set, in Miami "there were very complicated ramps, which made it impossible to operate like a clown because a clown basically needs an empty stage. First of all, the complicated set detracts from Bert's gestures; secondly, the whole attitude of the play with platforms seems fanciful and out of order." The bare space did not give Lahr license to clown, but it did allow him to play against himself. The new and unprecedented play, an "international tragicomedy hit," was performed by a known Broadway product. Berghof reported that Lahr "gave his best performance on opening night—it was his purest. He somehow felt that if he was really pure it would be acceptable. He's quite right because everybody is there waiting for the actor to send the laughs out; and he wasn't doing it."[35]

The quality of forces in conflict was also what most impressed Kenneth Tynan about the New York production, where "the eggheads were rolling in," and especially the business over which Lahr and Schneider differed: "Without [Lahr] the Broadway production of Mr. Beckett's play would be admirable; with him, it is transfigured. It is as if we, the audience, had elected him to represent our reactions, resentful and confused, to the lonely universe into which the author plunges us. 'I'm going,' says Mr. Lahr. 'We can't go,' snaps his partner. 'Why not?' pleads Mr. Lahr. 'We're waiting for Godot,' comes the reply. Whereat Mr. Lahr raises one finger with an 'Ah!' of comprehension which betokens its exact opposite, a totality of blankest ignorance."[36] On opening night, something of the production's tension between new and old forces, between high and low culture, could be found in the program. One page carried a new Cold War warning not entirely inappropriate for what would be called the play of the nuclear age: "In the event of an air raid alarm remain in your seats and obey the instructions of the management." The following page carried the traditional Rogers Peet clothiers advertisement composed, as usual, for the play: "Waiting for anybody can be a waste of time unless one waits in a convenient and useful and interesting place. That's why more and more husbands say to their wives or vice-versa: 'Meet me at Rogers Peet!'"[37]

Though the playwright could deny that the play had any particular social significance, the performance of it certainly had undeniable cultural significance. It had to be considered a success even by commercial standards. *Variety* immediately reported *Godot,* a "comedy-drama," as playing close to gross for its house, or taking in $10,000, high for a non-musical, in its first four performances during a "spotty" week on Broadway.[38] The first notices were divided, but even negative ones called attention to the uniqueness of the play. Great energies were spent "explaining" what the play was about, a kind of reaction that disappeared after *Godot* became ubiquitous and explanation for it bad taste. Brooks Atkinson warned his readers not to expect an explanation, but then he plunged on anyway: "It seems fairly certain that Godot stands for God. Those who are loitering by the withered tree are waiting for salvation, which never comes." John McClain of the *Journal-American,* like Atkinson writing a very favorable review, also hesitated and then ventured on anyway: "My guess is as good as any other, and I would say that the author is taking this tortuously oblique path to show us the futility of life." Reviewers who finally panned the play did so only after joining the game of speculation. John Chapman of the *Daily News,* whose verdict of the play as "merely a stunt" would rouse defenders, helpfully explained that "Godot never arrives because—if my symbols aren't clashing—Godot is Death."[39] These theories were supplemented by post-performance panel discussions in the theater with the cast. None of the audience who arrived with their Grove Press editions and stayed through the panels proposed that the play was a hoax. They were a self-selective group of, as Tynan put it, eggheads. Many noted and enjoyed the irony of the onstage and offstage cogitation. When Pozzo arrives with his slave Lucky in Act I, and assorted pastimes fail the four characters, "thinking" is the amusement of last resort.

> POZZO: "What do you prefer? Shall we have him dance, or sing, or recite, or think, or—":
> VLADIMIR: He thinks?
> POZZO: Certainly. Aloud. He even used to think very prettily once, I could listen to him for hours. Now . . . (*he shudders*). So much the worse for me. Well, would you like him to think something for us?
> ESTRAGON: I'd rather he'd dance, it'd be more fun. [26L-R]

Those who stayed through the panel discussions certainly preferred thinking to dancing. But Lahr, who attended some without contributing, evidently did not, whether as Estragon or as himself.

The hoax charge was mostly reserved for those who did not see the play. The most memorable party of that camp was Norman Mailer, who initially wrote in the *Village Voice* that without having read the play or seen a performance "what I smell in all this is that 'Waiting for Godot' is a poem to impotence" and so ineligible for the status of art. Nevertheless, Mailer offered a tutorial on its meanings: "Godot also means 'ot Dog, or the dog who is hot, and it means God-O, God as the female principle, just as Daddy-O in Hip means the father who has failed, the man who has become an O, a vagina."[40] Mailer's first pronouncement on *Godot* appeared on May 2, and, as in the case of Joyce's *Exiles* at the Neighborhood Playhouse in New York, the second wave of essays were more revealing than the initial reviews in the daily newspapers. On May 5, Harold Clurman's notice appeared in the *Nation*. He argued there that any resistance to *Godot* was a fundamentally American resistance to the intellectual climate of postwar Europe. "If this play is generally difficult for Americans to grasp as anything but an exasperatingly crazy concoction," Clurman wrote, "it is because there is no immediate point of reference for it in the conscious life of our people."[41]

A day later, on May 6, Israel Shenker's interview with Beckett appeared in the Sunday *Times* as "Moody Man of Letters" on the front of the entertainment section. There Beckett, among other things, attempted to explain the James Joyce connection. "'I was never Joyce's secretary, but, like all his friends, I helped him,'" Beckett told Shenker in a futile attempt to correct terminology that would persist for decades. On the artistic connection, in a statement that would be frequently quoted, Beckett said: "Joyce was a superb manipulator of material—perhaps the greatest. He was making words do the absolute maximum of work. There isn't a syllable that's superfluous. The kind of work I do is one in which I'm not master of my material. The more Joyce knew the more he could. He's tending toward omniscience and omnipotence as an artist. I'm working with impotence, ignorance. I don't think impotence has been exploited in the past."[42] That, of course, was of great interest to Norman Mailer, who began his second pronouncement on *Godot* with the Shenker story: "As I type this now—it is Sunday—there is an interview with Samuel Beckett in the *Times* drama section." In the course of that week, Mailer had resigned as columnist for the *Voice* because of editorial differences of opinion. Consequently, his second piece on *Godot* appeared as a paid advertisement under the title "A Public Notice by Norman Mailer." In it, by virtue of his payment now free to discuss topics "disproportionately difficult for a newspaper reader in a hurry," Mailer revealed that *Godot,* which he had by now read and seen, "is a play about impotence rather than an ode to it," that Bishop Berkeley "is the philosopher to whom the mysticism of Hip can be traced most directly," and that Vladimir and Estragon are "looking for the potency of the phallus and the testes."[43] In this deduction Mailer must have been influenced by Lucky, who, when he finally "thinks" onstage, includes in his annotations and documentation Bishop Berkeley, along with Puncher, Wattman, Fartov, and Belcher.

By the time Eric Bentley's piece appeared on May 14, he could describe the warring encampments. He dismissed what he called "intellectual anti-intellectualism," which he identified with Walter Kerr and which certainly included Mailer. His interest was in "non-intellectual pro-intellectualism," or those reviews that were bewildered but respectful of the play, and in "non-intellectual anti-intellectualism," or those like Chapman of the *News* who dismissed the play as a hoax. What this classification omitted, however, was "intellectual pro-intellectualism," or Bentley's own camp. Its position was to welcome European philosophy, or, in Bentley's words, "the 'existentialism' point of view"; to warn against excessive influence by Joyce, for "Irish litera-

ture is cut from those coats of many colors, *Ulysses* and *Finnegans Wake*";
and to praise the presence and the style of Bert Lahr, because "highbrow writers have been enthusiastic about clowns and vaudeville for
decades, but this impresses me as the first time that anything has successfully been done about the matter."[44] What is striking from today's
perspective is that Bentley and fellow intellectual pro-intellectualist
Harold Clurman were alone in speaking of production prerogatives over
the text. Moreover, they found these prerogatives underutilized. On
seeing the Berghof production, which he praised as being superior to
the play, Clurman wrote, "I can imagine a number of different ways of
staging the play." Bentley concurred. Though he allowed that "reverence toward the script is a good fault," he said of Berghof that "I have
less reverence for this play than he, and would have lopped off the last
bit of the first act. I would also have been tempted to make cuts at
several points where the dialogue stumbles."[45]

   This kind of discussion subsequently became very rare, and the
authority of the text was elevated far above the prerogatives of performance. There are many parallels with other works and other playwrights,
but Beckett's *Godot* in New York, in 1956 and after, is a salient example
of these shifting emphases. In 1956 *Godot* established a new kind of
intellectual drama in New York theater, a scene much more antithetical
to this kind of work than Paris, for example. It succeeded where O'Casey's
Within the Gates had not, on Broadway rather than "downtown," where
Bohemia did and does provide a more sympathetic audience for intellectual experiments. Beckett's play was much better received than is
generally remembered, and that degree of acceptance and even acclaim
required the critics to work against their quite defensible expectations,
especially on Broadway, for character development, conclusive action,
and a recognizable *mise en scène.* Berghof successfully staged what
Myerberg had set up: a performance with balanced tension between
high and low culture, between intellectual expectations and the ambi-
ence Bert Lahr brought to the stage. But what proved most memorable,
because it was most novel, was one side of the balance, the intellectual
side of the production. This quality overshadowed Lahr's very substantial presence because Beckett's association with Joyce extended the image in New York of the Irish playwright as intellectual, because shameless
solicitation of seventy thousand intellectuals made commercial theater
culture seem counterculture, and, of course, because the power of the
play text rose from a familiar to a metaphysical frame of reference that

required nightly "thinking" sessions. Both the volume and the tenor of critical response to Beckett's other works, including plays and novels, helped solidify a single impression of the playwright and of *Godot*. Alan Schneider's account of the Coconut Grove episode, which appeared in the "little magazine" *Chelsea* before being gathered into his autobiography in the 1980s was part of this phenomenon.

This kind of development was not surprising in Europe, where the play began in Parisian "pocket theater" and where, as Derek Mandel said, there soon was a single perception of "doing A BECKETT PLAY." That kind of Beckett play could visit New York, as, indeed, what became known as "Samuel Beckett's Production" did in 1978. This was the production that originated at the Schiller Theater in Berlin and provided prompt books with Beckett's perception of his play about twenty-five years after writing it. In revivals, it was directed by Walter Asmus, following the playwright's suggestions, and the program, in New York, included a long essay by Asmus describing working with Beckett. It recorded the very influential comment from Beckett: "Estragon is on the ground, he belongs to the stone. Vladimir is oriented towards the sky. He belongs to the tree." The production began with this metaphysical analogy, without a corresponding low, popular, or comic dimension. Asmus, summarizing Beckett, concludes: "The play should be done very simply, without long passages. To give confusion shape, [Beckett] says, a shape through repetition, repetition of themes. Not only themes in the script, but also themes of the body. When at the beginning Estragon is asleep leaning on the stone, that is a theme that repeats itself a few times. There are fixed points of waiting, where everything stands completely still, where silence threatens to swallow everything up. Then the action starts again."[46] The performance that resulted brought out dimensions of the text that a performer like Bert Lahr or site like Broadway could not possibly have illuminated in 1956. The Asmus production was powerful at particular moments, notably the famous poetic passage near the opening of Act II that begins:

ESTRAGON: All the dead voices.
VLADIMIR: They make a noise like wings.
ESTRAGON: Like leaves.
VLADIMIR: Like sand.
ESTRAGON: Like leaves.
Silence.

VLADIMIR: They all speak at once.
ESTRAGON: Each one to itself.
Silence. [40R]

The entire Asmus production, because it was built on conceptions and passages like these, was as solemn as the Berghof/Lahr production was not. It originated in Berlin and had to do with a German context where the critical discourse about Beckett had been dominated by Theodor Adorno and where theatrical images like Beckett's could not be presented without reference to World War II.[47]

Oddly, this scarcely universal conception of the play became the only fully accredited one wherever it was performed. During his life Beckett certainly assisted this narrowing of production possibilities by following his own increasing interests in the abstract and the patterned dramatic text and image. His direction of *Godot* was conceived after *Endgame, Krapp's Last Tape,* and many dramatic shorts that represent later development of his own work. At the time of his death in 1989, the authority of the playwright was unusually strong, and the conception of *Godot* that he had formed at a date later than the original conception was orthodoxy. In the newsletter of the Samuel Beckett Society, *The Beckett Circle,* correspondents continue to gauge the authenticity of individual productions against the author's last known intentions and remain alert to "revisionist productions." In 1994, for example, on the newsletter's first page, a production of *Godot* in Paris that took "liberties . . . with the rhythm of spoken lines" was judged against "the question of what would have been Beckett's reaction to this revisionist *relecture* of his text."[48]

As the conception of *Godot* narrowed, so did the conception of the Irish playwright. Emphasis on a *Godot* of generalization and repetition of themes had the effect of universalizing the play and the playwright, as can be seen in the Asmus report of discussions of stone and tree and themes of the body. In the 1950s there was no confusion at all in New York that Beckett was an Irish playwright and a direct descendant of James Joyce. Beckett was seen as an innovator, like Joyce, and an artist working beyond what Beckett himself, in a 1934 article on "Recent Irish Poetry," had described as the accredited themes of local Irish color. Once *Godot* was universalized, however, it existed outside the bounds of even the non-Irish Irish play, like *Exiles* or *Within the Gates.* The national origins of *Godot* became irrelevant, and its official designation became a term of international reference devised by Martin Esslin: Theater of the Absurd. The loss was Irish drama's, because without exceptional examples resources were circumscribed and its form appeared to the world to be rather monotonous. Outside Ireland, the Irish play remained a durable product, but after *Godot* anything eccentric to its familiar forms was considered irrelevant to it.

The result was a narrower conception of what constituted Irish drama. Immediately after the 1956 production of *Godot,* the provincialization of Irish drama was aided immensely by Brendan Behan, and especially in New York. Behan's work bears comparison with Beckett's. In particular, the offstage eponymous character of *The Quare Fellow,* and the ramifications of his absence on onstage characters, bears comparison with *Godot.* But the image of Behan as an Irish playwright, a creation by many hands, revoked images established in New York since Shaw and narrowed the role to a few familiar mannerisms of drink and song. Writing for the readers of the *New York Post* in 1959, Richard Watts could ask: "What will come of the Irish author, tosspot and frequent jailbird Brendan Behan? Will he, as many of his admirers insist, emerge as the legitimate inheriter [*sic*] of the great tradition of Synge and O'Casey?"[49] The great tradition Watts had in mind was Synge and the early O'Casey, and it did not include Shaw, Joyce, or Beckett. Behan contributed mightily to the extra-theatrical formation of this narrower image and tradition. Later in 1959 he appeared drunk on the Edward Murrow show on American television, and in 1960 he drunkenly joined onstage the actors performing *The Hostage* at the Cort Theatre. The image was rather lower than Boucicault's on the scale of artistic integrity. The work of "James Joyce's secretary" helped define the bounds of a known product by overstepping them, and the newly inscribed, narrower product was reenforced by Behan, productions of Behan's work, and the work of others. So well defined was the form that others could exploit it. One effect was a rebirth of that minor genre, the Irish play by a non-Irish author. A good contemporary example is *The Righteous Are Bold* by the American Frank Carney: it opened on Broadway in the same 1955-56 Broadway season as *Godot,* and it featured Dennis Day as the latest version of that mainstay of the New York stage, the Irish priest, which Boucicault originated and Shaw hoped to eradicate. These narrower confines are not a fact of Irish drama but of perception of it in New York and elsewhere and an important factor in the commercial process of theater that governs what gets produced and what does not.

Frank McGuinness's non-Irish Irish play *Someone Who'll Watch over Me* made an unusually long appearance on Broadway in 1992, and to a *New York Times* reporter McGuinness said, "I'm an Irishman. . . . After Beckett, nothing in the theater was the same, particularly for Irish playwrights. He gave me license to write about time."[50] The license, however, did not include rights to broaden the national drama in American eyes, and the obstacles to that are part of the production history in New York of McGuinness and, especially, Brian Friel.

These two corollary restrictive conceptions—the metaphysical quality of Beckett's play and the parochial form of Irish drama—were both evident in New York at the time of a conspicuous, for better or worse, revival of *Godot* in 1988. Directed by Mike Nichols, the production cast Robin Williams as Estragon and Steve Martin as Vladimir. Both brought to the stage their well-known personae as Hollywood comedians. This certainly returned to the play what Roger Blin had called "the director's share of freedom." As Myerberg had overcompensated for Bert Lahr by soliciting an audience of intellectuals, Nichols rather overcompensated for a rigidified recent tradition of "A BECKETT PLAY" by enlisting an excess of popular culture. But the production had some of the conceptual edge of the American premiere by working against expectations. While the critical expectations of 1956 were for kinds of coherence the play did not provide, the expectations of 1988 were for particular intellectual qualities associated with Beckett's later work that were equally reductive of *Godot*. Frank Rich of the *New York Times* railed that "Mr. Nichols has at times turned 'Godot' into exactly the sort of production that Beckett's theater rebels against," and William A. Henry III of *Time* magazine rued that "the supreme existentialist tragedy of the 20th century has been reduced to a heartwarming revue sketch about the homeless."[51] The interest of these representative statements is not their judgment of the success or failure of the production, but their assumption that only one possible production focus existed for *Godot*. At the same time, the impression that Beckett was Irish was returning by virtue of continuing volumes of critical work and some striking productions of Beckett material by Irish companies and solo actors. To accompany its Nichols production, the *New Theater Review,* a publication of Lincoln Center, where it was staged, devoted an issue to publicity material. The graphic motif of the issue was a green shamrock. The material included a note on Young Sam Beckett attending the Abbey Theatre by Hugh Kenner and an interview with Barry McGovern, then the best-known Irish interpreter of Beckett, under the title *Seanchai*. At a time when Irish cultural commentators were promoting the idea of "varieties of Irishness," the idea of Irishness, particularly concerning playwrights, was in New York focused almost entirely on a few familiar emblems of identity. One reviewer in 1988 repeated the stereotypes of 1956 by explaining that "Vladimir and Estragon's theological discourse on the fate of the thieves hung with Christ is a vermiform appendix of Beckett's Catholic upbringing."[52] He was not, of course, raised a Catholic, but that assumption could be made in a blooming New York culture of Irish kitsch, the culture into which Brian Friel's plays would venture a decade after *Godot* opened in New York.

Both the 1956 and the 1988 productions of *Godot* in New York were respected, as, indeed, was the Walter Asmus production. But New York still waits for a truly formative production of the play. However, while New York theater has colluded with propagation of a rather simplistic notion of Irishness and Irish drama, it also has contributed to the production history of a universally acclaimed play by challenging it, by producing secularized versions of sacred text. Both Berghof and Nichols insisted on what Roger Blin called the director's share of freedom, and both made decisions cognizant of the local setting of production, New York, and its relevance to the popular culture dimension of a high culture, intellectualized work. Both insisted on localized, provisional productions steeped in stage business rather than the universal and solemn style favored by those specializing in the playwright and his later work. Neither American director hoped to empty theaters. It can be said that the playwright's aloofness, rising from Shaw to O'Casey, was challenged in New York in 1956 and then again in 1988. There have been many unconventional productions of the play elsewhere, in America most notably at San Quentin prison in 1957. The year of the Nichols production, 1988, also saw two hotly debated productions of *Godot* with all-female casts. Other Beckett works have also become a testing grounds for notions of artistic privileges and who has prior claim to them. In America this has been especially evident in JoAnne Akalaitis's production of *Endgame* in Cambridge, Massachusetts, in 1984, or the publication history of the play not produced in Paris in 1953, *Eleuthéria*. The issue is international, of course, and has reference to artists other than Beckett. But on at least two notable occasions years apart, New York produced a kind of *Godot* not seen elsewhere and so made conspicuous parts of the text otherwise likely to be neglected.

These are not negligible parts of the text. The final image of the play is a moment not limited to generalized conceptions of tree and stone and themes of the body:

> ESTRAGON: Well? Shall we go?
> VLADIMIR: Pull on your trousers.
> ESTRAGON: What?
> VLADIMIR: Pull on your trousers.
> ESTRAGON: You want me to pull off my trousers?
> vladimir: Pull ON your trousers.
> ESTRAGON: (*realizing his trousers are down*). True.
> *He pulls up his trousers.*
> VLADIMIR: Well? Shall we go?
> ESTRAGON: Yes, Let's go.
> *They do not move.* [60R]

The Berghof and Nichols productions together make New York a site for *Godot*'s other than the narrowest purist versions of the play, and both of these indicated that limitation of the play to particular restrictions and expectations may be more reductive than protective. One New York theater director, writer, and historian, Gordon Rogoff, proposed as much in the *Village Voice*. His suggestion was that even the mixed results of the Nichols production opened the possibility "that *Godot*'s awesome, monochromatic presentation of one man's horrified glimpse into the abyss is no longer the only possible story."[53]

7

Brian Friel:
Erin on Broadway

In Brian Friel's *Philadelphia, Here I Come!*, Gar O'Donnell prepares to emigrate from Ireland for America. In 1966 Friel's play immigrated from Ireland to New York. The story in the play is a story of emigration, and the story about the play is one of immigration. The chief stage device of the play, which is very effective though not unprecedented, is representation of Gar O'Donnell by two actors, one playing the Public Gar that other characters know, and on playing the Private Gar that vocalizes personal fantasies and private desires. The two characters, memorably played in the New York premiere by the Irish actors Patrick Bedford (Public) and Donal Donnelly (Private), perform the dynamics of leavetaking in the deadly dull setting of the small town of Ballybeg and against the scene of the incommunicative O'Donnell family of widower shopkeeper father S.B. and housekeeper Madge. The effect is to put onstage both the real life of daily, silent routine and the private life of invention and eloquence. Though at the outset of a new life, as suggested by the play's title, Public Gar looks backward only, hoping to resolve unclear memories and to break through a longstanding emotional impasse with his father. Only Private Gar looks forward, to a new life, and his eloquence is produced by the prospects of America. Thus, in its two principal roles, *Philadelphia* dramatizes communication and failure of communication at the same time. By associating the first with America and the second with Ireland, the play mirrors the factors of reception affecting this play's fortunes in American theater and those of its predecessors as Irish plays in New York. *Philadelphia* dramatizes the optimism of eloquence leaving a small, familiar context for a foreign one, and its first production in New York illustrates some of the external factors hindering transmission of eloquence on arrival at a new scene.

The stage directions of *Philadelphia* state that "the two Gars, Public Gar and Private Gar, are two views of one man. Public Gar is the Gar people see, talk to, talk about. Private Gar is the unseen man, the man within, the conscience, the *alter ego,* the secret thought, the id."[1] The play opens with Public Gar onstage with Madge the housekeeper, and when she exits Private Gar enters:

> PUBLIC: It's all over.
> PRIVATE: (*off, in echo-chamber voice*): And it's all about to begin. It's all over.
> PUBLIC: And it's all about to begin.
> PRIVATE: Just think, Gar.
> PUBLIC: Think . . .
> PRIVATE: Think . . . Up in that big bugger of a jet, with its snout pointing straight for the States, and its tail belching smoke over Ireland; and you sitting up at the front (PUBLIC *acts this*) with your competent fingers poised over the controls; and then away down below in the Atlantic you see a bloody bugger of an Irish boat out fishing for bloody pollock and—(PUBLIC *nose-dives, engines screaming, machine guns stuttering.*) [31]

The America of destination is always imagined in the play as vulgar, "a profane, irreligious, pagan country of gross materialism" (32), and this image of America is constructed by Private Gar out of mass culture and Hollywood films. It is a derivative, selective, and distorted image, and in that resembles the image of Ireland constructed in America out of this play and others. However gross, the image of America is accepted by Private Gar as opportunity: "You're going to cut a bit of dash in them thar States," Private exhorts Public. "Great big sexy dames and night clubs and high living and films and dances" (55). But despite these thrilled apostrophes, Public Gar continually reverts to his habitual state of repression and mourning for what he is about to leave. He satisfies as best he can the ritual of farewells with a former love, Kate Doogan, his teacher, Master Boyle, and "the boys" (68). In the midst of this he recalls, and the play reenacts, his meeting at home with the loud, brassy Aunt Lizzy and docile Uncle Con, emigrants from Ballybeg themselves, who hope to sponsor his immigration to Philadelphia.

> CON: Honey! (*To* PUBLIC) You'll think about what we were discussing?

PUBLIC: I will, Uncle Con.
CON: The job's as good as you'll get and we'd be proud to have you.
LIZZY: Don't force him.
CON: I'm not forcing him. I'm only telling him.
LIZZY: Well now you've told him—a dozen times. So now desist, will you?
(CON *spreads his hands.*)
PUBLIC: I will think about it. Really.
LIZZY: Sure! Sure! Typical Irish! He will think about it! And while he's thinking about it the store falls in about his head! What age are you? Twenty-four? Twenty-five? What are you waiting for? For S.B. to run away to sea? Until the weather gets better?
CON: Honey!
LIZZY: I'm talking straight to the kid! He's Maire's boy and I've got an interest in him—the only nephew I have. [63]

Gar does choose to join his aunt and uncle in Philadelphia, as *Philadelphia* chose to join in New York those who had interests in it. Before going, Gar makes a final attempt to communicate with his father about a childhood memory of a fishing trip:

PUBLIC: D'you remember the blue boat?
S.B.: A blue one, eh?
PUBLIC: I don't know who owned it. But it was blue. And the paint was peeling.
S.B. (*Remembering*): I mind a brown one the doctor brought from somewhere up in the—
PUBLIC (*Quickly*): It doesn't matter who owned it. It doesn't even matter that it was blue. But d'you remember one afternoon in May—we were up there—the two of us—and it must have rained because you put your jacket round my shoulders and gave me your hat—
S.B.: Aye?
PUBLIC: And it wasn't that we were talking or anything— but suddenly—suddenly you sang "All round My Hat I'll Wear a Green Coloured Ribbon"—
S.B.: Me?

PUBLIC: —for no reason at all except that we—that you
were happy. D'you remember?
S.B.: No . . . no, then, I don't. . . [94-95]

Against this silence Private Gar posits the excitement abroad: "swaggering down 56th Street on Third at the junction of 29th and Seventh at 81st with this big blonde nuzzling up to you" (81). When asked at final curtain why he must go, Gar, caught between a familiar but disappointing home culture and an exotic one, can only answer, in the play's final line, "I don't know. I-I-I don't know" (99).

Private Gar was not far wrong about the States. In fact, *Philadelphia's* sponsor there exceeded Aunt Lizzy by several degrees of coarseness and possessiveness. *Philadelphia* had its premiere at the Gaiety Theatre in Dublin, with Bedford and Donnelly originating the two Gar roles, as part of the Theatre Festival of 1964. One of the leading Irish commentators on Friel, Richard Pine, has made an observation echoed by others, that "on September 28, 1964, with the premiere of *Philadelphia, Here I Come!*, [Friel] became the father of contemporary Irish drama."[2] At that moment Friel was thirty-five years old, with a degree from St. Patrick's College, Maynooth, and a brief term as primary- and secondary-school teacher in Derry, Northern Ireland, his childhood home. He already had logged a far longer term as a writer, especially of short stories, many of which appeared in the States in the *New Yorker,* and of BBC radio plays. After production of his first stage play, *The Enemy Within,* at the Abbey, Friel spent six months working with Tyrone Guthrie in Minneapolis, an experience, he would report much later, that "gave me courage and daring to attempt things."[3] What he attempted immediately after his work in America with Guthrie was *Philadelphia, Here I Come!,* which initiated the series of regularly appearing plays and regular productions in Ireland and elsewhere that for Pine and others underlie the project of contemporary Irish drama. After the 1964 Theatre Festival, *Philadelphia* was revived at the Gate Theatre specifically for the benefit of Broadway producers, and one who flew to Dublin, like Lizzy in search of progeny, was David Merrick.

At that point Merrick was near the zenith of his Broadway career. After his first great success with *Fanny* in 1954, he had spent the next decade importing to Broadway foreign plays, both commercial vehicles and artistically ambitious dramas such as *Look Back in Anger* and *The Entertainer.* By the time of *Philadelphia,* Merrick had also earned his reputation for publicity at any cost and for an aggressive posture toward newspaper critics. Examples of the first involving *Look Back* included advertisement illustrations with enough nudity to be rejected by newspapers and, when the play's shock value seemed to wane, hiring an actress to rise up out of the audience in outrage at the character of Jimmy Porter, climb onstage, and, in perfect profile for photographers, strike the actor, Kenneth Haigh, with an umbrella. One of the most legendary examples of Merrick's battles with reviewers was when, on lukewarm notices for the musical *Subways Are for Sleeping*, Merrick found New Yorkers in the telephone directory who had the same names as Howard Taubman, Walter Kerr, and Richard Watts, and in his advertisements quoted their purchased, proxy raves in the usual blurb style. When he flew to Dublin in the fall of 1965, Merrick was flush with a string of popular successes including *Oliver!* in 1963 and *Hello, Dolly!* in 1964, and he was about to enjoy the success of *Cactus Flower* in December.

To balance those enterprises, Merrick was also producing under the auspices of the David Merrick Arts Foundation. Founded in 1959, the foundation was sufficiently capitalized by the fall of 1965 to open its first production, John Osborne's *Inadmissible Evidence*. By various accounts the foundation was either an honorable attempt to reinvest commercial profits in serious drama or a tax dodge. On a personal level, the foundation was plainly Merrick's attempt to associate himself with high art and upper-crust society. On an institutional level, the nonprofit incorporation anticipated and perhaps partly inspired the spread of nonprofit theater in New York in subsequent decades. All these factors are evident in Merrick's own explanation for the foundation: "I have a theory that you can sell shows using the Madison Avenue technique. I reason—if you can sell all sorts of merchandise that they do sell with all these ridiculous campaigns—that I can certainly try that technique in selling my lovely plays. And I sold some rather literate and articulate plays that way. Believe it or not, they weren't all [*The World of*] *Suzie Wong.*"[4] After *Inadmissible Evidence,* the foundation produced in the same 1966-67 Broadway season both Peter Brooks's celebrated production known by the shortened title *Marat/Sade* and *Philadelphia, Here I Come!*

Under such auspices, the immigrant play *Philadelphia* met both high expectations and unexpected shenanigans in the New World. The first were effects of Merrick's publicity machine, and the second were

Merrick's personal effects. As early as December, positive reports began appearing in the press. Stuart Little of the *Herald Tribune* put the
best possible face on the foundation by letting readers know that "such
successes as *Cactus Flower,* which has been doing hit business at the
box office," enable Merrick "to embrace such projects as an Irish play
with a partly Irish cast by a writer known here only for some short
stories in the *New Yorker.*"[5] One indication of how rigid a genre Little
had in mind as an "Irish play" is the fact that his story about Friel's play
about Ballybeg appeared under the headline "Merrick's Next: Dublin
Comedy." The cast imported from the Gate revival were the five principal roles, with Americans filling the remaining supporting roles. Along
with the playwright, Merrick also summoned the director, Hilton
Edwards, founder with Micheál Mac Liammóir of the Gate Theatre as
an alternative in Dublin to the Abbey Theatre as a venue for international rather than national plays. While in rehearsal, Edwards was at
pains to make the point that this was not just another Irish play, a genre
he deplored. Before the new year, the *Herald Tribune* reported, "Edwards
expressed particular pleasure with the notion given him by Merrick
that the play needn't be considered specifically Irish, since its meaning
was rather more universal." Edwards certainly needed no help from
Merrick to reach this conclusion. He was, in fact, taking a lesson from
the debut of *Waiting for Godot* in New York and elsewhere by stressing
the universal reference of a work by a playwright always himself localized as "Irish." Edwards, actually, went further and took a lesson from
Shaw's defense of the artistic integrity of the Irish Players in 1911. Like
Shaw, he insisted that art, Ireland, and America never, ever conjoined
in Irish America. Shaw had defended Irish drama from Irish America
by warning that "America, being governed by a mysterious race—probably one of the last tribes of Israel—calling themselves American Gaels,
is a dangerous country for genuine Irishmen and Irishwomen."[6] A country, that is, which a young man like Gar O'Donnell or a play like *Philadelphia* visited at great peril. Edwards sounded this note before the New
York production. He proposed a different point of origin for the lost
tribe, but to the same effect. "There are three races, you know," he told
the *Herald Tribune:* "There are the Irish. There are the Americans. And
the third are the Irish-Americans. But in truth they have little to do
with America and still less to do with Ireland. My own theory is that
they came from that mythical country, Atlantis."[7] This was rather cruel,
especially in the context of theater. Only the month before, William

Alfred's play *Hogan's Goat* revived the genre of Irish American drama about power politics in New York. After a critical success and a run of more than six hundred performances, the play, written in blank verse, traveled to Dublin and an enthusiastic reception at the 1966 Theatre Festival.

Perhaps Edwards was revealing as his conception of *Philadelphia* a terrible destiny for Gar when he leaves Ballybeg for America. Private Gar never imagines an Irish America, only the mythic America of popular culture: "Let's git packin', boy. Let's git that li'l ole saddle bag opened and let's git packing" (36). The Irish America represented by Aunt Lizzie and Uncle Con is a limited, at best, prospect associated in rather patronizing terms with alcohol and bad grammar. In 1911, W.B. Yeats had contrived by ingenious logic the argument that *The Playboy of the Western World* would flatter the Irish American audience by suggesting that the quality men of Ireland emigrated, leaving the country with nothing but weak characters like the "mighty" men of Mayo in Synge's play. No one suggested the same for *Philadelphia, Here I Come!*, which put Irish America on stage in unflattering form. Gar O'Donnell offers to go to America "if you'll have me," and then Lizzie, drunk, exclaims: "If we'll have him, he says; he says if we'll have him! That's why I'm here! That's why I'm half-shot-up!" (66). The unpleasantness of Gar's prospects are underscored because at this moment in stage time Kate Doogan is marrying some other, much more successful, local boy. The logic on this occasion suggests that the quality stays in Ireland and the weak characters, like Public Gar, emigrate. *Philadelphia* does not flatter its Irish American audience. The play tests it, and the great success of *Philadelphia* in America in 1966 and afterward indicates that flattery is not required.

When Edwards was sharpening the edge of the play by disparaging Irish America in the press, he was also intent on distinguishing this play from the expectations associated with a product known as an Irish play. Part of this effort was to insist on *Philadelphia*'s universality: "it could just as well be about a boy leaving Russia," he told the *Herald Tribune*.[8] This particular analogy remained part of the publicity campaign even after opening, and it was helpfully propagated by a leading Irish American in the press, Pete Hamill. He warned readers of the *New York Post* against thinking "it is an 'Irish play'": "It is true that the play is set in Ireland, that it concerns the inner and outer life of a young Irishman bound for America, and that most of the players speak with brogues. But it is no more an Irish play than 'The Cherry Orchard' is a Russian play."[9] And no less. The nature of locality is central to Gar's dilemma and to the reception of *Philadelphia* in New York. When Lizzie and Con are on stage with Public Gar and Private Gar, the play text poses a rhetorical question: "Ireland—America—what's the difference?" (64). The difference is at that moment palpable on stage. The question is carelessly posed by Ben Burton, Lizzy and Con's American benefactor, and the only American in the play. He disqualifies himself from answering the question precisely because he is not an immigrant and so lacks personal experience with cultural contrast.

This kind of question was very prominent as the Merrick Arts Foundation production approached opening night. Nick LaPole of the *Journal American* quoted Friel three days before opening night in a fashion that purported universality and then immediately diminished that to local: "'An individual leaving behind him a whole culture is a universal theme,' says Friel, a 36-year-old former schoolteacher from Derry who makes his living mainly by writing short stories." LaPole also presented Edwards pursuing that prey of Shaw, the stage Irishman, and putting the hunt into the terms of the post-*Godot* Irish play. "The professional Irishman will play Ireland by ear," Edwards told LaPole. "He will ask people what they want him to be, and then act up to the role. Behan played the professional Irishman wherever he went, and it appears as if everyone was fascinated. But, as far as I'm concerned, Irishry is not even an interesting disease, so why bother to contract or cultivate it?"[10] Edwards's intention, at least, was with Friel to broaden the image of the Irish playwright lately shaped in dismal form in New York by Behan. With Friel's play, *Philadelphia,* the intention was to broaden expectations for an Irish play.

If there was any doubt about cultural contrasts in the context of this performance of an Irish play in New York, David Merrick provided proof. *Philadelphia* did the customary tryout in Philadelphia before opening in New York. There, at the Forest Theatre, a local television station was interviewing the preview audience as it exited. Merrick got in line, was not recognized, and so had his opportunity to explain to the television audience with total objectivity why this was one of the best plays ever written. However, he reserved his greatest intervention into the press for New York. The newspapers and the producers were then debating the merits of reviewing a final preview rather than the opening performance. For the reviewers, especially Stanley Kauffmann of the *Times,* additional time would allow a more thoughtful review. For Merrick, more time subverted enthusiasm and tempted overanalysis. Kauffmann followed the standing rules and requested tickets from Merrick for the final preview rather than the opening night. Merrick sent the tickets as requested with a note that read "At your peril." Kauffmann arrived on the night of February 15 to find the marquee of the Helen Hayes Theater dark and a sign on the door announcing that the performance was canceled. As Merrick told the press: "For about two weeks I had a premonition that something might go wrong with the last preview of *Philadelphia.* I guess I'm a mystic. By Monday I was really afraid something might happen, so we stopped selling tickets for Tuesday. My worst fears were confirmed. At 7:45 Tuesday night my technicians informed me that a large rat had gotten into the generator. It was, I discovered, a large white rat." It was plainly a lie, because lights other than the marquee were lit that night. Many thought the large white rat was an allusion to Kauffmann's physical appearance. The event, at any rate, was covered as a news story, and so, as Howard Kissel says in his book on Merrick: "Merrick put a play by an unknown writer from Dublin on the front page of the *New York Times.*"[11] This seemed to promise the kind of fantasy of reception that Private Gar in Ballybeg imagines for himself on arrival in America.

But the writer, of course, was not, as Cecil wrote, from Dublin, and the reception of *Philadelphia* in New York was not exactly a fantasy fulfilled. In an early dialogue with Public Gar, Private Gar imitates the father, S.B., extolling the benefits of travel. "Nothing like it to broaden the mind," he says in mimicry. "Man, how I'd love to travel. But there's some it doesn't agree with—like me" (45). There may be some plays it doesn't agree with either. In 1966 *Philadelphia* got a very positive reception but not the most productive kind of positive reception for the future of the Irish play in New York. Merrick's publicity machine and New York's predilection for its particular focus overwhelmed Edwards's intentions, and the work intended to broaden expectations for Irish plays, because of its own successes, inadvertently narrowed them. The play, and in particular the Donnelly-Bedford performance, was unquestionably a success. *Variety* immediately began running up numbers for the profits to the humble Irish playwright under headlines like "Ex-Teacher Friel Hits Cash Mark as 'Phil' Hits."[12] In the 1966 Drama Critics Award for Best Play, *Philadelphia* would have tied *Marat/Sade,* eleven ballots to eleven, if Whitney Bolton of the *Morning Telegraph* had remembered to vote. But the kind of praise *Philadelphia* received always referred back to the Irish play familiar in New York and deplored by Hilton Edwards. The only available form of praise seemed to be as addition to the tradition Friel and Edwards hoped to revise. For *Time* magazine, "Without O'Casey and Joyce, the play might have existed, but not so good a play," and the magazine's points of reference were Before the Silver Tassie O'Casey and all Joyce except *Exiles*.[13] Even the sole negative review built its verdict on the established conventions of the Irish play as it was known in New York and *Philadelphia*'s congruity with it. For *Newsweek,* the play "seems composed from half a hundred previous dramas, most of which were in turn composed from Ireland's continuing and somewhat narrow preoccupation with its own embattled sociology and beleaguered folkways."[14]

That reviewer did not admit the alter ego of this phenomenon: the narrow preoccupations of New York theater with Irish drama. *Philadelphia* represented some degree of change, but New York only recognized the familiar. The *New Yorker,* publisher of the playwright's short stories, reported that "although its author, Brian Friel, can hardly be hailed as a new-day O'Casey just yet, he has some of the master's ability."[15] An important complement to finding the familiar in the new play was to find the familiar in the young playwright. The figure of Friel added humble and rural to the well-known prototypes. The short stories, the BBC dramas, the Tyrone Guthrie were never mentioned. What was reported followed the direction of Stuart Little, whose review, under the title "Playwright Status for Ex-Teacher," explained that *Philadelphia* "got the best reception of any new play this season and made a playwright no longer unknown out of a 37-year-old former school teacher from the northernmost part of Ireland."[16] The failure of communication in the play consists largely of silence, but the failure of communication in the 1966 performance and reception of it consisted of simplification and reduction to familiar terms. A month after the opening, Walter Kerr referred to Donal Donnelly as "Donald," and on opening night the television correspondent Allan Jefferys, outside the Helen Hayes Theater, summoned local lore and called *Philadelphia* a "Gaelic Glass Menagerie."[17]

In *Philadelphia,* the past is always associated with Ireland and the future with America. Private Gar repeatedly evokes the eighteenth-century past of Edmund Burke by reciting bits of a famous speech memorized in Irish schools about meeting the Dauphiness at Versailles. The local teacher, Master Boyle, who taught Gar his history, tells Gar that America "is a vast restless place that doesn't give a curse about the past; and that's the way things should be" (52). Public Gar attempts to adopt just that alleged American attitude of disregard for the past, of indifference to cultural and historical conditions and obligations: "All this bloody yap about father and son and all this sentimental rubbish about 'homeland' and 'birthplace'—yap! Bloody yap! Impermanence—anonymity—that's what I'm looking for; a vast restless place that doesn't give a damn about the past. To hell with Ballybeg, that's what I say! (79). This is bravely declaimed to Kate Doogan, but it is clear that Public Gar cannot free himself completely from his past, even by leaving, and that his victory against circumstance by uprooting himself from Ballybeg entails considerable loss.

Ironically, the reception of *Philadelphia* in 1966 had less to do with the project of contemporary Irish drama than with the past history of Irish drama in New York. This became even more evident in the New York press after the popular and critical success of the play was secure. When plans were announced for a premiere production of Friel's next play, *The Loves of Cass Maguire,* in New York, James Davis of the *News* told readers that "should 'Philadelphia, Here I Come' still be on the Broadway boards come October—and there is little reason to doubt that this will not come to pass—young Irish playwright Brian Friel will be the first dramatist from the Emerald Isle to have two plays running simultaneously on Broadway since maybe the year of the big wind." After wielding the stereotype of the Emerald Isle and the allusion, without comparable humor or irony, to Buck Mulligan's joke in the opening chapter of *Ulysses* to the folklore publishing venture of the three weird sisters, Davis went on to state the record: "Friel's play has already run longer than John Millington Synge's 'Playboy of the Western World,' which ran for 81 performances at the Booth Theater in 1947, and Sean O'Casey's 'Within the Gates,' which lasted 141 [*sic*] performances in 1934."[18] In many successive revivals, *The Playboy,* once so vociferously protested, had secured status as the prototype of the Irish play. O'Casey could not revise the status of his own Dublin trilogy as exemplary Irish plays, and even a critical success like *Red Roses for Me* in 1955 was always measured against *Juno and the Paycock*. In fact the record *Philadelphia* broke in the category that James Davis called "longest-running play product of Erin on Broadway" was Paul Vincent Carroll's *Shadow and Substance,* which ran for 275 performances in 1938. It was a sturdy

Abbey product that Brooks Atkinson referred to, in an allusion to Joxer in *Juno,* and in praise, as "bright bits about the darlin' folks and their quaint manners."[19] *Philadelphia* broke the Erin on Broadway record with 362 performances.

Juno in particular was the kind of association that Hilton Edwards, vainly, hoped to avoid. In spring 1966, between the openings of *Philadelphia* and *Cass Maguire* in New York, Edwards told the *New York Post* that "no one these days is interested in such things as the Irish rebellion after two world wars and the H-bomb."[20] However, while evidently a "vast, restless place," the New York theater world was not, after all, careless of the past. It was, in fact, rather rooted in precedents for Irish drama and expectations shaped by Friel's predecessors and their various receptions in New York. Like Public Gar, Broadway looked back, and, also like Gar, *Philadelphia* incurred some losses in its brave beginning. The play was perceived less as the beginning of contemporary Irish drama than as the latest installment of a popular product from the Emerald Isle. The play itself contributed to this predicament because it included the familiar emblems of a Catholic, rural, repressed, and sexually puritanical Ireland. One very successful revival in New York nearly thirty years later was directed by Joe Dowling, who said of *Philadelphia* that "what [Friel] did so brilliantly was, he took all these stock elements of the old Abbey Theatre play—the father, son, housekeeper, priest, teacher—and then he turned up this extraordinary theatrical device of the private self. We'd never seen anything like it in the Irish theater before."[21] That evidently was too small a degree of innovation to communicate across the Atlantic. The peril of a radical departure from the familiar, like *Waiting for Godot,* was being perceived as not an Irish play at all and suffering from elevation to a high-art, international, and metaphysical event. But the perils of slight revisionist adjustment of the "stock elements of the old Abbey Theatre play," especially evident on migration to America, were that the familiar would obscure the innovative. This is a dimension of Irish drama especially evident from the American perspective: it frequently does rely on a rather small set of preoccupations. Certainly the New York stage does not represent fully the variety of dramas staged in Ireland. But Irish drama has a distinct status in America that French drama, for example, or German drama, does not. New York is narrow in its expectations for Irish drama, and Irish drama has fulfilled them.

All these dimensions of reception were in evidence in the next two Friel productions in New York after *Philadelphia*. The first was *The Loves of Cass Maguire,* which did indeed open at the Helen Hayes Theater while *Philadelphia* continued at the Plymouth. *Cass* opened in New York in October 1966 as another David Merrick Arts Foundation production directed by Hilton Edwards. The play reversed the situation of *Philadelphia* by returning an Irish emigrant to home, and if *Philadelphia* suggested that an Irish immigrant would be unhappy in America, *Cass* confirmed the costs of residence in that "vast, restless place." But too many distractions—in particular by Ruth Gordon in the title role—dissatisfied a New York eager for an "Irish play." Lee Jordan of WCBS regretted that the comic elements of *Cass* were derived "more from raunchy humor than rich Irish wit," and William Glover of Associated Press, apologizing for the play with the usual evocation of Joxer Daly, attempted high praise by calling *Cass* "a darlin' little play."[22] While *Philadelphia* ran in New York for two years, *Cass* struggled to run for two weeks. Its difficulties in New York had little to do with an unflattering—to Americans and Irish Americans—image of the effect of immigration to the States, because that was a prominent feature of *Philadelphia*. Its difficulties had much more to do with increasingly rigid expectation of what constituted an Irish play or an authentic Irish playwright.

The latter consideration was an important factor when the next Friel production, *Lovers,* opened in New York in 1968. This program of two one-act plays, "Winners" and "Losers," originated at the Gate Theatre rather than the Abbey, and it was not produced in New York by David Merrick. It was very well received and moved from Lincoln Center to the Music Box on Broadway to extend its run. But the positive reception had more to do with fulfillment of particular expectations than broadening the American sense of the Irish play, and those expectations had to do with valorizing the image of the genuine Irish playwright. Richard Watts, who thought that Art Carney as the narrator in "Winners" resembled Sean O'Casey, wrote that "there can no longer be any doubt that Brian Friel is the new top man in Irish dramatic writing and may well restore the theater of Ireland to the days of glory of Synge, Yeats, and O'Casey."[23] Offstage publicity at the time contributed to narrowing the pedigree acceptable for an Irish playwright. Friel, who has never courted personal publicity, attempted to offset that process. He had broken his arm and missed the Lincoln Center opening but came to New York to supervise movement of the production to the Music Box. "A thing of nothing, Broadway, isn't it?" he asked Alan Bunce of the

Christian Science Monitor. On arrival Friel announced that "Irish theater seems to be in a permanent state of senility. It isn't going to die,
and it certainly isn't getting rejuvenated in any way. Ireland doesn't
have the experimental theater you find here Off and Off-Off Broadway."
He repeated his warning that his work should not be understood as
local, that "drama can transcend these boundaries." But Bunce's own
commentary subverted that warning against the familiar emblems of
Ireland. "It's very easy to be fooled by Brian Friel's face," Bunce wrote.
"It fairly twinkles with self-deprecating glee. But the seriousness of his
statements belies the leprechaun smile."[24] Bunce apparently thought
that Friel's claim that he was not attempting to rejuvenate Irish drama
was just a joke.

Friel's work, by many estimations, was to be the rejuvenation of
Irish theater. For Richard Pine or Joe Dowling, that process began with
Philadelphia. For others, the process would begin later. Seamus Deane,
Irish critic, was collaborator with Friel and others on the Field Day
projects in theater and publications that began in 1980. For Deane, the
rejuvenating effect on Friel's work began in 1968, the year *Lovers* was
staged in New York, when issues in Northern Ireland erupted into pronounced violence. The rejuvenating effect of Friel's work on Irish theater began subsequently, in the mid-1970s, after his plays reflecting
this new context had their influence. According to Deane: "All of Friel's
major work dates from the mid-1970s. Before that, he had been an immensely skillful writer who had found himself being silently exploited
by the ease with which he could satisfy the taste for Irishness which
institutions like the *New Yorker* and the Irish Theatre had become so
expert in establishing. Although *Philadelphia* was a remarkable play,
prefiguring some of the later work in its preoccupations, it was a vir-
tuoso performance of the kind of Irish eloquence which had come to be
expected from Irish playwrights in particular."[25] This kind of effect
certainly was evident in the New York reception of *Philadelphia* and the
subsequent publicity that could describe an Irish playwright as a smil-
ing leprechaun.

Deane describes Friel after the mid-1970s as breaking patterns
associated with the Abbey Theatre, and he, along with many others,
points to the play *Translations* as an especially notable work in the new
direction. It was originally staged at the Guildhall in Derry as the first
production of the Field Day Company. While plays like *Philadelphia*
moved quickly to Broadway and plays like *Cass Maguire* and *Lovers*

originated there, *Translations* only opened in New York in a modest but excellent off-Broadway production by the Manhattan Theater Club in 1981. This off-Broadway venue and its association in Friel's mind with experimentation might suggest a significantly new artistic direction or audience for his work. However, there had been substantial debate in Ireland about whether there was a fundamental change in Friel's work after the 1970s, and in *Translations* in particular. That play's whole representation of the English ordnance survey in Ireland in the 1830s has been attacked for inaccuracies and improbabilities. For example, many have pointed to the unlikely and certainly unrepresentative image of a peasantry in full possession of several languages and an English officer corps with scarcely more than rudimentary command of one. Edna Longley has been especially vocal on the question of "Does *Translations* itself renew 'images of the past,' or does it recycle a familiar perspective?" She finds that *Translations* "does not so much *examine* myths of dispossession and oppression as repeat them."[26] Many more have joined this debate in Ireland.

In New York, which is demonstrably prone to celebration of what Deane called a particular kind of "Irish eloquence," the image of Friel and his work has not changed since the 1960s. Of course, he has moved from undiscovered schoolteacher to honored playwright, but the kind of praise in America for his work has not altered. This in itself does not settle debate about the direction of his work or changes in that direction. However, the quality of reception is one of many indications of drama in practice, of theater as transaction between artist and audience, and what Friel himself has called "a vulgar art form more dependent on the public than is poetry, or music, or visual arts."[27] The very long history of Friel productions in New York after *Lovers* is a rather repetitive record of familiar perspectives. When the Manhattan Theater Club production of *Translations* opened in 1981, Friel the playwright was celebrated for "mere Irishness," for Abbey Theatre associations, for anti-English sentiments, and for the "thin layer of chalk dust [that] tends to settle over the recent plays from the former schoolmaster."[28] When he was given a profile in the *New York Times* at about the time of the opening in New York of *Dancing at Lughnasa,* Mel Gussow reported Friel to be "at 62 very much in his prime, a writer on a level with Sean O'Casey and John Millington Synge."[29] When *Translations* was revived on Broadway in 1995, the positive and the negative reviews focused on the same familiar emblems of Irish drama. Clive Barnes's positive review praised the play for "eccentric Irish stereotypes who could have wandered in from imitations of Synge and O'Casey," and, in Donal Donnelly, "a lovely spot of Abbey-Irish for us to savor." John Heilpern dismissed the revival because "very little lives on the stage, except the worst of all possible things for an ensemble so fine on paper: a stage Irishness."[30] Friel has had his successes (*Dancing at Lughnasa,* 1991; *Molly Sweeny,* 1996) and failures (*Faith Healer,* 1979; *Wonderful Tennessee,* 1993) on the New York stage, but the terms of praise or blame continue to emphasize the Irish eloquence of his work and the satisfying taste of the requisite Irishness of his personal profile.

Part of this unvarying record can be attributed to continuing expectations in New York for the familiar patterns of Irish drama onstage. In 1980, Michiko Kakutani attempted a general overview of a revival of Irish drama and construction of a great debate in Ireland for the *New York Times.* But the poles of the debate were no further apart than Friel and Hugh Leonard, whose work also manipulates the stock elements of the old Abbey play. Emphasis remained on gleeful eloquence: for Friel, on "plays distinguished for their lyrical, elegiac prose."[31] The Friel-Leonard range is a predominant one in contemporary Irish drama and so draws most attention in America. New York illustrates this. There are many successful playwrights in Ireland working outside the Friel-Leonard range who are not produced in New York. There are exceptions, to be sure. For example, Stewart Parker's *Spokesong,* about a Belfast bicycle shop and the twin threats of bombings and urban renewal, had a successful production on Broadway in 1979. For it, Parker announced in New York his intention "to find a new form, not a copy of Behan or O'Casey."[32] But *Spokesong,* or Frank McGuinness's *Someone Who'll Watch over Me,* are unusual on Broadway or even in New York's smaller theaters. The Irish playwrights scarcely or most obscurely produced in New York include Tom Murphy, Thomas Kilroy, Christina Reid, Anne Devlin, Dermot Bolger, and Marina Carr. In the nineteenth century, Dion Boucicault stood on the apron at Walllack's on Broadway and Fourteenth Street and claimed with only slight exaggeration that his *Colleen Bawn* was the first Irish play. He told the audience that he hoped for a future of "plenty of Irish plays."[33] The quantity of Irish plays in New York has been plenty. But the kinds of Irish plays in New York have not been. Broader expectations that "Erin on Broadway" would provide an opportunity for plays outside the narrowest preoccupations, and that would have salutary effect on Irish drama and New York's perception of it.

Part of the blame for an American perception of a type of Irish drama as the whole of Irish drama can be attributed to the real successes of Irish Irish plays. Boucicault knew this quite well. He wrote and produced very different kinds of plays, such as melodramas on urban poverty. An Irish setting could support such a subject, because his play that began as *The Poor of New York,* and then became *The Poor of London* when it played there, and *The Poor of Chicago,* and so forth, became *The Poor of Dublin* when it played there. But for his Irish plays Boucicault relied on dramas of love and rebellion against picturesque scenes. So well established and successful was this convention that Shaw's challenge to it in *John Bull's Other Island* could not in New York even be recognized as a challenge. Synge's *Playboy* made the rural, peasant play the expectation of an Irish play by the elite audience as well as the popular audience. It did so in New York and the other cities the Irish Players visited in their long and formative American tour. O'Casey's B.T.S.T. plays expanded the convention to include urban settings, but, perhaps in part because O'Casey himself abandoned that genre, by the time of Friel's debut in New York the local notion of both Irish play and Irish playwright had become utterly rural again: a matter of darlin' folks and smilin' leprechauns. Ireland, of course, had become more urban. But New York's perception of it in the theater had not. To this day American audiences have minimal exposure to the Irish urban dramas of Tom Murphy or Dermot Bolger.

This fits larger patterns of the history of Irish culture in the twentieth century. Viewed from the end of the century, it is striking how, following national independence, a single, essential identity of Irish culture was successfully communicated by the Republic. Recent studies by Irish scholars like Declan Kiberd's *Inventing Ireland* and R.F. Foster's *Modern Ireland* have demonstrated the pervasive evidence of an essentialist image of a rural, Gaelic, Catholic, and nationalist Ireland. Against that image Kiberd, Foster, and others have placed the plural reality of "inventing Irelands" and "varieties of Irishness." The history of emigration from what became the Republic makes America naturally susceptible to a myth of a romantic Ireland. This helps account for the different and rather more diversified production history of Irish plays to be found in London than in New York. Further, the Catholic dimension of the essentialist image, with its resistance to feminist goals in regard to divorce law and abortion, for example, has made the New York stage especially resistant to playwrights like Christina Reid, Anne Devlin, and Marina Carr.

The economics of theater are no doubt another factor in the restricted sense of what can qualify as an Irish play in New York. The feasibility of a limited repertory of popular successes was recognized by the Abbey Theatre touring companies long ago. Independent productions, too, know the benefits of large audiences and the liabilities of repeating successes. But the interesting fact of the production history of Irish plays in New York is that the record disproves the perception that only formulas from an essentialist image can succeed. Of the principal playwrights represented in these chapters, only two of seven can be identified with some confidence as Catholic in background. The record of the most influential plays in New York by Irish playwrights is, in part, Shaw, Joyce, and Beckett, which is not the perception in New York of Irish drama. Isolated exceptions to the generally restrictive rule of what from Ireland gets produced on the American stage, like *Someone Who'll Watch over Me* and *Spokesong*, were successful. Audiences have demonstrated some appetite for new Irish plays, and critics are sometimes flexible. The fact of the record of Irish plays on the New York stage is that narrow expectations come not from production failures but from production timidity. The collective culture industry understands the benefits better than the dangers of repeating successes. Since a general revision of its essentialist image seems to be progressing in Ireland, the Republic may choose a different image to project, and the New York stage, which has proven itself receptive to change, could be a beneficiary.

It is ironic that Brian Friel's work, beginning with *Philadelphia*, should be celebrated for Irish eloquence. His plays record stories of repression and failure, and *Philadelphia* presents eloquence in Private Gar as an imaginary dimension in sharp contrast to the nearly mute reality of Ballybeg. In its public, real dimension, *Philadelphia* dramatizes a life without language as an effective medium for any task but passing time. In the era after Beckett, the frightening drama of inexpressiveness in *Philadelphia* is especially conspicuous. In the final act, S.B. O'Donnell sits down to checkers with Canon Mick O'Byrne, and Private Gar, invisible to them, mouths their predictable platitudes slightly before they utter them. The scene does not suggest the eloquence associated in New York with Irish Irish plays. Instead, it suggests images of repetition and helplessness not unlike *Waiting for Godot*. When Private Gar ceases his commentary, S.B. and the Canon continue:

CANON (*a major announcement*): D'you know what?

S.B.: What's that, Canon?

CANON: You'll have rain before morning.

S.B.: D'you think so?

CANON: It's in the bones. The leg's giving me the odd jab.

S.B.: We could do without the rain then.

CANON: Before morning you'll have it.

S.B.: Tch tch tch. We get our fill of it here.

CANON: The best barometer I know.

S.B.: Aye. No want of rain.

CANON: Before the morning.

S.B.: As if we don't get enough of it.

CANON: The jabs are never wrong. [85]

This is a bit of dialogue that can be staged as Brian Friel's parody, in his first important work, of the Irish Irish play he has subsequently been deemed to exemplify. In its onstage representation of communication and lack of it, of the stock elements of the old Abbey play, and of uncertainty on the prospect of immigration to America, *Philadelphia* provides an image of the predicament of the Irish play in New York.

The image resembles that of Gar looking to the past for sustenance and finding that past as uncertain as his future. In New York for the past three decades the past consistently evoked to describe Friel's work is an arbitrary and selective one. It makes the history of the Irish play in New York the history of Synge and B.T.S.T. O'Casey, when the record is quite otherwise. This is what Hilton Edwards would call the victory of the professional Irishman, and this history neglects an entirely different paradigm for Irish drama, one illustrated especially well in New York in productions of Shaw and Joyce and Beckett. Friel's work is intentionally local in reference, and so it invites categorization with Irish Irish plays of limited range in topic or characterization. His work helps demonstrate the formidability of stock elements of the Abbey legacy as it attempts to revise them. In Ireland, the revisionist dimension of his work is evident because the stock material is perceived as convention and because there are other playwrights with other projects that put his into a broad field. In America, where stories of rural Ireland can still seem exotic and where Friel's work appears to be the sole project of Irish drama, degrees of revision are not evident. In New York, Friel has been celebrated for fitting a popular mold not for altering it.

In 1966 Edwards and Friel hoped to broaden the range of Irish plays, and, instead, because of their success, they narrowed it. New York capitulated to a simplistic and reductive notion of Irish drama, and consequently of Ireland, that still prevails. The notion omits the record of Shaw, Joyce, Beckett, and others working in what, because of the narrowness of expectations, can be called non-Irish Irish drama.

All this testifies to the myriad factors other than play text controlling reception of performance, the "things" that genius is said by some to surpass. Friel himself writes acutely about the "things" that subvert text, and he has no illusion of genius in theater transmitting its individuality without interference. In the St. Patrick's Day 1972 essay in *TLS* that deplored the presence of Boucicault on the Irish stage, Friel also wrote about how "the theatre has always been susceptible to outside pressures."[35] He certainly could have drawn many examples from his experience in New York in 1966, and David Merrick's frequently hilarious interventions are proof that many factors outside the text control transmission of eloquence. In fact, because he recognizes outside pressures and responds to them, Friel bears some comparison with Boucicault. In choosing revision rather than radical departure from audience expectations, Boucicault and Friel, playwrights at the beginning and ending of this survey of productions, allow the audience an unusually pronounced role in theater. Consequently these two playwrights assume a much more amicable relation to audience than, for example, Shaw, or Lady Gregory producing Synge. The interior chapters of this survey record more hostile relations of playwright with audience and more inflated estimations of the privilege of art. Neither relation, on the basis of these productions in New York from 1874 to 1966, is an invariably reliable route to theater that is successful by all measures.

In the mid-1970s Friel was asking questions about these kinds of transactions of art and audience in theater in a diary that was later published. "Is there," he asked, "an anti-art element in theatre in that it doesn't speak to the individual in his absolute privacy and isolation but addresses him as an audience?"[36] Each episode in this history, including Friel's own, answers in the affirmative. The anti-art things in the history of these productions are such powerful factors in reception that it is not even useful to speak about a single "it" as a fundamental element of theater. Friel is under no illusion about that answer to his question. For this he is quite properly praised by Seamus Deane for not yielding to external pressures "or retreating into art's narcissistic alternative."[37] In *Philadelphia*'s two Gars, Friel represents just that productive opposition in theater between the anti-art, vulgar factors of the public world (well illustrated in New York in 1966) and creative powers prone to self-infatuation. He balanced these factors in his play and in his role in his first New York production. There, at a larger remove in all senses from Ballybeg than is possible in Ireland, the force of outside pressures contesting genius were especially visible. Later, in his diary, Friel wrote about the kind of transaction these balanced concerns produce, and he described very accurately the theatrical predicament underlying the reception of each of the Irish plays discussed in this study: "The dramatist has to recycle his experience through the pressure-chamber of his imagination. He has then to present this new reality to a public—300 diverse imaginations come together with no more serious intent than the casual wish to be 'entertained.' And he has got to forge those 300 imaginations into one perceiving faculty, dominate and condition them so that they become attuned to the tonality of the transmission and consequently to its meaning."[38] Because of the contrast allowed by transatlantic distance, Erin on Broadway delineates this drama of meaning and reception especially well.

NOTES

INTRODUCTION

1. W.H. Auden, *Selected Poetry of W.H. Auden* (New York: Vintage, 1971), pp. 174, 176.

2. George Steiner, *Language and Silence* (London: Faber and Faber, 1985), p. 47.

3. Quoted in Eileen O'Casey, *Cheerio, Titan: The Friendship between George Bernard Shaw and Eileen and Sean O'Casey* (New York: Scribner's, 1989), p. 90.

4. Emma Goldman, *The Social Significance of Modern Drama* (New York: Applause Books, 1987), p. 138.

5. Hallie Flanagan, *Shifting Scenes of the Modern European Theatre* (1929; New York: Benjamin Blom, 1972), p. 20.

6. George Jean Nathan, foreword to *Five Great Modern Irish Plays* (New York: Modern Library, 1941), p. ix.

7. William Butler Yeats, "A People's Theatre," in *Explorations* (New York: Collier Books, 1962), p. 250.

8. William Butler Yeats, "The Fascination of What's Difficult," in *Collected Poems* (New York: Macmillan, 1956), p. 91.

9. Loren Kruger, *The National Stage: Theatre and Cultural Legitimation in England, France, and America* (Chicago: Univ. of Chicago Press, 1992), p. 17.

10. Marvin Carlson, "Theatre Audiences and the Reading of Performance," in *Interpreting the Theatrical Past: Essays in the Historiography of Performance,* ed. Thomas Postlewait and Bruce A. McConachie (Iowa City: Univ. of Iowa Press, 1989), pp. 86-87.

11. Quoted in Edward L. Shaughnessy, *Eugene O'Neill in Ireland: The Critical Reception* (New York: Greenwood Press, 1988), p. 36.

1. DION BOUCICAULT, THE IRISH PLAY, AND THE POLITICS OF RECONCILIATION

1. Denis Donoghue, "The Problems of Being Irish," *Times Literary Supplement,* 17 March 1972, p. 292.

2. Brian Friel, "Plays Peasant and Unpeasant," *Times Literary Supplement,* 17 March 1972, pp. 305-6.

3. Review of *The Colleen Bawn, New York Tribune,* 30 March 1860, p. 8.

4. Dion Boucicault, "Leaves from a Dramatist's Diary," *North American Review* 149 (1889): 229.

5. Quoted in Pat M. Ryan, "The Hibernian Experience: John Brougham's Irish-American Plays," *MELUS* 10, no. 2 (summer 1983): 34.

6. Margaret G. Mayorga, *A Short History of the American Drama* (New York: Dodd, Mead, 1943), p. 247.

7. Maureen Murphy, "Irish-American Theatre," in *Ethnic Theatre in the United States,* ed. Maxine Schwartz (Westport, Conn.: Greenwood Press, 1983), p. 223.

8. See Mary C. Henderson, *The City and The Theatre: New York Playhouses from Bowling Green to Times Square* (Clifton, N.J.: James T. White), p. 114.

9. Boucicault, "Leaves from a Dramatist's Diary," p. 230.

10. Quoted in Kenneth R. Rossman, "The Irish in American Drama in the Mid-nineteenth Century," *New York History* (Cooperstown) 21 (1940): 45.

11. Boucicault, "Leaves from a Dramatist's Diary," p. 231.

12. Ibid., p. 232.

13. Alan Schneider, *Entrances: An American Director's Journey* (New York: Viking, 1986), p. 226.

14. Quoted in Montrose J. Moses, *The American Dramatist* (Boston: Little, Brown, 1925), p. 157.

15. Boucicault, "Leaves from a Dramatist's Diary," p. 235.

16. Dion Boucicault, "The Decline of the Drama," *North American Review* 125 (1877): 240. Subsequent references in this paragraph cited parenthetically.

17. Moses, *American Dramatist,* p. 171.

18. See Stephen J. Sullivan, "The Orange and Green Riots," *New York Irish History* 6 (1991-92): 7-8 and *passim.*

19. William Dean Howells, "Editor's Study," *Harper's New Monthly,* July 1886, p. 315.

20. On Harrigan and Hart, see Richard Moody, *Ned Harrigan: From Corlear's Hook to Herald Square* (Chicago: Nelson-Hall, 1980); and E.J. Kahn, Jr., *The Merry Partners: The Age and Stage of Harrigan and Hart* (New York: Random House, 1955).

21. Playbill reproduced in Moses, *American Dramatist,* p. 169.

22. Townsend Walsh, *The Career of Dion Boucicault* (New York: Dunlap Society, 1915), pp. 125, 126.

23. Boucicault, "Leaves from a Dramatist's Diary," pp. 235-36.

24. Dion Boucicault, *The Shaughraun* in *The Dolmen Boucicault,* ed. David Krause (Dublin: Dolmen Press, 1964), p. 187. All subsequent references to this edition are cited parenthetically in the text.

25. On the moon, see Boucicault, "Leaves From a Dramatist's Diary," p. 236, and Moses, *American Dramatist,* p. 169; on the curtain, see Walsh, *Career of Boucicault,* p. 133, n. 1.

26. "Amusements," *New York Times,* 15 Nov. 1875, p. 7.

27. "The Drama," *New York Daily Tribune,* 16 Nov. 1874, pp. 4, 5.

28. Henry James, "Fine Arts," *The Nation,* 11 March 1875, pp. 178-79.

29. *Boston Gazette,* 5 Feb. 1882. Townsend Walsh Collection, New York Public Library for the Performing Arts.

30. Quoted in Moody, p. 53; on the lawsuit, see Kahn, *Merry Partners,* pp. 179-84.

31. George C. D. Odell, *Annals of the New York Stage,* 1937 (New York: AMS, 1970), 9:522; Walsh, *Career of Boucicault,* p. 149.

32. "The Shaughraun," *New York Herald,* 7 March 1875, p. 5.

33. Bruce A. McConachie, *Melodramatic Formations: American Theatre and Drama, 1820-1870* (Iowa City: Univ. Iowa Press, 1992), p. 213, and Cheryl Herr, ed., *For the Land They Loved: Irish Political Melodrama, 1890-1925* (Syracuse: Syracuse Univ. Press, 1991), p. 14.

34. Krause, ed., *Dolmen Boucicault,* p. 36.

35. Letter to Disraeli quoted in Walsh, *Career of Boucicault,* pp. 137, 138-39. This letter and its context was the subject of an interesting exchange focused on theater in Dublin: Stephen M. Watt, "Boucicault and Whitbread: The Dublin Stage at the End of the Nineteenth Century," *Eire-Ireland* 18, no. 3 (1983): 23-53; Sven Eric Molin and Robin Goodefellowe, "Nationalism on the Dublin Stage," *Eire-Ireland* 21, no. 1 (1986): 135-38; Stephen M. Watt, "Nationalism on the Dublin Stage: A Postscript," 21, no. 4 (1987): 137-41.

36. Brian Friel, *Translations,* in *Selected Plays of Brian Friel* (Washington, D.C.: Catholic Univ. of America Press, 1984), pp. 409-10.

37. Friel, *Translations,* pp. 444, 447.

38. For Wilde in America, see Richard Ellmann, *Oscar Wilde* (New York: Knopf, 1988), pp. 160-67, 195-97.

39. J.M. Synge, *Prose,* vol. 3 of *Collected Works,* ed. Alan Price (Bucks: Colin Smythe, 1982), pp. 397-98.

40. Edward Stephens, *My Uncle John: Edward Stephens's Life of J.M. Synge,* ed. Andrew Carpenter (London: Oxford Univ. Press, 1974), p. 185.

41. Sean O'Casey, *Inishfallen Fare Thee Well* (New York: Macmillan, 1949), pp. 167, 395.

42. James Joyce, *Ulysses* (New York: Random House, 1986), pp. 134, 137.

43. Seamus Deane, ed., *The Field Day Anthology of Irish Writing* (Derry: Field Day Publications, 1991), 2:234.

44. Townsend Walsh, "In Praise of Boucicault," *The Gael,* December 1889, pp. 264, 263.

45. Brooks McNamara, *The Shuberts of Broadway: A History Drawn from the Collections of the Shubert Archive* (New York: Oxford Univ. Press, 1990), p. 20.

46. William Winter, *Other Days; Being Chronicles and Memories of the Stage* (1908; Freeport, N.Y.: Books for Libraries Press, 1970), pp. 138, 147, 149.

2. THE BERNARD SHAW CULT, NEW YORK, 1905

1. "Mr. Shaw a Success in Spite of Actors," *New York Times,* 10 Jan. 1905, p. 5.

2. Archibald Henderson, *George Bernard Shaw: Man of the Century* (New York: Appleton-Century-Crofts, 1956), p. 478.

3. Brooks Atkinson, *Broadway* (New York: Macmillan, 1970), p. 62.

4. B.H. Goldsmith, *Arnold Daly* (New York: James T. White, 1927), p. 24.

5. Quoted in ibid., p. 23.

6. Quoted in ibid., p. 25.

7. "John Bull's Other Island," *New York Evening Post,* 11 Oct. 1905, p. 9.

8. Archibald Henderson, "Arnold Daly and Bernard Shaw: A Bit of Dramatic History," *Arena* 32 (November 1904): 492.

9. Bernard Shaw, *Collected Letters, 1898-1910,* ed. Dan H. Laurence (New York: Dodd, Mead, 1972), p. 573.

10. Goldsmith, *Arnold Daly,* pp. 25, 26-27.

11. Bernard Shaw, *Plays Unpleasant* (London: Penguin, 1946), p. 7. Future references to this edition are cited parenthetically in the text.

12. Quoted in Dennis Kennedy, *Granville Barker and the Dream of Theatre* (Cambridge: Cambridge Univ. Press, 1985), p. 22.

13. "Preface for Politicians," *John Bull's Other Island* (London: Penguin, 1984), pp. 7-8. Future references to this edition are cited parenthetically in the text.

14. Quoted in Martin Miesel, *Shaw and the Nineteenth-Century Theater* (New York: Limelight Editions, 1984), p. 270.

15. "The Irish Players," *Evening Sun,* 9 Dec. 1911; George Bernard Shaw, *The Matter with Ireland,* ed. David H. Greene and Dan H. Laurence (London: Rupert Hart-Davis, 1962), p. 64.

16. "John Bull's Other Island," *New York Evening Post,* 11 Oct. 1905, p. 5.

17. "Garrick—John Bull's Other Island," *New York Dramatic Mirror,* 21 Oct. 1905, p. 3.

18. Quoted in Brooks Atkinson, *Broadway* (New York: Macmillan, 1970), p. 62.

19. Quoted in Michael Holroyd, *Bernard Shaw: The Search for Love* (New York: Random House, 1988), p. 296.

20. Laurence, *Collected Letters,* pp. 464, 465.

21. Timothy J. Gilfoyle, *City of Eros: New York City, Prostitution, and the Commercialization of Sex, 1790-1920* (New York: Norton, 1992), p. 205.

22. Quoted in Laurence, *Collected Letters,* p. 275.

23. Ibid., p. 465.

24. Quoted in ibid., p. 573.

25. Ibid., pp. 559, 562.

26. St. John Ervine, *Bernard Shaw: His Life, Work, and Friends* (New York: William Morrow, 1956), p. 349.

27. "Anthony Comstock Dies in His Crusade," *New York Times,* 22 Sept. 1915, p. 6.

28. "Vampire Literature," *North American Review* 153 (August 1891), p. 171.

29. "Shaw to Comstock: You Can't Intimidate Me," *New York Times,* 27 Oct. 1905, p. 9.

30. "Comstock Won't See Bernard Shaw's Play," *New York Times,* 26 Oct. 1905, p. 9.

31. Mary Shaw, "My 'Immoral' Play," *McClures,* April 1912, p. 685.

32. "Shaw Play Arouses New Haven Audience," *New York Times,* 28 Oct. 1905, p. 9.

33. Quoted in *New York Evening Post,* 28 Oct. 1905, p. 5.

34. "Pencil on Shaw's Play," *New York Times,* 30 Oct. 1905, p. 9.

35. Henderson, "Daly and Shaw," p. 511.

36. Quoted in Hesketh Pearson, *G.B.S.: A Full Length Portrait* (New York: Harper and Brothers, 1942), p. 165.

37. "Shaw Play Unfit," *New York Times,* 31 Oct. 1905, p. 9.

38. Mary Shaw, "My 'Immoral' Play," p. 688.

39. "Mrs. Warren Professes," *New York Sun,* 31 Oct. 1905, p. 7.

40. "Shaw Play Unfit," p. 9.

41. All quoted in "Critics Verdict Hostile," *New York Times,* 31 Oct. 1905, p. 9.

42. Quotations from "M'Adoo Stops the Shaw Play," *New York Sun,* 1 Nov. 1905, p. 6.

43. "The Court Approves Bernard Shaw's Play," *New York Times,* 7 July 1906, p. 7.

44. Laurence, *Collected Letters,* pp. 632, 633.

45. Goldsmith, *Arnold Daly,* p. 31.

46. Holroyd, *Bernard Shaw,* p. 294.

47. Atkinson, *Broadway,* p. 65.

3. SYNGE'S *PLAYBOY*, THE IRISH PLAYERS, AND THE ANTI-IRISH IRISH PLAYERS

1. Theodore Roosevelt, "The Irish Players," *Outlook,* 16 Dec. 1911, p. 915; "Anti-Irish Irish Players," *Gaelic American,* 16 Dec. 1911, p. 4.

2. Program, *The Rising of the Moon* and *The Playboy of the Western World,* Maxine Elliott Theatre, New York City, 27 Nov. 1911, pp. 1, 15; "Seamus M'Manus Raps 'The Playboy,'" *New York Times,* 27 Nov. 1911, p. 11.

3. William Butler Yeats, *Explorations* (New York: Collier Books, 1962), p. 414.

4. Conor Cruise O'Brien, *States of Ireland* (New York: Pantheon, 1972), p. 71. An even stronger case for the play's "assault" on the audience is made by Edward Hirsch in "The Gallous Story and the Dirty Deed: The Two *Playboys,*" *Modern Drama* 26 (March 1983): 85-102.

5. J.M. Synge, *Prose,* vol. 2 of *Collected Works,* ed. Alan Price (Gerrards Cross: Colin Smythe, 1982), p. 95.

6. J.M. Synge, *Plays Book II,* vol. 4 of *Collected Works,* ed. Ann Saddlemyer (Gerrards Cross: Colin Smythe, 1982), p. 117. Future references to this edition are cited parenthetically in the text.

7. Quoted in Peter Costello, *The Heart Grown Brutal: The Irish Revolution in Literature, from Parnell to the Death of Yeats, 1891-1939* (Dublin: Gill and Macmillan, 1977), p. 32.

8. Daniel Corkery, *Synge and Anglo-Irish Literature: A Study* (1931; New York: Russell and Russell, 1965), p. 2.

9. Seamus Deane, *Celtic Revivals: Essays on Modern Irish Literature* (Winston-Salem: Wake Forest Univ. Press, 1985), p. 53.

10. On the Dublin dispute over *The Playboy,* see Robert Hogan and James Kilroy, *The Abbey Theatre: The Years of Synge, 1905-1909,* vol. 3 of *Modern Irish Drama: A Documentary History* (Dublin: Dolmen Press, 1978), and David Cairns and Shaun

Richards, "Reading a Riot: The 'Reading Formation' of Synge's Abbey Audience," *Literature and History* 13, no. 2 (1987): 219-37.

11. Quoted in B. L. Reid, *The Man from New York: John Quinn and His Friends* (New York: Oxford Univ. Press, 1968), p. 49.

12. "McFadden's Row of Flats," *New York Times,* 10 March 1903, p. 9; Daniel J. Murphy, "The Reception of Synge's *Playboy* in Ireland and America, 1907-1912," *Bulletin of the New York Public Library* 64, no. 10 (1960): 526-27.

13. Thomas Flanagan, introduction to *The American Irish Revival: A Decade of "The Recorder," 1974-1983,* ed. Kevin M. Cahill, M.D. (Port Washington, N.Y.: Associated Faculty Press, 1984), p. xviii.

14. Quoted in "The Spectator," *Outlook,* 24 May 1913, p. 258.

15. Janet Egleson Dunleavy and Gareth W. Dunleavy, *Douglas Hyde: A Maker of Modern Ireland* (Berkeley: Univ. of California Press, 1991), pp. 317, 319.

16. Reid, *Man from New York,* p. 114.

17. Joseph Hone, *W.B. Yeats* (Harmondsworth: Penguin, 1971), p. 257.

18. Lawrence J. McCaffrey, *Textures of Irish America* (Syracuse: Syracuse Univ. Press, 1992), p. 147.

19. Quoted in Lady Augusta Gregory, *Our Irish Theatre: A Chapter in an Autobiography* (New York: Oxford Univ. Press, 1972), p. 222.

20. "Paints the Playboy in Glowing Colors," *Gaelic American,* 21 Oct. 1911, p. 1; "Ordure and Art in Drama," *Gaelic American,* 21 Oct. 1911, p. 4; "Bernard Shaw's Greatest Masterpiece," *Gaelic American,* 16 Dec. 1911, p. 4.

21. "Irish Plays and Players," *Outlook,* 29 July 1911, p. 704.

22. "Visitors from across the Sea," *New York World,* 26 Nov. 1911, p. M6.

23. Quoted in Robert Hogan, Richard Burnham, and Daniel P. Poteet, *Modern Irish Drama, A Documentary History: The Rise of the Realists 1910-1915* (Dublin: Dolmen Press, 1979), pp. 410-11.

24. "Seamus M'Manus Raps 'The Playboy,'" *New York Times,* 27 Nov. 1911, p. 11.

25. Gregory, *Our Irish Theatre,* pp. 104-5, 108-9, 110-11.

26. "Playboy Mobbed," *New York Sun,* 28 Nov. 1911, p. 1; "Riot in Theatre," *New York Times,* 28 Nov. 1911, 1.

27. "'Playboy' Mobbed," p. 2.

28. "Riot in Theatre," p. 2.

29. Ibid.

30. Ibid.

31. "Playboy Mobbed" and "'The Playboy' as Drama," *New York Sun,* 28 Nov. 1911, p. 2.

32. Gregory, *Our Irish Theatre,* p. 112.

33. "The 'Playboy' Row," *New York Times,* 29 Nov. 1911, p. 10.

34. Robert Edmond Jones, *The Dramatic Imagination: Reflections and Speculations on the Art of Theatre* (New York: Theatre Art Books, 1941), p. 75.

35. John Quinn, "Lady Gregory and the Abbey Theatre," *Outlook,* 16 Dec. 1911, p. 919.

36. Quoted in Dan H. Laurence and Nicholas Grene, eds., *Shaw, Lady Gregory and the Abbey: A Correspondence and a Record* (Gerrards Cross: Colin Smythe, 1993),

p. 67; George Bernard Shaw, *The Matter with Ireland,* ed. David H. Greene and Dan H. Laurence (London: Rupert Hart-Davis, 1962), p. 84.

37. Program, *The Rising of the Moon* and *The Playboy of the Western World,* Maxine Elliott Theatre, New York City, 27 Nov. 1911, n.p. On this program note, also see Synge, *Plays Book II,* pp. 363-64.

38. Adele M. Dalsimer, "Players in the Western World: The Abbey Theatre's American Tours," *Eire-Ireland* 16, no. 4 (1981): 87.

4. James Joyce Downtown

1. Richard Ellmann, *James Joyce* (New York: Oxford Univ. Press, 1959), p. 414.

2. Ludwig Lewisohn, *The Modern Drama: An Essay in Interpretation* (New York: B.W. Heubsch, 1916), pp. 267, 272-73.

3. Clayton Hamilton, "The Plays of Lord Dunsany," *Bookman* (New York) 44 (January 1917): 469; Lynde Denig, "The Most Talked of Playlet of the Year," *Theatre Magazine,* 1916, Billy Rose Theatre Collection, New York Public Library; "Lord Dunsany," *Theatre Magazine,* February 1917, Billy Rose Theatre Collection, New York Public Library; Edward Hale Bierstadt, *Dunsany the Dramatist* (Boston: Little, Brown, 1917), p. 9.

4. Alta May Coleman, "The Theatre Needs Reform, Says Dunsany," *Theatre Magazine,* December 1919, Billy Rose Theater Collection, New York Public Library.

5. Hamilton, p. 470.

6. Alice Lewisohn Crowley, *The Neighborhood Playhouse: Leaves from a Theatre Scrapbook* (New York: Theatre Arts Books, 1959, pp. 66, 70, 71.

7. Harry Esty Dounce, "Latest of the Irish Dramatists," *New York Sun,* 11 March 1917, Billy Rose Theatre Collection, New York Public Library.

8. Hamilton, "Plays of Lord Dunsany," p. 478.

9. Crowley, *Neighborhood Playhouse,* p. 68.

10. St. John Ervine, *Bernard Shaw: His Life, Work, and Friends* (New York: William Morrow, 1956), p. 372.

11. John Corbin, "North of Ireland Drama," *New York Times,* 13 May 1919, p. 18.

12. An accurate account of this episode can be found in Walter Prichard Eaton, *The Theatre Guild: The First Ten Years* (New York: Brentano's, 1929), pp. 30-40.

13. Moses, *American Dramatist,* pp. 401, 404.

14. Quoted in Sheldon Cheney, *The Art Theater* (New York: Knopf, 1925), p. 6.

15. Quoted in Eaton, *Theatre Guild,* pp. 185-86.

16. Crowley, *Neighborhood Playhouse,* p. 7; Elmer Rice, *The Living Theatre* (New York: Harper Brothers, 1959).

17. Arthur Pollack, "Plays and Things," *Brooklyn Eagle,* 9 March 1925, Billy Rose Theatre Collection, New York Public Library; Gilbert W. Gabriel, "The Joyce 'Exiles,'" *New York Telegram,* 20 Feb. 1925, p. 24.

18. Crowley, *Neighborhood Playhouse,* pp. 170, 171.

19. Frank Wright Tuttle, "Lord Dunsany in New York," *Vanity Fair,* March 1919, Billy Rose Theatre Collection, New York Public Library.

20. "Exiles," *Neighborhood Playbill* (Neighborhood Playhouse) no. 3 (1924-25), p. 6.

21. Quoted in Robert H. Deming, ed., *James Joyce: The Critical Heritage* (London: Routledge and Kegan Paul, 1970), 1:97.

22. Quoted in ibid., 1:104.

23. Quoted in ibid., 1:144.

24. Margaret Anderson, ed., *The Little Review Anthology* (New York: Hermitage House, 1953), pp. 217-18.

25. Ann Douglas, *Terrible Honesty: Mongrel Manhattan in the 1920's* (New York: Farrar, Straus, Giroux, 1995), p. 124.

26. James Joyce, *Exiles* (New York: Viking, 1961), p. 123. Future references to this edition are cited parenthetically in the text.

27. Margaret Anderson, *My Thirty Years' War* (New York: Covici, Friede, 1930), pp. 216, 175.

28. Ellmann, *James Joyce,* p. 517.

29. Anderson, *My Thirty Years' War,* p. 215.

30. Reid, *Man from New York,* pp. 447, 453.

31. Ibid., p. 446.

32. Anderson, *My Thirty Years' War,* p. 218.

33. Quoted in Ellmann, *James Joyce,* p. 518.

34. James Joyce, *Ulysses* (New York: Random House, 1961), p. xii.

35. Quoted in Edward de Grazia, *Girls Lean Back Everywhere: The Law of Obscenity and the Assault on Genius* (New York: Random House, 1992), p. 14.

36. Quoted in Deming, *James Joyce,* 1:253, 1:302. See also Boyd, "Concerning James Joyce," *New York World,* 25 Jan. 1925, quoted in Deming, *James Joyce,* 1: 320-22; and "'Ulysses' and Its Author," *New York Times Book Review,* 2 March 1924, 7.

37. Ernest Boyd, "Order Established in the Literary Choas [*sic*] of James Joyce," *New York Times Book Review,* 2 March 1924, 7.

38. Richard Ellmann, ed., *Letters of James Joyce* (New York: Viking Press, 1966), 3:91.

39. Malcolm Cowley, "James Joyce," *Bookman* (New York) 59 (July 1924): 520.

40. Ellmann, ed., *Letters,* 3:80, 100.

41. Anderson, *Little Review Anthology,* p. 221.

42. Crowley, *Neighborhood Playhouse,* p. 197.

43. Ernest Boyd, "James Joyce," *Neighborhood Playbill,* pp. 1, 2; James Joyce, "The Day of the Rabblement," *The Critical Writings of James Joyce,* ed. Ellsworth Mason and Richard Ellmann (New York: Viking, 1959), p. 69.

44. George Jean Nathan, "The Theatre," *American Mercury* 4 (April 1925): 501; Robert Benchley, "Drama," *Life,* 12 March 1925, p. 20; Robert Littell, "Three Shades of Black," *New Republic,* 4 March 1925, p. 45; Louis K. Feder, "Exiles," *New York Graphic,* 20 Feb. 1925, p. 20.

45. Joseph Wood Krutch, "Figures of the Dawn," *Nation,* 11 March 1925, p. 272.

46. Nathan, "Theatre," p. 501.

47. Stark Young, "Joyce at the Neighborhood," *New York Times,* 20 Feb. 1925, p. 20.

48. Ellmann, ed., *Letters,* 3:114, 115.

49. Louis Shaeffer, *O'Neill: Son and Artist* (Boston: Little, Brown, 1973), p. 147.

50. Quoted in Sylvia Beach, *Shakespeare and Company* (New York: Harcourt, Brace, 1959), p. 167.

51. John MacNicholas, "The Stage History of *Exiles,*" *James Joyce Quarterly* 19, no.1 (1981): 23.

52. Brooks Atkinson, "Joyce's Credo," *New York Times,* 24 March 1957, sec. 2, p. 1.

53. Marvin Magalaner and Richard M. Kain, *Joyce: The Man, the Work, the Reputation* (New York: New York Univ. Press, 1956), p. 135.

54. Martin Esslin, "Exiles," *Plays and Players,* 18 Jan. 1971: 52.

5. Sean O'Casey and *Within the Gates*

1. Brooks Atkinson, "W.B. Yeats and J. Swift," *New York Times,* 29 Oct. 1932, Billy Rose Theatre Collection, New York Public Library.

2. "Norah O'Neale," *Gaelic American,* 27 Oct. 1934, p. 2.

3. Adele M. Dalsimer, "Players in the Western World: The Abbey Theatre's American Tours," *Eire-Ireland* 16, no. 4 (1981): 87, 91.

4. A.J. Liebling, "Sean O'Casey Comes Over to Hear American Plaudits," *New York World-Telegram,* 17 Sept. 1934, Billy Rose Theatre Collection, New York Public Library.

5. Sean O'Casey, *Autobiographies* (New York: Carroll and Graf, 1984), 2:281, 279.

6. Eileen O'Casey, *Sean* (New York: Coward, McCann, Geoghegan, 1972), p. 89.

7. Eileen O'Casey, *Cheerio, Titan: The Friendship between George Bernard Shaw and Sean O'Casey* (New York: Scribner's Sons, 1989), p. 58-59.

8. Sean O'Casey, "Tender Tears for Poor O'Casey," in *The Green Crow* (New York: George Braziller, 1956), p. 177.

9. Brooks Atkinson, "The Play," *New York Times,* 12 Nov. 1934; Robert Garland, "Dubliners at Best in O'Casey Classic," *New York World Telegram,* 23 Nov. 1934; both Billy Rose Theatre Collection, New York Public Library.

10. O'Casey, *Autobiographies,* 2:352.

11. Sean O'Casey, "No Flowers for Films," in *Green Crow,* p. 194-95.

12. O'Casey, *Autobiographies,* 2:251-52.

13. Sean O'Casey, *Within the Gates: A Play of Four Scenes in a London Park* (New York: Macmillan, 1935), p. v. Future references to this edition are cited parenthetically in the text.

14. O'Casey, *Autobiographies,* 2:418.

15. David Krause, ed., *The Letters of Sean O'Casey* (New York: Macmillan, 1975), 1:503.

16. Quoted in ibid., 1:491-92, 496.

17. Quoted in ibid., 1:494, 502.

18. "Coward Codology: I" and "Coward Codology: III," in *Green Crow,* pp. 96, 113.

19. A brief, effective summary of these contrary positions can be found in

Stephen Watt, *Joyce, O'Casey, and the Irish Popular Theater* (Syracuse: Syracuse Univ. Press, 1991), 143-49.

20. David Krause, *Sean O'Casey: The Man and His Work,* enlarged ed. (New York: Macmillan, 1975), pp. 143-44.

21. Krause, ed., *Letters,* 1:312.

22. Quoted in E. O'Casey, *Sean,* pp. 129-30.

23. O'Casey, *Autobiographies,* 2:154.

24. Robert G. Lowery and Patricia Angelin, eds., *My Very Dear Sean: George Jean Nathan to Sean O'Casey, Letters and Articles* (Rutherford, N.J.: Fairleigh Dickinson Univ. Press, 1985), p. 32.

25. E. O'Casey, *Sean,* pp. 130-31.

26. Lowery and Angelin, eds., *My Very Dear Sean,* pp. 140-41, 36.

27. Joseph W. Alsop, Jr., "Sean O'Casey Arrives to See New Play Done," *New York Herald Tribune,* 18 Sept. 1934, p. 20.

28. O'Casey, *Autobiographies,* 2:403.

29. E. O'Casey, *Sean,* p. 136.

30. O'Casey, *Autobiographies,* 2:404.

31. "Leaves from a Dramatist's Diary," p. 233.

32. *New York Times,* 15 Nov. 1934; *New York Herald Tribune,* 22 Nov. 1934; both Billy Rose Theatre Collection, New York Public Library.

33. Joseph W. Alsop, Jr., "Sean O'Casey Leads the Singing," *New York Herald Tribune,* 21 Oct. 1934, sec. 5, p. 2.

34. E. O'Casey, *Sean,* p. 139.

35. See Lowery and Angelin, eds., *My Very Dear Sean,* p. 37.

36. Bosley Crowther, "Who Is Then the Gentleman?" *New York Times,* 14 Oct. 1934, sec. 10, p. 1.

37. Arthur Gelb and Barbara Gelb, *O'Neill* (New York: Harper and Brothers, 1962), pp. 788-89, 790; Louis Shaeffer, *O'Neill: Son and Artist* (Boston: Little, Brown, 1973), p. 437.

38. Lowery and Angelin, eds., *My Very Dear Sean,* p. 145.

39. Richard Watts, Jr., "Sight and Sound," *New York Herald Tribune,* 28 Oct. 1934, Billy Rose Theatre Collection, New York Public Library.

40. Cecelia Ager, "O'Casey Dissects the N.Y. Critics; Tells about Art," *Variety* 6 Nov. 1934; John Anderson, "O'Casey Drama Scales Peak of Greatness; Audience Awestruck," *New York Evening Journal,* 23 Oct. 1934; both Billy Rose Theatre Collection, New York Public Library.

41. E. O'Casey, *Sean,* p. 136; "Within the Gates," *Variety,* 30 Oct. 1934; John Anderson, "Divided Opinion on O'Casey," *New York Evening Journal,* 27 Oct. 1934; latter two Billy Rose Theatre Collection, New York Public Library.

42. See E. O'Casey, *Sean,* p. 137.

43. Sean O'Casey, "From 'Within the Gates,'" *New York Times,* 21 Oct. 1934, sec. 10, p. 1.

44. "From 'Within the Gates,'" p. 3.

45. E. O'Casey, *Sean,* p. 138.

46. Brooks Atkinson, review of *Within the Gates, New York Times,* 23 Oct. 1934, p. 23; Stark Young, "Theatre Gates," *New Republic,* 7 Nov. 1934, p. 369.

47. "Within the Gates," *New Republic,* 7 Nov. 1934, p. 369.

48. O'Casey, *Autobiographies,* 2:421.

49. Robert Garland, "'Within the Gates' Surges with Power," *New York World-Telegram,* 23 Oct. 1934; Gilbert W. Gabriel, "Within the Gates," *New York American,* 23 Oct. 1934; both Billy Rose Theatre collection, New York Public Library.

50. Stark Young, "Theatre Gates," *New Republic,* 7 Nov. 1934, p. 369.

51. Joseph Wood Krutch, "Mr. O'Casey's Charade," *Nation* 7 Nov. 1934, p. 546.

52. George Jean Nathan, "The Theatre," in Lowery and Angelin, eds., *My Very Dear Sean,* pp. 142-44.

53. E. O'Casey, *Sean,* p. 138.

54. Lowery and Angelin, eds., *My Very Dear Sean,* p. 40.

55. Ervine quoted in George Jean Nathan, "The Best of the Irish," Lowery and Angelin, eds., *My Very Dear Sean,* p. 148; Katharine J. Worth, *Revolutions in Modern English Drama* (London: G. Bell, 1972), p. 112.

6. *Waiting for Godot* in New York

1. "The Shaughraun," *New York Herald,* 7 March 1975, p. 5.

2. Letter to Alan Schneider, 11 Jan. 1956; published in "Beckett's Letters on Endgame," in Daniel Wolf and Edwin Fancher, eds., *The Village Voice Reader: A Mixed Bag from the Greenwich Village Newspaper* (New York: Doubleday, 1962), p. 183. Bracketed interpolations as printed in the published text.

3. Alan Schneider, *Entrances* (New York: Viking, 1986), p. 225.

4. Quoted in Dierdre Bair, *Samuel Beckett: A Biography* (New York: Harcourt Brace Jovanovich, 1978), p. 462.

5. "Waiting for Godot," *Variety,* 23 April 1956, p. 72.

6. Brooks Atkinson, "Beckett's 'Waiting for Godot,'" *New York Times,* 20 April 1956, p. 21; Israel Shenker, "Moody Man of Letters," *New York Times,* 6 May 1956, sec. 2, p. 1.

7. Schneider, *Entrances,* p. 224; Wolf and Fancher, eds., *Village Voice Reader,* p. 185.

8. Quoted in Lawrence Graver, *Beckett: Waiting for Godot* (New York: Cambridge Univ. Press, 1989), p. 6.

9. Bair, *Samuel Beckett,* 403-4.

10. *Waiting for Godot: A Tragicomedy in Two Acts* (New York: Grove Press, 1954), p. 6R. Future references to this edition are cited parenthetically in the text; because of the pagination of alternate pages in the Grove Press edition, page references are distinguished as R (right) and L (left).

11. Dougald McMillan and Martha Fehsenfeld, *Beckett in the Theatre* (New York: Riverrun Press, 1988), pp. 76, 68.

12. See ibid., pp. 87-91. This description further simplifies Beckett's reduction of the action of the play.

13. Kenneth Tynan, "At Three Minutes Past Eight You Must Dream," *New Yorker,* 21 Feb. 1977, pp. 45-46.

14. Quoted in Graver, *Beckett,* p. 13.

15. Schneider, *Entrances,* p. 225.

16. Quoted in McMillan and Fehsenfeld, *Beckett in the Theatre*, p. 82.

17. [G.S. Fraser], "They Also Serve," *Times Literary Supplement*, 10 Feb. 1956, p. 84; William Empson, "Waiting for Godot," *Times Literary Supplement*, 30 March 1956, p. 195; "Puzzling about Godot," *Times Literary Supplement*, 13 April 1956, p. 221.

18. Schneider, *Entrances*, p. 227.

19. Quoted in John Lahr, *Notes on a Cowardly Lion: The Biography of Bert Lahr* (New York: Knopf, 1969), pp. 262, 261.

20. Schneider, *Entrances*, p. 236, 227.

21. Lahr, *Notes on a Cowardly Lion*, p. 255.

22. Schneider, *Entrances*, p. 228; Lahr, *Notes on a Cowardly Lion*, p. 266.

23. Lahr, *Notes on a Cowardly Lion*, p. 264-65; Schneider, p. 230.

24. Quoted in McMillan and Fehsenfeld, *Beckett in the Theatre*, pp. 90, 85.

25. Schneider, *Entrances*, p. 229.

26. Quoted in Lahr, *Notes on a Cowardly Lion*, p. 263.

27. Schneider, *Entrances*, p. 235.

28. Quoted in McMillan and Fehsenfeld, *Beckett in the Theatre*, p. 69.

29. Bair, *Samuel Beckett*, p. 461-62.

30. Lahr, *Notes on a Cowardly Lion*, p. 273.

31. Samuel Beckett quoted by Alec Reid, Graver, *Beckett*, p. 19.

32. Quoted in McMillan and Fehsenfeld, *Beckett in the Theatre*, p. 85.

33. Arthur Gelb, "Wanted: Intellects," *New York Times*, 15 April 1956, sec. 2, p. 1.

34. McMillan and Fehsenfeld, *Beckett in the Theatre*, p. 180.

35. Quoted in Lahr, *Notes on a Cowardly Lion*, pp. 274, 279.

36. Kenneth Tynan, *Curtains: Selections from the Drama Criticism and Related Writings* (New York: Atheneum, 1961), p. 272.

37. *Waiting for Godot* program, 19 April 1956, John Golden Theatre, New York City, pp. 9, 10.

38. "B'way Uneven," *Variety*, 23 April 1956, p. 75.

39. Reviews of *Waiting for Godot, New York Dramatic Mirror* microfilm, pp. 320-322.

40. Norman Mailer, "The Hip and the Square," *Village Voice*, 2 May 1956, p. 5.

41. Harold Clurman, *Nation*, 5 May 1956, p. 390.

42. Shenker, "Moody Man," sec. 2, p. 3.

43. Norman Mailer, "A Public Notice by Norman Mailer," *Village Voice*, 9 May 1956, p. 12.

44. Eric Bentley, "The Talent of Samuel Beckett," *New Republic*, 14 May 1956; reprinted in Ruby Cohn, ed., *Casebook on "Waiting for Godot"* (New York: Grove Press, 1967), pp. 59, 61-62.

45. Clurman, p. 390; Bentley, "Talent of Beckett," p. 64.

46. Program, *Waiting for Godot*, 3 June 1978, Brooklyn Academy of Music, New York City.

47. Excellent discussion of the German Beckett can be found in Jack Zipes, "Beckett in Germany/Germany in Beckett," *New German Critique* 26 (Spring/Summer 1982): 151-58.

48. Rosette C. Lamont, "*En attendant Godot* in Paris," *The Beckett Circle* 16, no. 1 (1994): 1.

49. Richard Watts, "The Perverse Art of Brendan Behan," *New York Post,* 3 July 1959, 14.

50. Bruce Weber, "On Stage, and Off," *New York Times,* 26 Feb. 1993, p. C2.

51. Frank Rich, review of *Waiting for Godot, New York Times,* 7 Nov. 1988, p. C15; William A. Henry III, review of *Waiting for Godot, Time,* 21 Nov. 1988, p. 125.

52. Thomas M. Disch, review of *Waiting for Godot, Nation,* 19 Dec. 1988, p. 695.

53. Gordon Rogoff, "Pacifying the Terror," *Village Voice,* 15 Nov. 1988, p. 104.

7. BRIAN FRIEL

1. *Selected Plays of Brian Friel* (Washington, D.C.: Catholic University of America Press, 1986), p. 27. Future references to this edition are cited parenthetically in the text.

2. Richard Pine, "Brian Friel and Contemporary Irish Drama," *Colby Quarterly* 27, no. 4 (1991): 190.

3. Mel Gussow, "From Ballybeg to Broadway," *New York Times Magazine,* 29 Sept. 1991, p. 56.

4. Howard Kissel, *David Merrick: The Abominable Showman* (New York: Applause Books, 1993), p. 281.

5. Stuart W. Little, "Merrick's Next: Dublin Comedy," *New York Herald Tribune,* 14 Dec. 1965, p. 17.

6. Quoted in Dan H. Laurence and Nicholas Grene, eds., *Shaw, Lady Gregory, and the Abbey: A Correspondence and a Record* (Gerrards Cross: Colin Smythe, 1993), p. 67.

7. Stuart W. Little, "Theater News," *New York Herald-Tribune,* 30 Dec. 1965, p. 11.

8. Ibid., p. 11.

9. Pete Hamill, "A Night at the Theater," *New York Post,* 14 April 1966, Billy Rose Theatre Collection, New York Public Library.

10. Nick LaPole, "Dublin Tries Broadway," *New York Journal-American,* 13 Feb. 1966, Billy Rose Theatre Collection, New York Public Library.

11. Kissel, *David Merrick,* p. 331.

12. "Ex-Teacher Friel Hits Cash Mark as 'Phil' Hits," *Variety,* 2 March 1966, Billy Rose Theatre Collection, New York Public Library.

13. "Goodbye to Ballybeg," *Time,* 25 Feb. 1966, Billy Rose Theatre Collection, New York Public Library.

14. "Irish Mist," *Newsweek,* 28 Feb. 1966, Billy Rose Theatre Collection, New York Public Library.

15. John McCarten, "Vigil in Ballybeg," *New Yorker,* 26 Feb. 1966, p. 71.

16. Stuart W. Little, "Playwright Status for Ex-Teacher," *New York Herald Tribune,* 18 Feb. 1966, p. 15.

17. Walter Kerr, "The Public Face and the Private Self," *New York Herald Tribune,* 6 March 1966, p. 17; transcript, Allan Jefferys on WABC 16 Feb. 1966, Billy Rose Theatre Collection, New York Public Library.

18. James Davis, "'I Shall Return'—B. Friel," *New York Sunday News*, 7 Aug. 1966, p. 53.

19. Brooks Atkinson, review of *Shadow and Substance, New York Times*, 27 Jan. 1938, p. 16.

20. Frances Herridge, "'Philadelphia' Director Prepares New Friel Play," *New York Post*, 14 May 1966, Billy Rose Theatre Collection, New York Public Library.

21. Wendy Smith, "Joe Dowling Likes His Actors to Feel Free," *New York Times*, 4 Sept. 1994, sec. 2, p. 5.

22. Lee Jordan, WCBS, 7 Oct. 1966, and William Glover, Associated Press, 7 Oct. 1966, transcripts Billy Rose Theatre Collection, New York Public Library.

23. Richard Watts, "The Ireland of Brian Friel," *New York Post*, 15 Aug. 1968, p. 24.

24. Alan N. Bunce, "Frank Talk from Friel," *Christian Science Monitor*, 27 Nov. 1968, sec. 2, p. 13.

25. Seamus Deane, "Introduction," *Selected Plays of Brian Friel* (Washington, D.C.: Catholic University of America Press, 1986), p. 16.

26. Edna Longley, "Poetry in the Wars," *Field Day Anthology of Irish Writing* (Derry: Field Day, 1991), 3:649, 650.

27. Brian Friel, "Plays Peasant and Unpeasant," *Times Literary Supplement*, 17 March 1972, p. 305.

28. Joseph Hurley, "The Troubles According to Brian Friel," *Soho News* (New York), 15 April 1981, p. 63.

29. Gussow, "From Ballybeg to Broadway," p. 55.

30. Clive Barnes, "Nothing Is Lost in 'Translations,'" *New York Post*, 20 March 1995, p. 25; John Heilpern, "Translations," *New York Observer*, 18 April 1995, p. 22.

31. Michiko Kakutani, "Today's Irish Dramatists," *New York Times*, 2 Nov. 1980, sec. 2, p. 1.

32. Frances Herridge, "Belfast and Bagels," *New York Post*, 9 March 1979, p. 29.

33. Review of *The Colleen Bawn, New York Tribune*, 30 March 1860, p. 8.

34. Declan Kiberd, *Inventing Ireland* (Cambridge: Harvard Univ. Press, 1995), and R.F. Foster, *Modern Ireland* (New York: Oxford Univ. Press, 1988).

35. Friel, "Plays Peasant and Unpeasant," p. 305.

36. Brian Friel, "Extracts from a Sporadic Diary," *The Writers: A Sense of Ireland*, ed. Andrew Carpenter and Peter Fallon (New York: Braziller, 1980), pp. 41-42.

37. "Introduction," *Selected Plays*, p. 22.

38. Friel, "Extracts," p. 43.

INDEX